FOR PERSONAL and FA...

Our Daily Bread

ANNUAL EDITION

INTRODUCTION

We're glad you've picked up a copy of the 2022 Annual Edition of *Our Daily Bread,* which has been published to encourage believers in Jesus.

We hope the devotionals and feature articles will assist you in your walk with God. Several articles each month address a specific topic to help you grow in your understanding of it and in your faith in Christ. These articles feature a header that presents the monthly topic.

Please share these devotionals with others who need to know more about the hope found in Jesus Christ.

If we can serve you, feel free to contact us.

The Our Daily Bread staff

COVERS PHOTOS:
Landscape: *Lavender field, England* © Shutterstock
Flower: *Roses* © Shutterstock
EDITORIAL TEAM: Tom Felten, Tim Gustafson, Regie Keller, Alyson Kieda, Becky Knapp, Monica La Rose, Julie Schwab, and Peggy Willison
ACKNOWLEDGMENTS: Scripture taken from Holy Bible, New International Version®, NIV® Copyright © 1973, 1978, 1984, 2011 by Biblica, Inc.® Used by permission. All rights reserved worldwide.

© 2020 Our Daily Bread Ministries®, Grand Rapids, Michigan, USA

Internet address: ourdailybread.org • email: odb@odb.org

ISBN: 978-1-64641-113-9 (Landscape)
ISBN: 978-1-64641-114-6 (Flower)

Printed in China.

THE PEACE JESUS OFFERS

Peace is a reality few people experience these days. But in the midst of our chaotic world, God offers a peace that goes far beyond human understanding. This hope of peace lies at the heart of the story of the Bible.

Because of Adam and Eve's rebellion in the garden of Eden, all of us are born in need of a restored relationship with our Creator. But God has addressed this relationship problem. He promised to send someone who would offer salvation to everyone. This person is Jesus, "the Lamb of God, who takes away the sin of the world!" (JOHN 1:29). By faith we identify and trust in Jesus' offer of Himself for our sins so we can experience salvation and, as a result, peace with God.

But daily events threaten this peace. Anger, jealousy, stress, relationships, and job and health issues leave us feeling anything but peaceful. There's another kind of peace that Jesus offers us—the peace of God.

> *We can let the peace of God rule in our hearts.*

Jesus said, "Peace I leave with you; my peace I give you. I do not give to you as the world gives. Do not let your hearts be troubled and do not be afraid" (JOHN 14:27).

The apostle Paul encouraged his readers with these words: "Let the peace of Christ rule in your hearts, since as members of one body you were called to peace. And be thankful" (COLOSSIANS 3:15).

The big story of the Bible is that Jesus has conquered death and promises us eternal life. Because of this wonderful truth, we don't need to be consumed by the world's uncertainty. Instead, we can let the peace of God rule in our hearts.

DAVID FREES, *DIGITAL PUBLISHER & DIRECTOR OF ONLINE LEARNING*

Wisdom is like honey for you: If you find it,
there is a future hope. [PROVERBS 24:14]

★ *JANUARY TOPIC: THE BIG STORY OF THE BIBLE*

GOOD FOR YOU

People the world over spent an estimated $98.2 billion on
chocolate in 2016. The number is staggering, yet at the
same time not all that surprising. Chocolate, after all, tastes
delicious and we enjoy consuming it. So the world rejoiced col-
lectively when the sweet treat was found to have significant
health benefits as well. Chocolate contains flavonoids that help
safeguard the body against aging and heart disease. Never has a
prescription for health been so well received or heeded (in mod-
eration, of course!).

Solomon suggested there's another "sweet" worthy of our
investment: wisdom. He recommended his son eat honey "for it
is good" (PROVERBS 24:13) and compared its sweetness to wisdom.
The person who feeds on God's wisdom in Scripture finds it not
only sweet to the soul but beneficial for teaching and training,
equipping us for "every good work" we'll need to accomplish in
life (2 TIMOTHY 3:16–17).

Wisdom is what allows us to make smart choices and understand the world around us. And it's worth investing in and sharing with those we love—as Solomon wished to do for his son. We
can feel good about feasting on God's wisdom in the Bible. It's a
sweet treat that we can enjoy without limit—in fact, we're encouraged to! God, thank You for the sweetness of Your Scriptures!

KIRSTEN HOLMBERG

What wisdom do you need to consume today?
How has God's wisdom been sweet to you?

God, please nourish us with Your wisdom.

I constantly remember you in
my prayers. [2 TIMOTHY 1:3]

PROMPTED TO PRAY

"**S**everal years ago I was prompted to pray for you often, and I wonder why."

That text message from an old friend came with a photo of a note she'd kept in her Bible: "Pray for James. Cover mind, thoughts, words." Beside my name she'd recorded three separate years.

I looked at the years and caught my breath. I wrote back and asked what month she began to pray. She responded, "Sometime around July."

That was the month I was preparing to leave home for extended study abroad. I would be facing an unfamiliar culture and language and have my faith challenged like never before. As I looked at the note, I realized I'd received the precious gift of generous prayer.

My friend's kindness reminded me of another "prompting" to pray, Paul's instruction to his young missionary friend Timothy: "I urge, then, *first of all*, that petitions, prayers, intercession and thanksgiving be made for all people" (1 TIMOTHY 2:1). The phrase "first of all" indicates highest priority. Our prayers matter, Paul explains, because God "wants all people to be saved and to come to a knowledge of the truth" about Jesus (V. 4).

God moves through faithful prayer in countless ways to encourage others and draw them near to Himself. We may not know someone's circumstances when they come to mind, but God does. And He'll help that person as we pray!   JAMES BANKS

**Who comes to mind that needs your prayers in this new year?
How can you remind yourself to pray for them often?**

Loving God, please help me to pray often and to make a lasting difference in others' lives through my intercession for them.

BIBLE IN A YEAR | GENESIS 4–6; MATTHEW 2   5

I know that my redeemer lives,
and that in the end he will stand on the earth.
[JOB 19:25]

A HUNDRED YEARS FROM NOW

"**I** just want people to remember me a hundred years from now," said screenwriter Rod Serling in 1975. Creator of the TV series *The Twilight Zone*, Serling wanted people to say of him, "He was a writer." Most of us can identify with Serling's desire to leave a legacy—something to give our lives a sense of meaning and permanence.

The story of Job shows us a man struggling with meaning amid life's fleeting days. In a moment, not just his possessions but those most precious to him, his children, were taken. Then his friends accused him of *deserving* this fate. Job cried out: "Oh, that my words were recorded, that they were written on a scroll, that they were inscribed with an iron tool on lead, or engraved in rock forever!" (JOB 19:23–24).

Job's words *have* been "engraved in rock forever." We have them in the Bible. Yet Job needed even more meaning in his life than the legacy he'd leave behind. He discovered it in the character of God. "I know that my redeemer lives," Job declared, "and that in the end he will stand on the earth" (19:25). This knowledge gave him the right longing. "I myself will see him," Job said. "How my heart yearns within me!" (V. 27).

In the end, Job didn't find what he expected. He found much more—the Source of all meaning and permanence (42:1–6).

TIM GUSTAFSON

Why do you think Job wanted his words preserved forever? How do you want people to remember you one hundred years from now?

God, everything is fleeting except for You. We praise You for Your unshakable character. Show us what is truly important.

Walk by the Spirit, and you will not
gratify the desires of the flesh. [GALATIANS 5:16]

WALKING WITH THE SPIRIT

Ten thousand hours. That's how long author Malcolm Gladwell suggests it takes to become skillful at any craft. Even for the greatest artists and musicians of all time, their tremendous inborn talent wasn't enough to achieve the level of expertise that they would eventually attain. They needed to immerse themselves in their craft every single day.

As strange as it might seem, we need a similar mentality when it comes to learning to live in the power of the Holy Spirit. In Galatians, Paul encourages the church to be set apart for God. But Paul explained that this couldn't be achieved through merely obeying a set of rules. Instead we're called to walk with the Holy Spirit. The Greek word that Paul uses for "walk" in Galatians 5:16 literally means to walk around and around something, or to journey *(peripateo)*. So for Paul, walking with the Spirit meant journeying with the Spirit each day—it's not just a one-time experience of His power.

May we pray to be filled with the Spirit daily—to yield to the Spirit's work as He counsels, guides, comforts, and is simply there with us. And as we're "led by the Spirit" in this way (V. 18), we become better and better at hearing His voice and following His leading. Holy Spirit, may I walk with You today, and every day!

PETER CHIN

While being indwelt by the Holy Spirit when we receive salvation is a one-time event, how does this differ from being filled or walking with the Spirit? How have you been exhibiting the fruit of the Spirit?

Father, help me to experience the presence and leading of the Holy Spirit today, so that I might walk with You and live in a way that pleases You.

You are the light of the world. A town
built on a hill cannot be hidden. [MATTHEW 5:14]

SHINING THE LIGHT

Stephen told his parents that he needed to get to school early every day, but for some reason he never explained why it was so important. Yet they made sure he arrived at Northview High School by 7:15 each morning.

On a wintry day during his junior year, Stephen was in a car accident that sadly took his life. Later, his mom and dad found out why he'd been going to school so early. Each morning he and some friends had gathered at the school entrance to greet other students with a smile, a wave, and a kind word. It made all students—even those who weren't popular—feel welcomed and accepted.

A believer in Jesus, Stephen wanted to share His joy with those who desperately needed it. His example lives on as a reminder that one of the best ways to shine the light of Christ's love is by gestures of kindness and through a welcoming spirit.

In Matthew 5:14–16, Jesus reveals that in Him we're "the light of the world" and "a town built on a hill" (V. 14). Ancient cities were often built of white limestone, truly standing out as they reflected the blazing sun. May we choose not to be hidden but to give light "to everyone in the house" (V. 15).

And as we "let [our] light shine before others" (V. 16), may they experience the welcoming love of Christ.   *DAVE BRANON*

What's one way you could be more welcoming to the lonely and needy around you? How can the Holy Spirit help you be a city set on a hill for others to see?

Heavenly Father, thank You for Stephen's example. Like him, help me to show kindness and a welcoming spirit to everyone I meet.

Do not forget to show hospitality to strangers,
for by so doing some people have shown hospitality
to angels without knowing it. [HEBREWS 13:2]

MYSTERIOUS HELPERS

L
ouise suffers from muscular dystrophy. While trying to exit
a train station one day, she found herself facing a large flight
of stairs without an elevator or escalator. On the verge of
tears, Louise saw a man suddenly appear, pick up her bag, and
gently help her up the stairs. When she turned to thank him, he
was gone.

Michael was late for a meeting. Already stressed from a relationship breakdown, he started battling London's traffic only to get
a flat tire. As he stood helplessly in the rain, a man stepped out of
the crowd, opened the boot (trunk), jacked up the car, and changed
the wheel. When Michael turned to thank him, he was gone.

Who were these mysterious helpers? Kind strangers, or something more?

The popular image we have of angels as radiant or winged crea-
tures is only half true. While some appear this way (ISAIAH 6:2;
MATTHEW 28:3), others come with dusty feet, ready for a meal
(GENESIS 18:1–5) and are easily mistaken for everyday people
(JUDGES 13:16). The writer of Hebrews says that by showing hospital-
ity to strangers, we can entertain angels without realizing it (13:2).

We don't know if Louise and Michael's helpers were angels.
But according to Scripture, they could have been. Angels are at
work right now, helping God's people (HEBREWS 1:14). And they
can appear as ordinary as a person on the street.   *SHERIDAN VOYSEY*

**What do you know about angels? Can you think of an instance when
you may have encountered one without realizing it at the time?**

*Thank You, God, for the angels You send,
meeting us in our time of need.*

When you give to the needy,
do not let your left hand know what
your right hand is doing. [MATTHEW 6:3]

SECRET DELIVERY

A clear, glass vase with bell-shaped lilies of the valley, pink tulips, and yellow daffodils greeted Kim at her front door. For seven months, an anonymous believer in Jesus sent Kim beautiful bouquets from a local flower shop. Each monthly gift arrived with a note filled with scriptural encouragement and signed: "Love, Jesus."

Kim shared photos of these secret deliveries on Facebook. The flowers gave her opportunity to celebrate an individual's kindness and to acknowledge the way God expressed His love to her through His people. As she trusted Him through her battle with a terminal disease, every colorful blossom and handwritten note affirmed God's loving compassion for her.

The sender's anonymity reflects the heart motive Jesus encourages His people to adopt when giving. He warns against practicing righteous acts "to be seen" by others (MATTHEW 6:1). Good deeds are intended to be expressions of worship overflowing from hearts grateful for all God's done for us. Highlighting our own generosity with the hope or expectation of being honored can take the focus off the Giver of all good things—Jesus.

God knows when we give with good intentions (V. 4). He simply wants our generosity motivated by love as we give Him the glory, the honor, and the praise.   *XOCHITL DIXON*

How can you place the spotlight on Jesus by giving to someone in secret this week? How can you give God credit while still accepting appreciation?

Jesus, thank You for reminding us that giving to others is a privilege and a wonderful way to thank You for all You've given us.

The Lord longs to be gracious to you. [ISAIAH 30:18]

★ *JANUARY TOPIC: THE BIG STORY OF THE BIBLE*

GOD WAITED

When Denise Levertov was just twelve, long before she became a renowned poet, she had the gumption to mail a package of poetry to the great poet T. S. Eliot. She then waited for a reply. Surprisingly, Eliot sent two pages of handwritten encouragement. In the preface to her collection *The Stream and the Sapphire*, she explained how the poems "trace [her] own movement from agnosticism to Christian faith." It's powerful, then, to recognize how one of the later poems ("Annunciation") narrates Mary's surrender to God. Noting the Holy Spirit's refusal to overwhelm Mary and His desire for Mary to freely receive the Christ child, these two words blaze at the poem's center: "God waited."

In Mary's story, Levertov recognized her own. God waited, eager to love her. He would not force anything upon her. He waited. Isaiah described this same reality, how God stood ready, eager with anticipation, to shower Israel with tender love. "The LORD longs to be gracious to you . . . to show you compassion" (30:18). He was ready to flood His people with kindness, and yet *God waited* for them to willingly receive what He offered (V. 19).

It's a wonder that our Creator, the Savior of the world, chooses to wait for us to welcome *Him*. The God who could so easily overpower us practices humble patience. The Holy One waits for us.

WINN COLLIER

In what areas of your life has God been waiting for you? How might you surrender to Him?

God, it boggles my mind that You wait for me. Wait? For me? This makes me trust You, desire You. Please come. Give me Your full self.

BIBLE IN A YEAR | GENESIS 20–22; MATTHEW 6:19–34   11

Everyone who hears these words of mine
and puts them into practice is like a wise man
who built his house on the rock. [MATTHEW 7:24]

THE LEANING TOWER

You've probably heard of the famous Leaning Tower of Pisa in Italy, but have you heard of the leaning tower of San Francisco? It's called the Millennium Tower. Built in 2008, this fifty-eight-story skyscraper stands proudly—but slightly crookedly—in downtown San Francisco.

The problem? Its engineers didn't dig a deep enough foundation. So now they're being forced to retrofit the foundation with repairs that may cost more than the entire tower did when it was originally built—a fix that some believe is necessary to keep it from collapsing during an earthquake.

The painful lesson here? Foundations matter. When your foundation isn't solid, catastrophe could ensue. Jesus taught something similar near the end of His Sermon on the Mount. In Matthew 7:24–27, He contrasts two builders, one who built on a rock, another on sand. When a storm inevitably came, only the house with a solid foundation was left standing.

What does this mean for us? Jesus clearly states that our lives must be built through obedience and trust upon Him (V. 24). When we rest in Him, our lives can find solid ground through God's power and unending grace.

Christ doesn't promise us that we'll never face storms. But He does say that when He's our rock, those storms will never wash away our faith-fortified foundation in Him.   *ADAM R. HOLZ*

How has your faith helped you to weather the worst storms you've faced? What are some practical ways you can strengthen your faith each day?

Father, storms are inevitable in life. Help us to choose to dwell daily in Scripture and strengthen our strong foundation in You.

The Spirit God gave us does not make us timid, but gives us power, love and self-discipline. [2 TIMOTHY 1:7]

HERE BE DRAGONS?

Legend has it that at the edges of medieval maps, marking the boundaries of the world the maps' creators knew at the time, there'd be inscribed the words "Here be dragons"—often alongside vivid illustrations of the terrifying beasts supposedly lurking there.

There's not much evidence medieval cartographers actually wrote these words, but I like to think they could have. Maybe because "here be dragons" sounds like something I might've written at the time—a grim warning that even if I didn't know exactly what would happen if I ventured into the great unknown, it likely wouldn't be good!

But there's one glaring problem with my preferred policy of self-protection and risk-aversion: it's the opposite of the courage to which I'm called as a believer in Jesus (2 TIMOTHY 1:7).

One might even say I'm misguided about what's really dangerous. As Paul explained, in a broken world bravely following Christ will sometimes be painful (V. 8). But as those brought from death to life and entrusted with the Spirit's life flowing in and through us (VV. 9–10,14), how could we not?

When God gives us a gift this staggering, to fearfully shrink back would be the real tragedy—far worse than anything we might face when we follow Christ's leading into uncharted territory (VV. 6–8, 12). He can be trusted with our hearts and our future (V. 12).

MONICA LA ROSE

Is there a particularly debilitating fear God may be calling you to confront? How might the support of other believers encourage you?

Loving God, thank You for the new life You've given us, for freedom from all that would cripple us in fear and shame. Help us to find peace in You.

They bowed down and worshiped him.
[MATTHEW 2:11]

THE ONLY KING

As five-year-old Eldon listened to the pastor talk about Jesus leaving heaven and coming to earth, he gasped when the pastor thanked Him in prayer for dying for our sins. "Oh, no! He died?" the boy said in surprise.

From the start of Christ's life on earth, there were people who wanted Him dead. Wise men came to Jerusalem during the reign of King Herod inquiring, "Where is the one who has been born king of the Jews? We saw his star when it rose and have come to worship him" (MATTHEW 2:2). When the king heard this, he became fearful of one day losing his position to Jesus. So he sent soldiers to kill all the boys two years old and younger around Bethlehem. But God protected His Son and sent an angel to warn His parents to leave the area. They fled, and He was saved (VV. 13–18).

When Jesus completed His ministry, He was crucified for the sins of the world. The sign placed above His cross, though meant in mockery, read, "This is Jesus, the King of the Jews" (27:37). Yet three days later He rose in victory from the grave. After ascending to heaven, He sat down on the throne as King of kings and Lord of lords (PHILIPPIANS 2:8–11).

The King died for our sins—yours, mine, and Eldon's. Let's allow Him to rule in our hearts.   *ANNE CETAS*

**What does it mean for you to have Jesus as your King?
Are there areas of your life where He's not?**

*Jesus, thank You for willingly dying for our sins and offering
forgiveness. Teach us to submit to Your rule.*

I will sing praise to my God
as long as I live. [PSALM 146:2]

A LIFESTYLE OF PRAISE

Wallace Stegner's mother died at the age of fifty. When Wallace was eighty, he finally wrote her a note—"Letter, Much Too Late"—in which he praised the virtues of a woman who grew up, married, and raised two sons in the harshness of the early Western United States. She was the kind of wife and mother who was an encourager, even to those that were less than desirable. Wallace remembered the strength his mother displayed by way of her voice. Stegner wrote: "You never lost an opportunity to sing." As long as she lived, Stegner's mother sang, grateful for blessings large and small.

The psalmist too took opportunities to sing. He sang when the days were good, and when they weren't so good. The songs were not forced or coerced, but a natural response to the "Maker of heaven and earth" (146:6) and how He "gives food to the hungry" (V. 7) and "gives sight to the blind" (V. 8) and "sustains the fatherless and the widow" (V. 9). This is really a lifestyle of singing, one that builds strength over time as daily trust is placed in "the God of Jacob" who "remains faithful forever" (VV. 5–6).

The quality of our voices isn't the point, but our response to God's sustaining goodness—a lifestyle of praise. As the old hymn puts it: "There's within my heart a melody." *JOHN BLASE*

How can you make singing praises to God a regular part of your day? What's your favorite song of praise?

Maker of heaven and earth, when I pause and reflect, Your provision for and protection of me is overwhelming. May my life be a continuous song of praise to You for as long as I live.

When he saw the crowds, he had compassion
on them, because they were harassed and helpless,
like sheep without a shepherd. [MATTHEW 9:36]

EVERYONE NEEDS COMPASSION

When Jeff was a new believer in Jesus and fresh out of college, he worked for a major oil company. In his role as a salesman, he traveled; and in his travels he heard people's stories—many of them heartbreaking. He realized that what his customers most needed wasn't oil, but compassion. They needed God. This led Jeff to attend seminary to learn more about the heart of God and eventually to become a pastor.

Jeff's compassion had its source in Jesus. In Matthew 9:27–33 we get a glimpse of Christ's compassion in the miraculous healing of two blind men and one demon-possessed man. Throughout His earthly ministry, He went about preaching the gospel and healing "through all the towns and villages" (V. 35). Why? "When he saw the crowds, he had compassion on them, because they were harassed and helpless, like sheep without a shepherd" (V. 36).

The world today is still full of troubled and hurting people who need the Savior's gentle care. Like a shepherd who leads, protects, and cares for his sheep, Jesus extends His compassion to all who come to Him (11:28). No matter where we are in life and what we're experiencing, in Him we find a heart overflowing with tenderness and care. And when we've been a beneficiary of God's loving compassion, we can't help but want to extend it to others.   *ALYSON KIEDA*

**When have you experienced God's tender care?
Who can you reach out to in compassion?**

*Heavenly Father, we're so grateful You had compassion on us!
We would be lost without You. Help us to extend Your overflowing
compassion to others.*

Teach us to number our days,
that we may gain a heart of wisdom. [PSALM 90:12]

SLOWING DOWN TIME

A lot has changed since the electric clock was invented in the 1840s. We now keep time on smart watches, smart phones, and laptops. The entire pace of life seems faster—with even our "leisurely" walking speeding up. This is especially true in cities and can have a negative effect on health, scholars say. "We're just moving faster and faster and getting back to people as quickly as we can," Professor Richard Wiseman observed. "That's driving us to think everything has to happen now."

Moses, the writer of one of the oldest of the Bible's psalms, reflected on time. He reminds us that God controls life's pace. "A thousand years in your sight are like a day that has just gone by, or like a watch in the night," he wrote (PSALM 90:4).

The secret to time management, therefore, isn't to go faster or slower. It's to abide in God, spending more time with Him. Then we get in step with each other, but first with Him—the One who formed us (139:13) and knows our purpose and plans (V. 16).

Our time on earth won't last forever. Yet we can manage it wisely, not by watching the clock, but by giving each day to God. As Moses said, "Teach us to number our days, that we may gain a heart of wisdom" (90:12). Then, with God we'll always be on time, now and forever.　　　　　　　　　　　*PATRICIA RAYBON*

What's your pace in life? How could you spend more time with God, getting in step with Him?

*Gracious God, when we fall out of step with You,
draw us closer to abide in You.*

Where were you when I laid
the earth's foundation? [JOB 38:4]

★ *JANUARY TOPIC: THE BIG STORY OF THE BIBLE*

PERFECTLY PLACED

Scientists know our planet is precisely the right distance from the sun to benefit from its heat. A little closer and all the water would evaporate, as on Venus. Only a bit farther and everything would freeze like it does on Mars. Earth is also just the right size to generate the right amount of gravity. Less would make everything weightlessly sterile like our moon, while more gravity would trap poisonous gases that suffocate life as on Jupiter.

The intricate physical, chemical, and biological interactions that comprise our world bear the imprint of a sophisticated Designer. We catch a glimpse of this complex craftsmanship when God speaks to Job about things beyond our understanding. "Where were you when I laid the earth's foundation?" God asks. "Who marked off its dimensions? Surely you know! Who stretched a measuring line across it? On what were its footings set, or who laid its cornerstone?" (JOB 38:4–6).

This glimpse of creation's magnitude causes us to wonder at Earth's mighty oceans bowing before the One who "shut up the sea behind doors when it burst forth from the womb, . . . [who said] 'This far you may come and no farther' " (VV. 8–11). In wonder may we sing with the morning stars and shout for joy with the angels (V. 7), for this elaborate world was made for us that we might know and trust God.   *REMI OYEDELE*

How does God's amazing creation cause you to praise Him today? What about its design reveals a Maker?

Thank You, Creator God, for this elaborate world You designed for us.

"Bring them here to me," [Jesus] said.
[MATTHEW 14:18]

BRING WHAT YOU HAVE

"**S**tone Soup," an old tale with many versions, tells of a starving man who comes to a village, but no one there can spare a crumb of food for him. He puts a stone and water in a pot over a fire. Intrigued, the villagers watch him as he begins to stir his "soup." Eventually, one brings a couple of potatoes to add to the mix; another has a few carrots. One person adds an onion, another a handful of barley. A farmer donates some milk. Eventually, the "stone soup" becomes a tasty chowder.

That tale illustrates the value of sharing, but it also reminds us to bring what we have, even when it seems to be insignificant. In John 6:1–14 we read of a boy who appears to be the only person in a huge crowd who thought about bringing some food. Christ's disciples had little use for the boy's sparse lunch of five loaves and two fishes. But when it was surrendered, Jesus increased it and fed thousands of hungry people!

I once heard someone say, "*You* don't have to feed the five thousand. You just have to bring your loaves and fishes." Just as Jesus took one person's meal and multiplied it far beyond anyone's expectations or imagination (V. 11), He'll accept our surrendered efforts, talents, and service. He just wants us to be willing to bring what we have to Him.   *CINDY HESS KASPER*

What have you been holding back from God?
Why is it difficult to bring that area of your life to Him?

Jesus, help me to surrender whatever I have to You,
knowing You can multiply a little into a lot.

He stilled the storm to a whisper;
the waves of the sea were hushed. [PSALM 107:29]

STORM CHASERS

"**C**hasing tornadoes," says Warren Faidley, "is often like a giant game of 3D-chess played out over thousands of square miles." The photojournalist and storm-chaser adds: "Being in the right place at the right time is a symphony of forecasting and navigation while dodging everything from softball-sized hailstones to dust storms and slow-moving farm equipment."

Faidley's words make my palms sweat and heart beat faster. While admiring the raw courage and scientific hunger storm chasers display, I balk at throwing myself into the middle of potentially fatal weather events.

In my experience, however, I don't have to chase storms in life—they seem to be chasing *me*. That experience is mirrored by Psalm 107 as it describes sailors trapped in a storm. They were being chased by the consequences of their wrong choices but the psalmist says, "They cried out to the Lord in their trouble, and he brought them out of their distress. He stilled the storm to a whisper; the waves of the sea were hushed. They were glad when it grew calm" (PSALM 107:28–30).

Whether the storms of life are of our own making or the result of living in a broken world, our Father is greater. When we are being chased by storms, He alone is able to calm them—or to calm the storm within us.   *BILL CROWDER*

When facing difficulties, where do you turn for help? How might you trust your heavenly Father today, who is greater than your storms?

Thank You, Father, that You're with me in my struggles and Your power is greater than any storm on my horizon.

If your enemy is hungry, feed him.
[ROMANS 12:20]

INSTEAD OF REVENGE

After Jim Elliot and four other missionaries were killed by Huaorani tribesmen in 1956, no one expected what happened next. Jim's wife, Elisabeth, their young daughter, and another missionary's sister willingly chose to make their home among the very people who killed their loved ones. They spent several years living in the Huaorani community, learning their language, and translating the Bible for them. These women's testimony of forgiveness and kindness convinced the Huaorani of God's love for them and many received Jesus as their Savior.

What Elisabeth and her friend did is an incredible example of not repaying evil with evil but with good (ROMANS 12:17). The apostle Paul encouraged the church in Rome to show through their actions the transformation that God had brought into their own lives. What did Paul have in mind? They were to go beyond the natural desire to take revenge; instead, they were to show love to their enemies by meeting their needs, such as providing food or water.

Why do this? Paul quotes a proverb from the Old Testament: "If your enemy is hungry, feed him; if he is thirsty, give him something to drink" (V. 20; PROVERBS 25:21–22). The apostle was revealing that the kindness shown by believers to their enemies could win them over and light the fire of repentance in their hearts.

ESTERA PIROSCA ESCOBAR

How did Jesus live out the command to love one's enemies? What will you do today to show God's love to those who have harmed you?

Abba, Father, it's difficult, even impossible, for us to love others in our own strength. Help us through Your Spirit to truly love our enemies, and use us to bring them to You.

Do not touch my anointed ones;
do my prophets no harm. [PSALM 105:15]

WHEN GOD INTERVENES

In a poem titled "This Child Is Beloved," Omawumi Efueye, known affectionately as Pastor O, writes about his parents' attempts to end the pregnancy that would result in his birth. After several unusual events that prevented them from aborting him, they decided to welcome their child instead. The knowledge of God's preservation of his life motivated Omawumi to give up a lucrative career in favor of full-time ministry. Today, he faithfully pastors a London church.

Like Pastor O, the Israelites experienced God's intervention at a vulnerable time in their history. While traveling through the wilderness, they came within sight of King Balak of Moab. Terrified of their conquests and their vast population, Balak engaged a seer named Balaam to place a curse on the unsuspecting travelers (NUMBERS 22:2–6).

But something amazing happened. Whenever Balaam opened his mouth to curse, a blessing issued instead. "I have received a command to bless; he has blessed, and I cannot change it," he declared. "No misfortune is seen in Jacob, no misery observed in Israel. The Lord their God is with them; . . . God brought them out of Egypt" (NUMBERS 23:20–22). God preserved the Israelites from a battle they didn't even know was raging!

Whether we see it or not, God still watches over His people today. May we worship in gratitude and awe the One who calls us blessed.   *REMI OYEDELE*

How often do you stop to consider the daily protection God extends over you? What does the knowledge that He saves you from unseen dangers mean to you?

Father in heaven, forgive us for the many times we take Your care and protection for granted. Give us eyes to see how much You bless us.

Hatred stirs up conflict, but love
covers over all wrongs. [PROVERBS 10:12]

CLEAN CONTAINERS

"**H**atred corrodes the container that carries it." These words were spoken by former Senator Alan Simpson at the funeral of George H. W. Bush. Attempting to describe his dear friend's kindness, Senator Simpson recalled how the forty-first president of the United States embraced humor and love rather than hatred in his professional leadership and personal relationships.

I relate to the senator's quote, don't you? Oh, the damage done to *me* when I harbor hatred!

Medical research reveals the damage done to our bodies when we cling to the negative or release bursts of anger. Our blood pressure rises. Our hearts pound. Our spirits sag. Our containers corrode.

In Proverbs 10:12, King Solomon observes, "Hatred stirs up conflict, but love covers over all wrongs." The conflict that results from hatred here is a blood feud between rivaling peoples of different tribes and races. Such hatred fuels the drive for revenge so that people who despise each other can't connect.

By contrast, God's way of love covers—*draws a veil over, conceals, or forgives*—all wrongs. That doesn't mean we overlook errors or enable a wrongdoer. But we don't nurse the wrong when someone is truly remorseful. And if they never apologize, we still release our feelings to God. We who know the Great Lover are to "love each other deeply, because love covers over a multitude of sins" (1 PETER 4:8).   *ELISA MORGAN*

What things cause you to hate? How might the hard-hearted heat of hostility eat away at our personal joy and our world's peace?

O God, help me surrender to Your great love that covers all sins and makes me into a clean container in which You dwell in love.

BIBLE IN A YEAR | GENESIS 49–50; MATTHEW 13:31–58

Then Nathan said to David,
"You are the man!" [2 SAMUEL 12:7]

WHERE ARE YOU HEADED?

I n northern Thailand, the Wild Boars youth soccer team decided to explore a cave together. After an hour they turned to go back and found that the entrance to the cave was flooded. Rising water pushed them deeper into the cave, day after day, until they were finally trapped more than two miles (four kilometers) inside. When they were heroically rescued two weeks later, many wondered how they had become so hopelessly trapped. Answer: one step at a time.

In Israel, Nathan confronted David for killing his loyal soldier, Uriah. How did the man "after [God's] own heart" (1 SAMUEL 13:14) become guilty of murder? *One step at a time*. David didn't go from zero to murder in one afternoon. He warmed up to it, over time, as one bad decision bled into others. It started with a second glance that turned into a lustful stare. He abused his kingly power by sending for Bathsheba, then tried to cover up her pregnancy by calling her husband home from the front. When Uriah refused to visit his wife while his comrades were at war, David decided he would have to die.

We may not be guilty of murder or trapped in a cave of our own making, but we're either moving toward Jesus or toward trouble. Big problems don't develop overnight. They break upon us gradually, one step at a time.   *MIKE WITTMER*

**What decision can you make right now to move toward Jesus
and away from trouble? What must you do to confirm
this decision?**

Jesus, I'm running to You!

The Son is the image of the invisible God,
the firstborn over all creation. [COLOSSIANS 1:15]

★ *JANUARY TOPIC: THE BIG STORY OF THE BIBLE*

THE GREATEST MYSTERY

Before I came to faith in Jesus, I'd heard the gospel preached but wrestled with His identity. How could He offer forgiveness for my sins when the Bible says only God can forgive sins? I discovered I wasn't alone in my struggles after reading J. I. Packer's *Knowing God*. Packer suggests that for many unbelievers the "really staggering Christian claim is that Jesus of Nazareth was God made man . . . as truly and fully divine as He was human." Yet this is the truth that makes salvation possible.

When the apostle Paul refers to Christ as "the image of the invisible God," he's saying Jesus is completely and perfectly God—Creator and Sustainer of all things in heaven and earth—but *also* fully human (COLOSSIANS 1:15–17). Because of this truth, we can be confident that through Christ's death and resurrection, He's not only carried the consequences for our sins but has also redeemed human nature, so that we—and all of creation—can be reconciled to God (VV. 20–22).

In an amazing, initiating act of love, God the Father reveals Himself in and through Scripture by the power of God the Holy Spirit and through the life of God the Son. Those who believe in Jesus are saved because He *is* Emmanuel—God with us. Hallelujah!   *XOCHITL DIXON*

When have you wrestled with your understanding of Jesus? What was the result?

Loving God, thank You for revealing Yourself and reconciling us through Jesus.

I waited patiently for the LORD;
he turned to me and heard my cry. [PSALM 40:1]

WAITING WITH THE TURTLE

Every fall, when the painted turtle senses winter coming, she dives to the bottom of her pond, burying herself in the muck and mud. She pulls into her shell and goes still: her heart rate slows, almost stopping. Her body temperature drops, staying just above freezing. She stops breathing, and she waits. For six months, she stays buried, and her body releases calcium from her bones into her bloodstream, so that she slowly begins even to lose her shape.

But when the pond thaws, she will float up and breathe again. Her bones will reform, and she will feel the warmth of the sun on her shell.

I think of the painted turtle when I read the psalmist's description of waiting for God. The psalmist is in a "slimy pit" of "mud and mire," but God hears him (PSALM 40:2). God lifts him out, and gives him a firm place to stand. God is "my help and my deliverer," he sings (V. 17).

Perhaps it feels like you've been waiting forever for something to change—for a new direction in your career, for a relationship to be restored, for the willpower to break a bad habit, or for deliverance from a difficult situation. The painted turtle and the psalmist are here to remind us to trust in God: He hears, and He will deliver.　　　　　　　　　　　　　　*AMY PETERSON*

What do you need to trust God with?
What might that look like today?

*God, sometimes it's hard to wait. But we trust in You and in
Your deliverance. Please give us patience, and allow Your greatness
and glory to be evident in our lives.*

I have made you and I will carry you.
[ISAIAH 46:4]

NO LINE TO LOVE

Sometimes when my Labrador retriever wants attention, he'll take something of mine and parade it in front of me. One morning as I was writing at the desk with my back turned, Max snatched my wallet and ran off. But realizing I hadn't seen him do it, he returned and nudged me with his nose—wallet in mouth, eyes dancing, tail wagging, taunting me to play.

Max's antics made me laugh, but they also reminded me of my limitations when it comes to being attentive to others. So often I've intended to spend time with family or friends, but other things occupy my time and awareness; and before I know it the day slips away and love is left undone.

How comforting to know that our heavenly Father is so great that He's able to attend to each of us in the most intimate ways— even sustaining every breath in our lungs for as long as we live. He promises His people, "Even to your old age and gray hairs I am he, I am he who will sustain you. I have made you and I will carry you" (ISAIAH 46:4).

God always has time for us. He understands every detail of our circumstances—no matter how complex or difficult—and is there whenever we call on Him in prayer. We never have to wait in line for our Savior's unlimited love. *JAMES BANKS*

**In what ways does God take care of your daily needs?
How can you share His love with others?**

*You always have time for me, Jesus.
Please help me to live every moment for You!*

You will tread our sins underfoot and hurl all our iniquities into the depths of the sea. [MICAH 7:19]

DEMONSTRATING GRACE

❝ **I**n moments where tragedy happens or even hurt, there are opportunities to demonstrate grace or to exact vengeance," the recently bereaved man remarked. "I chose to demonstrate grace." Pastor Erik Fitzgerald's wife had been killed in a car accident caused by an exhausted firefighter who fell asleep while driving home, and legal prosecutors wanted to know whether he would seek the maximum sentence. The pastor chose to practice the forgiveness he often preached about. To the surprise of both him and the firefighter, the men eventually became friends.

Pastor Erik was living out of the grace he'd received from God, who'd forgiven him all of his sins. Through his actions he echoed the words of the prophet Micah, who praised God for pardoning sin and forgiving when we do wrong (MICAH 7:18). The prophet uses wonderfully visual language to show just how far God goes in forgiving His people, saying that He will "tread our sins underfoot" and hurl our wrongdoings into the deep sea (V. 19). The firefighter received a gift of freedom that day, which brought him closer to God.

Whatever difficulty we face, we know that God reaches out to us with loving, open arms, welcoming us into His safe embrace. He "delights to show mercy" (V. 18). As we receive His love and grace, He gives us the strength to forgive those who hurt us— even as Pastor Erik did. 　　　　*AMY BOUCHER PYE*

How do you respond to this story of amazing forgiveness? Can you think of someone you need to forgive? If so, ask God to help you.

Father God, You love us without ceasing, and You delight to forgive us when we return to You. Envelop us with Your love, that we might demonstrate grace to those who hurt us.

Continue in what you have learned . . .
how from infancy you have known the
Holy Scriptures. [2 TIMOTHY 3:14–15]

GUIDING CHILDREN TO GOD

An outspoken atheist believes it's immoral for parents to teach their children religion as though it were actually true. He even claims that parents who pass along their faith to their children are committing child abuse. Though these views are extreme, I do hear from parents who are hesitant to boldly encourage their children toward faith. While most of us readily hope to influence our children with our view of politics or nutrition or sports, for some reason some of us treat our convictions about God differently.

In contrast, Paul wrote of how Timothy had been taught "from infancy . . . the Holy Scriptures, which are able to make you wise for salvation through faith in Christ Jesus" (2 TIMOTHY 3:15). Timothy didn't arrive at faith as an adult through the power of his own, unaided reason. Rather, his mother nurtured his heart toward God; then he continued in what he had learned (V. 14). If God is life, the source of true wisdom, then it's vital for us to tenderly cultivate a love for God in our families.

There are many belief systems that are influencing our children. TV shows, movies, music, teachers, friends, the media— each of these carry assumptions (either obvious or under the radar) about faith that exert real influence. May we choose not to be silent. The beauty and grace we've experienced compels us to guide our children toward God.   *WINN COLLIER*

Reflect on the myriad influences and messages children (or all of us) receive in a given day. How do these forces shape you and those you love?

Dear Father, thank You for the joy and privilege to gracefully nurture children's hearts toward You.

The LORD would speak to Moses face to face,
as one speaks to a friend. [EXODUS 33:11]

FRIENDSHIP BENCH

I n the African country of Zimbabwe, war trauma and high unemployment can leave people in despair—until they find hope on a "friendship bench." Hopeless people can go there to talk with trained "grandmothers"—elderly women taught to listen to people struggling with depression, known in that nation's Shona language as *kufungisisa*, or "thinking too much."

The Friendship Bench Project is being launched in other places, including Zanzibar, London, and New York City. "We were thrilled to bits with the results," said one London researcher. A New York counselor agreed. "Before you know it, you're not on a bench, you're just inside a warm conversation with someone who cares."

The project evokes the warmth and wonder of talking with our Almighty God. Moses put up not a bench but a tent to commune with God, calling it the tent of meeting. There, "the LORD would speak to Moses face to face, as one speaks to a friend" (EXODUS 33:11). Joshua, his assistant, wouldn't even leave the tent, perhaps because he so valued his time with God (V. 11).

Today we no longer need a tent of meeting. Jesus has brought the Father near. As He told His disciples, "I have called you friends, for everything that I learned from my Father I have made known to you" (JOHN 15:15). Yes, our God awaits us. He's our heart's wisest helper, our understanding Friend. Talk with Him now.

PATRICIA RAYBON

What worries consume your thoughts today? As you talk to God about these concerns, what good thoughts about Him can you focus on instead?

Dear God, thank You for encouraging our hearts with noble thoughts of You. When we're sick with worry, point our minds back to You.

We have this treasure in jars of clay
to show that this all-surpassing power
is from God and not from us. [2 CORINTHIANS 4:7]

AN OLD CLAY POT

I've acquired a number of old clay pots over the years. My favorite was excavated from a site dated during Abraham's time. It's at least one item in our home that is older than I! It's not much to look at: stained, cracked, chipped, and in need of a good scrubbing. I keep it to remind me that I'm just a man made out of mud. Though fragile and weak, I carry an immeasurably precious treasure—Jesus. "We have this treasure [Jesus] in jars of clay" (2 CORINTHIANS 4:7).

Paul continues: "We are hard pressed on every side, but not crushed; perplexed, but not in despair; persecuted, but not abandoned; struck down, but not destroyed" (VV. 8–9). *Hard pressed, perplexed, persecuted, struck down.* These are the pressures the pot must bear. *Not crushed, in despair, abandoned, destroyed.* These are the effects of the counteracting strength of Jesus in us.

"We always carry around in our body the death of Jesus" (V. 10). This is the attitude that characterized Jesus who died to Himself every day. And this is the attitude that can characterize us—a willingness to die to self-effort, trusting solely in the sufficiency of the One who lives in us.

"So that the life of Jesus may also be revealed in our mortal body" (V. 10). This is the outcome: *the beauty of Jesus made visible in an old clay pot.*

DAVID H. ROPER

How can you meet the demands placed on you?
Where does your strength come from?

God, I'm weak and fragile. Thank You for living in me.
I want You and Your strength to be seen.

The thief comes only to steal and kill and destroy;
I have come that they may have life,
and have it to the full. [JOHN 10:10]

LIFE TO THE FULL

The year was 1918, near the end of World War I, and photographer Eric Enstrom was putting together a portfolio of his work. He wanted to include one that communicated a sense of fullness in a time that felt quite empty to so many people. In his now much-loved photo, a bearded old man sits at a table with his head bowed and his hands clasped in prayer. On the surface before him there is only a book, spectacles, a bowl of gruel, a loaf of bread, and a knife. Nothing more, but also nothing less.

Some might say the photograph reveals scarcity. But Enstrom's point was quite the opposite: Here is a full life, one lived in gratitude, one you and I can experience as well regardless of our circumstances. Jesus announces the good news in John 10: "life . . . to the full" (V. 10). We do a grave disservice to such good news when we equate *full* with *many things*. The fullness Jesus speaks of isn't measured in worldly categories like riches or real estate, but rather a heart, mind, soul, and strength brimming in gratitude that the Good Shepherd gave "his life for the sheep" (V. 11), and cares for us and our daily needs. This is a full life—enjoying relationship with God—that's possible for every one of us.   *JOHN BLASE*

**Would you say that right now you're living "life to the full"?
Why or why not? Have you had a tendency to equate *full*
with *many things*?**

*Good Shepherd, thank You for laying down Your life for me, one of
the sheep. And thank You for Your promise to provide nothing less
than the daily bread I need, both literally and figuratively.*

Strengthen the feeble hands,
steady the knees that give way. [ISAIAH 35:3]

STRENGTHENING WEAK KNEES

W hen I was a kid, I thought the song title "He Looked Beyond My Fault and Saw My Need," written by Dottie Rambo in 1967, was "He Looked Beyond My Faults and Saw My Knees." Employing the logic of a child, I wondered why God would look at knees. Was it because they were weak? I knew that weak-kneed meant "afraid." I later discovered that Dottie had written the song about God's unconditional love in response to her brother Eddie's belief that he was unlovable because of the wrong things he'd done. Dottie assured him that God saw his weakness but loved him anyway.

God's unconditional love is apparent throughout the many *weak-kneed* moments of the people of Israel and Judah. He sent prophets like Isaiah with messages for His wayward people. In Isaiah 35, the prophet shares the hope of God's restoration. The encouragement that would come as a result of embracing hope would "strengthen the feeble hands, steady the knees that give way" (V. 3). Through the encouragement they received, God's people would in turn be able to encourage others. This is why Isaiah instructs in verse 4, "Say to those with fearful hearts, 'Be strong, do not fear.' "

Feeling weak-kneed? Talk to your heavenly Father. He strengthens weak knees through the truth of the Scriptures and the power of His presence. You'll then be able to encourage others.

LINDA WASHINGTON

What are some of the ways you've been encouraged recently? How will you encourage someone who's facing hard times?

Father, I need Your strength and Your grace today.

Cast but a glance at riches,
and they are gone. [PROVERBS 23:5]

GOING, GOING, GONE

The mischievous artist Banksy pulled off another practical joke. His painting *Girl with Balloon* sold for one million pounds at Sotheby's auction house in London. Moments after the auctioneer yelled "Sold," an alarm sounded and the painting slipped halfway through a shredder mounted inside the bottom of the frame. Banksy tweeted a picture of bidders gasping at his ruined masterpiece, with the caption, "Going, going, gone."

Banksy relished pulling one over on the wealthy, but he need not have bothered. Wealth itself has plenty of pranks up its sleeve. God says, "Do not wear yourself out to get rich . . . . Cast but a glance at riches, and they are gone, for they will surely sprout wings and fly off to the sky like an eagle" (VV. 4–5).

Few things are less secure than money. We work hard to earn it, yet there are many ways to lose it. Investments go sour, inflation erodes, bills come, thieves steal, and fire and flood destroy. Even if we manage to keep our money, the time we have to spend it continually flies. Blink, and your life is going, going, gone.

What to do? God tells us a few verses later: "always be zealous for the fear of the LORD. There is surely a future hope for you, and your hope will not be cut off" (VV. 17–18). Invest your life in Jesus; He alone will keep you forever.　　*MIKE WITTMER*

**Where does your life feel insecure?
How might that lead you to Jesus?**

*God, help me to give my insecurities to You and to trust in
Your goodness and faithfulness.*

THE WAY OF LOVE

I n one of my favorite scenes in Jerry Bock's *Fiddler on the Roof,* the main character, Teyve, impulsively asks his wife Golde (whom he'd married in an arranged marriage) if she loves him. "Do I *what?*" she responds, flustered. So begins an exchange that leads to Golde conceding that if twenty-five years of working and struggling together and raising children together isn't love, she doesn't know what is! The scene closes as the two together soak in the wonder of knowing they were loved.

I treasure that scene because it both reflects the joy of being loved *and* a commitment to living out the kind of love that is *forged* through discipline and commitment. That's a perspective on love that's much bigger than romance; it's the kind of active, self-giving love that, in the New Testament, believers are invited, over and over, to live out. It's worth emphasizing that 1 Corinthians 13's breathtaking vision of love, so often

> *It's a way of life that believers in Jesus can choose each day.*

read at weddings, is addressed to a *community,* calling them to cultivate this kind of love—not just with one special person, but with the entire fellowship of believers with whom they share life.

The kind of lifestyle that 1 Corinthians 13 describes—a life of love that's "not self-seeking" (V. 5) but "always protects, always trusts, always hopes, [and] always perseveres" (V. 7)— doesn't come naturally to any of us. Instead, it's a way of life that believers in Jesus can choose each day as the Holy Spirit empowers us to let go of the envy and anger and self-seeking that would naturally drive us (EPHESIANS 4:31) in exchange for the grace and freedom of the "way of love" (5:2) that our Savior made possible.

MONICA LA ROSE, OUR DAILY BREAD *AUTHOR*

If you love those who love you,
what reward will you get? [MATTHEW 5:46]

★ *FEBRUARY TOPIC: DEVELOPING A LOVING CHARACTER*

GOD-SIZED LOVE

I once visited an impoverished neighborhood of Santo Domingo in the Dominican Republic. Homes were made of corrugated iron, with electrical wires dangling live above them. There I had the privilege of interviewing families and hearing how churches were helping to combat unemployment, drug use, and crime.

In one alleyway I climbed a rickety ladder to a small room to interview a mother and her son. But just a moment later someone rushed up, saying, "We must leave *now*." A machete-wielding gang leader was apparently gathering a mob to ambush us.

We visited a second neighborhood, but there we had no problem. Later I discovered why. As I visited each home, a gang leader stood outside guarding us. It turned out his daughter was being fed and educated by the church, and because believers were standing by her, he stood by us.

In the Sermon on the Mount, Jesus presents a standard of love that's beyond comparison. This kind of love embraces not just the "worthy" but the undeserving (MATTHEW 5:43–45), reaching beyond family and friends to touch those who can't or won't love us back (VV. 46–47). This is God-sized love (V. 48)—the kind that blesses everyone.

As believers in Santo Domingo live out this love, neighborhoods are starting to change. Tough hearts are warming to their cause. That's what happens when God-sized love comes to town.

SHERIDAN VOYSEY

How would you describe the difference between human love and godly love? Who can you bless today who can't repay you?

Jesus, pour Your love into me so I may pour it out to others—even to those who can't repay the favor.

A crown of beauty instead of ashes,
the oil of joy instead of mourning. [ISAIAH 61:3]

A TIME FOR BEAUTY

One January morning I woke expecting to see the same dreary midwinter landscape that had greeted me for several weeks: beige grass poking through patches of snow, gray skies, and skeletal trees. Something unusual had happened overnight, though. A frost had coated everything with ice crystals. The lifeless and depressing landscape had become a beautiful scene that glistened in the sun and dazzled me.

Sometimes we view problems without the imagination it takes to have faith. We expect pain, fear, and despair to greet us every morning, but overlook the possibility of something different ever happening. We don't expect recovery, growth, or victory through God's power. Yet the Bible says God is the one who helps us through difficult times. He repairs broken hearts and liberates people in bondage. He comforts the grieving with "a crown of beauty instead of ashes, the oil of joy instead of mourning, and a garment of praise instead of a spirit of despair" (ISAIAH 61:3).

It isn't that God just wants to cheer us up when we have problems. It's that He Himself is our hope during trials. Even if we have to wait for heaven to find ultimate relief, God is present with us, encouraging us and often giving us glimpses of Himself. In our journey through life, may we come to understand St. Augustine's words: "In my deepest wound I saw your glory, and it dazzled me."

JENNIFER BENSON SCHULDT

**How can you turn to God when you're in trouble?
What rewards can come from this practice?**

*Faithful God, give me the faith I need to make it through today
and help me to see You at work as I face adversity.*

BIBLE IN A YEAR | EXODUS 29-30; MATTHEW 21:23-46

He will baptize you with the Holy Spirit
and fire. [LUKE 3:16]

A FIRE CALLED HOLY

After several years of drought, the wildfires of Southern California left some residents thinking of them as acts of God. This disturbing impression was reinforced when news sources began referring to one as the Holy Fire. Many unfamiliar with the area didn't realize it was a reference to the Holy Jim Canyon region. But who was Holy Jim? According to local history, he was a nineteenth-century beekeeper so irreligious and cantankerous that neighbors tagged him with that ironic nickname.

John the Baptist's reference to a baptism of "the Holy Spirit and fire" also came with its own story and explanation (LUKE 3:16). Looking back, he was likely thinking of the kind of Messiah and refining fire foreseen by the prophet Malachi (3:1–3; 4:1). But only after the Spirit of God came like wind and fire on the followers of Jesus did the words of Malachi and John come into focus (ACTS 2:1–4).

The fire John predicted wasn't what was expected. As a true act of God, it came with boldness to proclaim a different kind of Messiah and holy flame. In the Spirit of Jesus, it exposed and consumed our futile human efforts—while making room for the love, joy, peace, patience, goodness, kindness, faithfulness, gentleness, and self-control of the Holy Spirit (SEE GALATIANS 5:22–23). Those are the acts of God that He would like to work in us.   *MART DEHAAN*

How has your life been affected by the work of the Holy Spirit? What does it mean for you to pursue a holy—set apart—life before God?

Father in heaven, please replace our fear of Your Holy Spirit with a love, joy, and peace that is as priceless as our stubborn ways are worthless.

Rejoice always, pray continually, give thanks in all circumstances. [1 THESSALONIANS 5:16–18]

FULL ATTENTION

Technology today seems to demand our constant attention. The modern "miracle" of the internet gives us the amazing capacity to access humanity's collective learning in the palm of our hand. But for many, such constant access can come at a cost.

Writer Linda Stone has coined the phrase "continual partial attention" to describe the modern impulse to always need to know what's happening "out there," to make sure we're not missing anything. If that sounds like it could produce chronic anxiety, you're right!

Although the apostle Paul struggled with different reasons for anxiety, he knew our souls are wired to find peace in God. Which is why, in a letter to new believers who'd endured persecution (1 THESSALONIANS 2:14), Paul concluded by urging the believers to "rejoice always, pray continually, give thanks in all circumstances" (5:16–18).

Praying "continually" might seem pretty daunting. But then, how often do we check our phones? What if we instead let that urge be a prompt to talk to God?

More important, what if we learned to exchange a need to always be in "the know" for continual, prayerful rest in God's presence? Through relying on Christ's Spirit, we can learn to give our heavenly Father our continual *full* attention as we make our way through each day.   ADAM R. HOLZ

How would you say technology impacts your faith, both negatively and positively? What might help you grow in undivided focus on God?

Father, thank You for inviting us into a relationship with You, one in which You long to hear from us continually.

The Spirit teaches you everything you need to
know, and what he teaches is true—it is not a lie.
[1 JOHN 2:27 NLT]

HOW TO STAY ON TRACK

As the world's fastest blind runner, David Brown of the U.S. Paralympic Team credits his wins to God, his mother's early advice ("no sitting around"), and his running guide—veteran sprinter Jerome Avery. Tethered to Brown by a string tied to their fingers, Avery guides Brown's winning races with words and touches.

"It's all about listening to *his* cues," says Brown, who says he could "swing out wide" on 200-meter races where the track curves. "Day in and day out, we're going over race strategies," Brown says, "communicating with each other—not only verbal cues, but physical cues."

In our own life's race, we're blessed with a Divine Guide. Our Helper, the Holy Spirit, leads our steps when we follow Him. "I am writing these things to you about those who are trying to lead you astray," wrote John (1 JOHN 2:26). "But you have received the Holy Spirit, and he lives within you, so you don't need anyone to teach you what is true. For the Spirit teaches you everything you need to know" (V. 27 NLT).

John stressed this wisdom to the believers of his day who faced "antichrists" who denied the Father and that Jesus is the Messiah (V. 22). We face such deniers today as well. But the Holy Spirit, our Guide, leads us in following Jesus. We can trust His guidance to touch us with truth, keeping us on track.   *PATRICIA RAYBON*

**How attuned are you to the Holy Spirit's guidance? How can you
listen better when He guides, warns, and directs?**

*Dear God, attune our hearts to Your Holy Spirit's guidance so we'll
run to Your truth and not to lies.*

My heart is poured out on the ground
...because children and infants faint
in the streets of the city. [LAMENTATIONS 2:11]

MERCY'S LAMENT

Her father blamed his illness on witchcraft. It was AIDS. When he died, his daughter, ten-year-old Mercy, grew even closer to her mother. But her mother was sick too, and three years later she died. From then on, Mercy's sister raised the five siblings. That's when Mercy began to keep a journal of her deep pain.

The prophet Jeremiah kept a record of his pain too. In the grim book of Lamentations, he wrote of atrocities done to Judah by the Babylonian army. Jeremiah's heart was especially grieved for the youngest victims. "My heart is poured out on the ground," he cried, "because my people are destroyed, because children and infants faint in the streets of the city" (2:11). The people of Judah had a history of ignoring God, but their children were paying the price too. "Their lives ebb away in their mothers' arms," wrote Jeremiah (V. 12).

We might have expected Jeremiah to reject God in the face of such suffering. Instead, he urged the survivors, "Pour out your heart like water in the presence of the LORD. Lift up your hands to him for the *lives of your children*" (V. 19).

It's good, as Mercy and Jeremiah did, to pour out our hearts to God. Lament is a crucial part of being human. Even when God permits such pain, He grieves with us. Made as we are in His image, He must lament too!   *TIM GUSTAFSON*

How do you handle the painful situations in your life? How might it help you to write it down and share your journal with a friend?

Dear God, I'm hurting because of _____.
You see my grief. Please show Your strength in my life today.

Father, if you are willing, take this cup from me;
yet not my will, but yours be done. [LUKE 22:42]

PRAYING LIKE JESUS

Every coin has two sides. The front is called "heads" and, from early Roman times, usually depicts a country's head of state. The back is called "tails," a term possibly originating from the British ten pence depicting the raised tail of a heraldic lion.

Like a coin, Christ's prayer in the garden of Gethsemane possesses two sides. In the deepest hours of His life, on the night before He died on a cross, Jesus prayed, "Father, if you are willing, take this cup from me; yet not my will, but yours be done" (LUKE 22:42). When Christ says, "take this cup," that's the raw honesty of prayer. He reveals His personal desire, "This is what *I* want."

Then Jesus turns the coin, praying "not my will." That's the side of abandon. Abandoning ourselves to God begins when we simply say, "But what do *You* want, God?"

This two-sided prayer is also included in Matthew 26 and Mark 14 and is mentioned in John 18. Jesus prayed both sides of prayer: take this cup (what I want, God), yet not My will (what do You want, God?), pivoting between them.

Two sides of Jesus. Two sides of prayer.　　　　*ELISA MORGAN*

What might we learn if we prayed honestly and with complete abandon, as Jesus did? What situation are you facing right now where you can pray honestly yet with abandon to God?

Father, help me follow the example of Your Son, who spent everything so that I might possess real life that includes experiencing intimate prayer with You.

This happened that we might not rely on ourselves
but on God, who raises the dead. [2 CORINTHIANS 1:9]

★ *FEBRUARY TOPIC: DEVELOPING A LOVING CHARACTER*
LOVING OTHERS WITH OUR PRAYERS

"Are people still praying for me?"
That was one of the first questions a missionary asked
his wife whenever she was allowed to visit him in prison. He
had been falsely accused and incarcerated for his faith for two years.
His life was frequently in danger because of the conditions and hostility in the prison, and believers around the world were earnestly
praying for him. He wanted to be assured they wouldn't stop,
because he believed God was using their prayers in a powerful way.

Our prayers for others—especially those who are persecuted
for their faith—are a vital gift. Paul made this clear when he wrote
the believers in Corinth about hardships he faced during his missionary journey. He "was under great pressure," so much that he
"despaired of life itself" (2 CORINTHIANS 1:8). But then he told them
God had delivered him and described the tool He'd used to do it:
"We have set our hope that he will continue to deliver us, as you
help us by your *prayers*" (VV. 10–11, EMPHASIS ADDED).

God moves through our prayers to accomplish great good in the
lives of His people. One of the best ways to love others is to pray for
them, because through our prayers we open the door to the help
only God can provide. When we pray for others, we love them in
His strength. There's none greater or more loving than He.

JAMES BANKS

**How do you love others with your prayers? In what ways can you
encourage prayer for those who are persecuted for their faith?**

*Loving and Almighty God, thank You for the amazing gift of prayer
and the ways You move through it. Please help me to pray faithfully
for others today!*

He remembers that we are dust.
[PSALM 103:14]

WE ARE DUST

The young father was at the end of his rope. "Ice cream! Ice cream!" his toddler screamed. The meltdown in the middle of the crowded mall began drawing the attention of shoppers nearby. "Fine, but we just need to do something for mommy first, okay?" the father said. "Nooooo! Ice cream!" And then she approached them: a small, well-dressed woman with shoes that matched her handbag. "He's having a big fit," the father said. The woman smiled and responded, "Actually, it looks like a big fit is having your little boy. Don't forget he's so small. He needs you to be patient and stay close." The situation didn't magically resolve itself, but it was just the kind of pause the father and son needed in the moment.

Echoes of the wise woman's words are heard in Psalm 103. David writes of our God who is "compassionate and gracious, slow to anger, abounding in love" (V. 8). He then continues by invoking the image of an earthly father who "has compassion on his children," and even more so "the LORD has compassion on those who fear him" (V. 13). God our Father "knows how we are formed, he remembers that we are dust" (V. 14). He knows we're small and fragile.

We often fail and are overwhelmed by what this big world hands us. What an amazing assurance to know of our Father's patient, ever-present, abounding love.   *JOHN BLASE*

**When have you felt overwhelmed like a little child?
How do you believe God the Father responded to you in that moment?**

Thank You for being our patient, present Father who remembers who and what we are.

I have loved you with an everlasting love.
[JEREMIAH 31:3]

RUNNING INTO LOVE

Nora was tiny, but "Bridget"—the belligerent, six-foot-tall woman glowering down at her—didn't intimidate her. Bridget couldn't even say why she had stopped at the crisis pregnancy center; she'd already made up her mind to "get rid of this . . . kid." So Nora gently asked questions, and Bridget rudely deflected them with profanity-laced tirades. Soon Bridget got up to leave, defiantly declaring her intent to end her pregnancy.

Slipping her small frame between Bridget and the door, Nora asked, "Before you go, may I give you a hug, and may I pray for you?" No one had ever hugged her before—not with healthy intentions, anyway. Suddenly, unexpectedly, the tears came.

Nora beautifully reflects the heart of our God who loved His people Israel "with an everlasting love" (JEREMIAH 31:3). The people had stumbled into the hard consequences of their persistent violation of His guidelines. Yet God told them, "I have drawn you with unfailing kindness. I will build you up again" (VV. 3–4).

Bridget's history is complex. (Many of us can relate.) Until she ran into real love that day, her belief had been that God and His followers would only condemn her. Nora showed her something different: the God who won't ignore our sin because He loves us beyond imagination. He welcomes us with open arms. We don't have to keep running. *TIM GUSTAFSON*

What's your perception of God? How does it line up with the God you read about in today's Scripture reading?

Father, I so often take Your incredible love for granted. Forgive me, and help me to reflect that love to someone today.

Better a neighbor nearby than
a relative far away. [PROVERBS 27:10]

NEARBY NEIGHBORS

Our neighborhood, like many others, uses a website to help neighbors connect immediately with those surrounding them. In my community, members warn one another of mountain lion sightings and wildfire evacuation orders, as well as supply one another with child care when the need arises. It has even proven to be a resource for locating runaway pets. By leveraging the power of the internet, those living near one another are connecting again in ways that are often lost in today's fast-paced world.

Being in relationship with those who live nearby was also important long ago in the days of King Solomon. While family relationships are truly important and can be a source of great support, Solomon indicates that the role of a *friend* is vital—especially when "disaster strikes" (PROVERBS 27:10). Relatives might care deeply for their family members and desire to be of help in such circumstances. But if they're far away, there's little they can do in the moments when calamity strikes. Neighbors, however, because they're close by, are likely to know of the need quickly and can assist more readily.

Because technology has made it easier than ever to remain connected with loved ones across the globe, we may be tempted to overlook those living nearby. *Jesus, help us invest in relationships with the people You've placed around us!*　　KIRSTEN HOLMBERG

**Who has brought you aid in your times of need?
How can you come alongside those living nearest you?**

*Thank You, God, for giving us neighbors to show care
for one another.*

Though your sins are like scarlet,
they shall be as white as snow. [ISAIAH 1:18]

THE MIRACLE OF WHITE SNOW

I n the seventeenth century, Sir Isaac Newton used a prism to study how light helps us see different colors. He found that when light passes through an object, the object appears to possess a specific color. While a single ice crystal looks translucent, snow is made up of many ice crystals smashed together. When light passes through all of the crystals, snow appears to be white.

The Bible mentions something else that has a certain color—sin. Through the prophet Isaiah, God confronted the sins of the people of Judah and described their sin as "like scarlet" and as "red as crimson." But God promised they would "be as white as snow" (ISAIAH 1:18). How? Judah needed to turn away from wrongdoing and seek God's forgiveness.

Thanks to Jesus, we have permanent access to God's forgiveness. Jesus called Himself "the light of the world" and said whoever follows Him "will never walk in darkness, but will have the light of life" (JOHN 8:12). When we confess our sins, God forgives us and we're seen through the light of Christ's sacrifice on the cross. This means that God sees us as He sees Jesus—blameless.

We don't have to wallow in the guilt and shame of what we've done wrong. Instead, we can hold on to the truth of God's forgiveness, which makes us "white as snow."　　　　　*LINDA WASHINGTON*

What does it mean to be completely forgiven?
What helps you remember that God has forgiven you?

Heavenly Father, thank You for the forgiveness You freely offer.

[God] brought me out into a spacious place.
[PSALM 18:19]

FREED FROM OUR CAGE

While out taking walks, writer Martin Laird would often encounter a man with four Kerry Blue Terriers. Three of the dogs ran wild through the open fields, but one stayed near its owner, running in tight circles. When Laird finally stopped and asked about this odd behavior, the owner explained that it was a rescue dog that had spent most of his life locked in a cage. The terrier continued to run in circles as though contained inside a confined box.

The Scriptures reveal that we're trapped and hopeless unless God rescues us. The psalmist spoke of being afflicted by an enemy, entrapped by "the snares of death" with the "cords of death . . . coiled around" him (PSALM 18:4–5). Enclosed and shackled, he cried to God for help (V. 6). And with thundering power, He "reached down . . . and took hold" of him (V. 16).

God can do the same for us. He can break the chains and release us from our confining cages. He can set us free and carry us "out into a spacious place" (V. 19). How sad it is, then, when we keep running in small circles, as if we're still confined in our old prisons. In His strength, may we no longer be bound by fear, shame, or oppression. God has rescued us from those cages of death. We can run free.   *WINN COLLIER*

What are the cages that have you confined?
How are you living as though an old cage still traps and holds you?

God, You say You set the captives free. Help me to believe it.
Help me to live it. I want to be free. I want to be in Your
spacious place.

I say to the LORD, "You are my Lord;
apart from you I have no good thing." [PSALM 16:2]

WHEN LIFE IS HARD

Physically, mentally, and emotionally exhausted, I curled up in my recliner. Our family had followed God's leading and had moved from California to Wisconsin. After we arrived, our car broke down and left us without a vehicle for two months. Meanwhile, my husband's limited mobility after an unexpected back surgery and my chronic pain complicated our unpacking. We uncovered costly problems with our new-to-us, old home. Our senior dog suffered with health issues. And though our new pup brought great joy, raising a furry ball of energy was far more work than anticipated. My attitude soured. How was I supposed to have unshakeable faith while traveling on a bumpy road of hardships?

As I prayed, God reminded me of the psalmist whose praise didn't depend on circumstances. David poured out his emotions, often with great vulnerability, and sought refuge in the presence of God (PSALM 16:1). Acknowledging God as provider and protector (VV. 5–6), he praised Him and followed His counsel (V. 7). David affirmed that he would "not be shaken" because he kept his eyes "always on the LORD" (V. 8). So, he rejoiced and rested secure in the joy of God's presence (VV. 9–11).

We too can delight in knowing our peace doesn't depend on our present situation. As we thank our unchanging God for who He is and always will be, His presence will fuel our steadfast faith.

XOCHITL DIXON

How can offering God praise for His unchanging character and wondrous works increase your faith during challenging circumstances? What situations do you need to place in God's trustworthy hands?

Thanks for being You, Father!

He put his hands on her, and immediately she straightened up and praised God. [LUKE 13:13]

★ *FEBRUARY TOPIC: DEVELOPING A LOVING CHARACTER*

TOUCH THE NEEDY

I t wasn't surprising when Mother Teresa received the Nobel Peace Prize. True to form, she received the award "in the name of the hungry, of the naked, of the homeless, of the blind, of the lepers, of all those who feel unwanted, unloved, uncared for throughout society." Those were the people she ministered to for most of her life.

Jesus modeled how to care for and love the marginalized, regardless of circumstances. Unlike the synagogue leaders who respected the Sabbath law more than the sick (LUKE 13:14), when Jesus saw an ill woman at the temple, He was moved with compassion. He looked beyond the physical impairment and saw God's beautiful creation in bondage. He called her to Him and said she was healed. Then He "put his hands on her, and immediately she straightened up and praised God" (V. 13). By touching her, He upset the leader of the synagogue because it was the Sabbath. Jesus, the Lord of the Sabbath (LUKE 6:5), compassionately chose to heal the woman—a person who had faced discomfort and humiliation for nearly two decades.

I wonder how often we see someone as underserving of our compassion. Or maybe we've experienced rejection because we didn't meet somebody else's standard. May we not be like the religious elite who cared more about rules than fellow humans. Instead, let's follow Jesus' example and treat others with compassion, love, and dignity.　　　　*ESTERA PIROSCA ESCOBAR*

How have you experienced God's healing and touch? Who can you show compassion to this week?

Jesus, thank You for Your infinite love and incredible compassion for all humans, including those marred by disease and difficulties.

Be completely humble and gentle; be patient,
bearing with one another in love. [EPHESIANS 4:2]

DIVIDED IN LOVE

When public debate erupted over a controversial Singapore law, it divided believers with differing views. Some called others "narrow-minded" or accused them of compromising their faith.

Controversies can cause sharp divisions among God's family, bringing much hurt and discouraging people. I've been made to feel small over personal convictions on how I apply the Bible's teachings to my life. And I'm sure I've been equally guilty of criticizing others I disagree with.

I wonder if the problem lies not in what or even in how we express our views, but in the attitudes of our hearts when we do so. Are we just disagreeing with views or seeking to tear down the people behind them?

Yet there are times when we need to address false teaching or explain our stand. Ephesians 4:2–6 reminds us to do so with humility, gentleness, patience, and love. And, above all else, to make every effort "to keep the unity of the Spirit" (V. 3).

Some controversies will remain unresolved. God's Word, however, reminds us that our goal should always be to build up people's faith, not tear them down (V. 29). Are we putting others down to win an argument? Or are we allowing God to help us understand His truths in His time and His way, remembering that we share one faith in one Lord? (VV. 4–6).   *LESLIE KOH*

How can you explain your stand on sensitive issues humbly, gently, and lovingly? What will you pray for those who seem to disagree?

God, guide me as I speak the truth so that I do so out of love and seek only to build up, not to tear down.

Surely I am with you always,
to the very end of the age. [MATTHEW 28:20]

EVER-PRESENT PRESENCE

During the 2018 World Cup, Colombian forward Radamel Falcao scored in the seventieth minute against Poland, securing a victory. The dramatic goal was Falcao's thirtieth in international play, earning him the distinction of scoring the most goals by a Colombian player in international competition.

Falcao has often used his success on the soccer pitch to share his faith, frequently lifting his jersey after a score to reveal a shirt with the words, *Con Jesus nunca estara solo*: "With Jesus you'll never be alone."

Falcao's statement points us to the reassuring promise from Jesus, "I am with you always, to the very end of the age" (MATTHEW 28:20). Knowing He was about to return to heaven, Jesus comforted His disciples by assuring them He'd always be with them, through the presence of His Spirit (V. 20; JOHN 14:16–18). Christ's Spirit would comfort, guide, protect, and empower them as they took the message of Jesus to cities both near and far. And when they experienced periods of intense loneliness in unfamiliar places, Christ's words would likely echo in their ears, a reminder of His presence with them.

No matter where we go, whether close to home or faraway, as we follow Jesus into the unknown we too can cling to this same promise. Even when we experience feelings of loneliness, as we reach out in prayer to Jesus, we can receive comfort knowing He's with us.   *LISA M. SAMRA*

How does the assurance that Jesus is always with you provide comfort? How has He comforted you when you felt alone?

Jesus, thank You that I'm never alone because You're with me.

Though I walk through the darkest valley,
I will fear no evil, for you are with me. [PSALM 23:4]

UNIMAGINABLE

Bart Millard penned a megahit in 2001 when he wrote, "I Can Only Imagine." The song pictures how amazing it will be to be in Christ's presence. Millard's lyrics offered comfort to our family that next year when our seventeen-year-old daughter, Melissa, died in a car accident and we imagined what it was like for her to be in God's presence.

But *imagine* spoke to me in a different way in the days following Mell's death. As fathers of Melissa's friends approached me, full of concern and pain, they said, "I can't imagine what you're going through."

Their expressions were helpful, showing that they were grappling with our loss in an empathetic way—finding it *unimaginable*.

David pinpointed the depth of great loss when he described walking through "the darkest valley" (PSALM 23:4). The death of a loved one certainly is that, and we sometimes have no idea how we're going to navigate the darkness. We can't imagine ever being able to come out on the other side.

But as God promised to be with us in our darkest valley now, He also provides great hope for the future by assuring us that beyond the valley we'll be in His presence. For the believer, to be "away from the body" means being present with Him (2 CORINTHIANS 5:8). That can help us navigate the unimaginable as we imagine our future reunion with Him and others.   *DAVE BRANON*

What's the best thing you can say to friends who've suffered the loss of someone they loved? How can you prepare for those times?

Thank You, God, for being with us even in the darkest valley as we imagine the glories of heaven.

The LORD opened the servant's eyes,
and he [saw] chariots of fire all around Elisha.
[2 KINGS 6:17]

THE REALITY OF GOD

I n C. S. Lewis's *The Chronicles of Narnia: The Lion, the Witch and the Wardrobe,* all of Narnia is thrilled when the mighty lion Aslan reappears after a long absence. Their joy turns to sorrow, however, when Aslan concedes to a demand made by the evil White Witch. Faced with Aslan's apparent defeat, the Narnians experience his power when he emits an earsplitting roar that causes the witch to flee in terror. Although all seems to have been lost, Aslan ultimately proves to be greater than the villainous witch.

Like Aslan's followers in Lewis's allegory, Elisha's servant despaired when he got up one morning to see himself and Elisha surrounded by an enemy army. "Oh no, my lord! What shall we do?" he exclaimed (2 KINGS 6:15). The prophet's response was calm: "Don't be afraid . . . . Those who are with us are more than those who are with them" (V. 16). Elisha then prayed, "Open his eyes, LORD, so that he may see" (V. 17). So, "the LORD opened the servant's eyes, and he looked and saw the hills full of horses and chariots of fire all around Elisha" (V. 17). Although things at first seemed bleak to the servant's eye, God's power ultimately proved greater than the enemy horde.

Our difficult circumstances may lead us to believe all is lost, but God desires to open our eyes and reveal that He is greater.

REMI OYEDELE

What difficult times are you facing? How have you experienced that God is greater than any evil you face?

Thank You, God, for Your faithfulness.

Joseph stored up huge quantities of grain,
like the sand of the sea. [GENESIS 41:49]

THE HARDEST PLACES

Geoff is a youth pastor today in the same city where he once abused heroin. God transformed both his heart and his circumstances in a breathtaking way. "I want to keep kids from making the same mistakes and suffering the pain I went through," Geoff said. "And Jesus will help them." Over time, God set him free from the slavery of addiction and has given him a vital ministry in spite of his past.

God has ways of bringing unexpected good out of situations where hope seems lost. Joseph was sold into slavery in Egypt and falsely accused and sent to prison, where he was forgotten for years. But God restored him and placed him in a position of authority directly under Pharaoh, where he was able to save many lives—including the lives of his brothers who'd abandoned him. There in Egypt Joseph married and had children. He named the second Ephraim (drawn from the Hebrew term for "twice fruitful"), and gave this reason: "It is because God has made me fruitful in the land of my suffering" (GENESIS 41:52).

Geoff's and Joseph's stories, while separated by three to four thousand years, point to the same unchanging truth: even the hardest places in our lives can become fertile ground for God to help and bless many. Our Savior's love and power never change, and He's always faithful to those who trust in Him.   *JAMES BANKS*

When have you seen God bring something good out of difficulty in your life? How can you use your past problems to encourage others today?

All-powerful Father, I praise You that nothing is too hard for You! Thank You for Your perfect faithfulness, today and forever.

So that Christ may dwell in your hearts
through faith. [EPHESIANS 3:17]

A PLACE OF BELONGING

Some years after the tragic loss of their first spouses, Robbie and Sabrina fell in love, married, and combined their two families. They built a new home and named it Havilah (a Hebrew word meaning "writhing in pain" and "to bring forth"). It signifies the making of something beautiful through pain. The couple says they didn't build the home to forget their past but "to bring life from the ashes, to celebrate hope." For them, "it is a place of belonging, a place to celebrate life and where we all cling to the promise of a future."

That's a beautiful picture of our life in Jesus. He pulls our lives from the ashes and becomes for us a place of belonging. When we receive Him, He makes His home in our hearts (EPHESIANS 3:17). God adopts us into His family through Jesus so that we belong to Him (1:5–6). Although we'll go through painful times, He can use even those to bring good purposes in our lives.

Daily we have opportunity to grow in our understanding of God as we enjoy His love and celebrate what He's given us. In Him, there's a fullness to life that we couldn't have without Him (3:19). And we have the promise that this relationship will last forever. Jesus is our place of belonging, our reason to celebrate life, and our hope now and forever.   *ANNE CETAS*

In what ways has Jesus changed your life?
What does it mean for you to belong to Jesus?

I'm grateful that I belong to You, Jesus.
Thank You for a life of hope for now and forever.

Father, forgive them, for they do not know
what they are doing. [LUKE 23:34]

★ *FEBRUARY TOPIC: DEVELOPING A LOVING CHARACTER*

STRONGER THAN HATE

Within twenty-four hours of his mother Sharonda's tragic death, Chris found himself uttering these powerful, grace-filled words: "Love is stronger than hate." His mother, along with eight others, had been killed at a Wednesday night Bible study in Charleston, South Carolina. What was it that had so shaped this teenager's life that these words could flow from his lips and his heart? Chris is a believer in Jesus whose mother had "loved everybody with all her heart."

In Luke 23:26–49 we get a front row seat to an execution scene that included two criminals and the innocent Jesus (V. 32). All three were crucified (V. 33). Amid the gasps and sighs and the likely groans from those hanging on the crosses, the following words of Jesus could be heard: "Father, forgive them, for they do not know what they are doing" (V. 34). The hate-filled initiative of the religious leaders had resulted in the crucifixion of the very One who championed love. Though in agony, Jesus' love continued to triumph.

How have you or someone you love been the target of hate, ill-will, bitterness, or ugliness? May your pain prompt your prayers, and may the example of Jesus and people like Chris encourage you by the power of the Spirit to choose love over hate.   *ARTHUR JACKSON*

When have you found it hard to love someone? Is there someone you find it hard to forgive now? What steps might you take?

Father, forgive me when I find it hard to forgive others. Help me to demonstrate that love is stronger than hate.

But he was pierced for our transgressions,
he was crushed for our iniquities. [ISAIAH 53:5]

PIERCED LOVE

She'd called. She'd texted. Now Carla stood outside her brother's gated entry, unable to rouse him to answer. Burdened with depression and fighting addiction, her brother had hidden himself away in his home. In a desperate attempt to penetrate his isolation, Carla gathered several of his favorite foods along with encouraging Scriptures and lowered the bundle over the fence.

But as the package left her grip, it snagged on one of the gate spikes, tearing an opening and sending its contents onto the gravel below. Her well-intended, love-filled offering spilled out in seeming waste. Would her brother even notice her gift? Would it accomplish the mission of hope she'd intended? She can only hope and pray as she waits for his healing.

God so loved the world that—in essence—He lowered His one and only Son over the wall of our sin, bringing gifts of love and healing into our weary and withdrawn world (JOHN 3:16). The prophet Isaiah predicted the cost of this act of love in Isaiah 53:5. This very Son would be "pierced for our transgressions, . . . crushed for our iniquities." His wounds would bring the hope of ultimate healing. He took on Himself "the iniquity of us all" (V. 6).

Pierced by spikes for our sin and need, God's gift of Jesus enters our days today with fresh power and perspective. What does His gift mean to you?   *ELISA MORGAN*

**How have you experienced God's pierced love?
How have you seen Him transform a broken life by His
amazing grace?**

*Dear God, thank You for Your gift of Jesus, sent over the fences in my
heart to meet my need today.*

[He] began to tell . . . how much
Jesus had done for him. [MARK 5:20]

LIBERATED BY JESUS

66 **I** lived with my mother so long that she moved out!" Those
were the words of KC, whose life before sobriety and surrender to Jesus was not pretty. He candidly admits supporting his drug habit by stealing—even from loved ones. That life is
behind him now and he rehearses this by noting the years,
months, and days he's been clean. When KC and I regularly sit
down to study God's Word together, I'm looking at a changed man.

Mark 5:15 speaks of a former demon-possessed individual
who had also been changed. Prior to his healing, *helpless, hopeless, homeless,* and *desperate* are words that fit the man (VV. 3–5).
But all of that changed after Jesus liberated him (V. 13). But, as
with KC, his life before Jesus was far from normal. His internal
turmoil that he expressed externally is not unlike what people
experience today. Some hurting people dwell in abandoned
buildings, vehicles, or other places; some live in their own homes
but are emotionally alone. Invisible chains shackle hearts and
minds to the point that they distance themselves from others.

In Jesus, we have the One who can be trusted with our pain
and the shame of the past and present. And, as with Legion and
KC, He waits with open arms of mercy for all who run to Him
today (V. 19).   *ARTHUR JACKSON*

How has Jesus changed you?
Who do you know that needs to hear it?

*God, I'm so grateful that, through Jesus, things that controlled me
in the past can indeed remain in the past.*

Godliness with contentment
is great gain. [1 TIMOTHY 6:6]

RICH TOWARD GOD

Growing up during the Great Depression, my parents knew deep hardship as children. As a result, they were hard-working and grateful money stewards. But they were never greedy. They gave time, talent, and treasury to their church, charity groups, and the needy. Indeed, they handled their money wisely and gave cheerfully.

As believers in Jesus, my parents took to heart the apostle Paul's warning: "Those who want to get rich fall into temptation and a trap and into many foolish and harmful desires that plunge people into ruin and destruction" (1 TIMOTHY 6:9).

Paul gave this advice to Timothy, the young pastor of the city of Ephesus, a wealthy city where riches tempted all.

"The love of money is a root of all kinds of evil," Paul warned. "Some people, eager for money, have wandered from the faith and pierced themselves with many griefs" (V. 10).

What, then, is the antidote to greed? Being "rich toward God," said Jesus (SEE LUKE 12:13–21). By pursuing, appreciating, and loving our heavenly Father above all, He remains our chief delight. As the psalmist wrote, "Satisfy us in the morning with your unfailing love, that we may sing for joy and be glad all our days" (PSALM 90:14).

Rejoicing in Him daily relieves us of coveting, leaving us contented. May Jesus redeem our heart's desires, making us rich toward God!   *PATRICIA RAYBON*

How have you mishandled money, or made it more than it ought to be? How might you give your financial concerns to God this day?

Satisfy us in the morning, God, with Your unfailing love—replacing our greed with holy hunger for You.

Rejoice in the Lord always.
I will say it again: Rejoice! [PHILIPPIANS 4:4]

THOUGHTS OF JOY

I n *What We Keep,* a collection of interviews by Bill Shapiro, each person tells of a single item that holds such importance and joy that he or she would never part with it.

This caused me to reflect on the possessions that mean the most to me and bring me joy. One is a simple forty-year-old recipe card in my mom's handwriting. Another is one of my grandma's pink teacups. Other people may value treasured memories—a compliment that encouraged them, a grandchild's giggle, or a special insight they gleaned from Scripture.

What we often keep stashed away in our hearts, though, are things that have brought us great unhappiness: Anxiety—hidden, but easily retrieved. Anger—below the surface, but ready to strike. Resentment—silently corroding the core of our thoughts.

The apostle Paul addressed a more positive way to "think" in a letter to the church at Philippi. He encouraged the people of the church to always rejoice, to be gentle, and to bring everything to God in prayer (PHILIPPIANS 4:4–9).

Paul's uplifting words on what to think about helps us see that it's possible to push out dark thoughts and allow the peace of God to guard our hearts and minds in Christ Jesus (V. 7). It's when the thoughts that fill up our minds are true, noble, right, pure, lovely, admirable, and praiseworthy that we keep His peace in our hearts (V. 8).　　　　　　　　*CINDY HESS KASPER*

What unwelcome thoughts have stubbornly taken residence in my mind and heart? What's one way I can daily fill up my mind with good things?

Guide my thoughts this day, O God, as You hold my heart and life in Your care.

You do not even know what will
happen tomorrow. [JAMES 4:14]

UNEXPECTED CHANGE

In January 1943, warm Chinook winds hit Spearfish, South Dakota, quickly raising the temperatures from −4° to 45°F (−20° to 7°C). That drastic weather change—a swing of 49 degrees—took place in just two minutes. The widest temperature change recorded in the USA over a twenty-four-hour period is an incredible 103 degrees! On January 15, 1972, Loma, Montana, saw the temperature jump from −54° to 49°F (−48° to 9°C).

Sudden change, however, is not simply a weather phenomenon. It's sometimes the very nature of life. James reminds us, "Now listen, you who say, 'Today or tomorrow we will go to this or that city, spend a year there, carry on business and make money.' Why, you do not even know what will happen tomorrow" (4:13–14). An unexpected loss. A surprise diagnosis. A financial reversal. Sudden changes.

Life is a journey with many unpredictable elements. This is precisely why James warns us to turn from "arrogant schemes" (V. 16) that do not take the Almighty into account. As he advised us, "You ought to say, 'If it is the Lord's will, we will live and do this or that' " (V. 15). The events of our lives may be uncertain, but one thing is sure: through all of life's unexpected moments, our God will never leave us. He's our one constant throughout life.

BILL CROWDER

When facing sudden change, how do you respond? What do you think an appropriate faith response to life's surprises should look like?

Father, forgive me for the times I worry over things I couldn't anticipate or can't control, and help me to find my rest in You.

Suffering produces endurance.
[ROMANS 5:3 ESV]

THE FAITH TO ENDURE

Ernest Shackleton (1874–1922) led an unsuccessful expedition to cross Antarctica in 1914. When his ship, aptly named *Endurance*, became trapped in heavy ice in the Weddell Sea, it became an endurance race just to survive. With no means of communicating with the rest of the world, Shackleton and his crew used lifeboats to make the journey to the nearest shore— Elephant Island. While most of the crew stayed behind on the island, Shackleton and five crewmen spent two weeks traveling 800 miles across the ocean to South Georgia to get help for those left behind. The "failed" expedition became a victorious entry in the history books when all of Shackleton's men survived, thanks to their courage and endurance.

The apostle Paul knew what it meant to endure. During a stormy sea voyage to Rome to face trial for his belief in Jesus, Paul learned from an angel of God that the ship would sink. But the apostle kept the men aboard encouraged, thanks to God's promise that all would survive, despite the loss of the ship (ACTS 27:23–24).

When disaster strikes, we tend to want God to immediately make everything better. But God gives us the faith to endure and grow. As Paul wrote to the Romans, "Suffering produces endurance" (ROMANS 5:3 ESV). Knowing that, we can encourage each other to keep trusting God in hard times.　　*LINDA WASHINGTON*

**What's your usual response to hardship?
How can you encourage someone who's going through difficult times?**

*Heavenly Father, I need Your help to keep going,
even when it's tough.*

PRAY FIRST

Jack was a rough-spoken plumber who worked on our church building project several years ago. After he learned I was praying for him, he sometimes asked me to pray for his friends. I prayed daily for seven years for God to draw Jack near and save him.

One Saturday during my morning devotional time, I was convicted about a need for more people to come to Christ at our church, and I prayed a simple prayer: "Please, Lord, just give us one!" That afternoon my cell phone rang. It was Jack. "I've just been diagnosed with pancreatic cancer, and I'm not ready." We agreed to meet the following Wednesday, and he consented to have others pray for him. At our church's prayer meeting that Sunday evening we prayed for Jack's healing and salvation.

> *Prayer emphasizes God's ability.*

The following week, after a heartfelt conversation, Jack received Jesus as his Lord and Savior and was baptized the following Sunday.

Prayer emphasizes God's ability to make things happen. When we humbly admit we can't force others to come to Him, we open the door for God to accomplish what we could never do. When we pray for God's Spirit to draw others near, we invite His power, and He's able to overcome odds that seem insurmountable to us.

Because of God's kindness to us through Jesus, we can "approach God's throne of grace with confidence" (HEBREWS 4:16), as we cry out with compassion for those lost in darkness and facing eternity apart from Him. And as we love others with our prayers, we can be assured that our Savior "is also interceding for us" (ROMANS 8:34).

ADAPTED FROM PRAY FIRST: THE POWER OF PRAYER IN SHARING THE GOSPEL, *BY **JAMES BANKS**. © OUR DAILY BREAD MINISTRIES.*

Be wise in the way you act toward outsiders;
make the most of every opportunity. [COLOSSIANS 4:5]

★ *MARCH TOPIC: EVANGELISM*

EVERY OPPORTUNITY

Ever caught a dragon? I hadn't until my son convinced me to download a game on my phone. Producing a digital map mirroring the real world, the game allows you to catch colorful creatures near you.

Unlike most mobile games, this one *requires* movement. Anywhere you go is part of the game's playing field. The result? I'm doing a lot more walking! Anytime my son and I play, we strive to maximize every opportunity to nab the critters that pop up around us.

It's easy to focus on, even obsess over, a game that's crafted to captivate users. But as I played the game, I was convicted with this question: *Am I this intentional about maximizing the spiritual opportunities around me?*

Paul knew the need to be alert to God's work around us. In Colossians 4, he asked for prayer for an opportunity to share the gospel (V. 3). Then he challenged, "Be wise in the way you act toward outsiders; make the most of every opportunity" (V. 5). Paul didn't want the Colossians to miss any chance of influencing others toward Christ. But doing so would require truly seeing them and their needs, then engaging in ways "full of grace" (V. 6).

In our world, far more things vie for our time and attention than a game's imaginary dragons. But God invites us to navigate a real-world adventure, every day seeking opportunities to point to Him.

ADAM R. HOLZ

When did God use someone to bring you into deeper relationship with Him? When has He used you to impact someone?

Jesus, thank You that You're constantly at work in the people around me. Help me to make the most of every opportunity I have to demonstrate Your love and grace.

BIBLE IN A YEAR | NUMBERS 23–25; MARK 7:14–37　　　65

At once they left their nets and followed him. [MATTHEW 4:20]

A CALL TO LEAVE

As a young woman, I imagined myself married to my high school sweetheart—until we broke up. My future yawned emptily before me and I struggled with what to do with my life. At last I sensed God leading me to serve Him by serving others and enrolled in seminary. Then the reality crashed through that I'd be moving away from my roots, friends, and family. In order to respond to God's call, I had to leave.

Jesus was walking beside the Sea of Galilee when He saw Peter and his brother Andrew casting nets into the sea, fishing for a living. He invited them to "Come, follow me...and I will send you out to fish for people" (MATTHEW 4:19). Then Jesus saw two other fishermen, James and his brother John, and offered them a similar invitation (V. 21).

When these disciples came to Jesus, they also left something. Peter and Andrew "left their nets" (V. 20). James and John "left the boat and their father and followed him" (V. 22). Luke puts it this way: "So they pulled their boats up on shore, left *everything* and followed him" (LUKE 5:11).

Every call *to* Jesus also includes a call *from* something else. Net. Boat. Father. Friends. Home. God calls all of us to a relationship with Himself. Then He calls each of us to serve.   *ELISA MORGAN*

How could God's call to follow Him also call you from something else? In what ways can you trust Him with what you may be leaving?

Loving God, help me understand what I might need to leave in order to respond to Your call.

Before I formed you . . . I knew you.
[JEREMIAH 1:5]

FULLY KNOWN

"**Y**ou shouldn't be here right now. Someone up there was looking out for you," the tow truck driver told my mother after he had pulled her car from the edge of a steep mountain ravine and studied the tire tracks leading up to the wreck. Mom was pregnant with me at the time. As I grew, she often recounted the story of how God saved *both* our lives that day, and she assured me that God valued me even before I was born.

None of us escape our omniscient (all-knowing) Creator's notice. More than 2,500 years ago He told the prophet Jeremiah, "Before I formed you in the womb I knew you" (JEREMIAH 1:5). God knows us more intimately than any person ever could and is able to give our lives purpose and meaning unlike any other. He not only formed us through His wisdom and power, but He also sustains every moment of our existence—including the personal details that occur every moment without our awareness: from the beating of our hearts to the intricate functioning of our brains. Reflecting on how our heavenly Father holds together every aspect of our existence, David exclaimed, "How precious to me are your thoughts, God!" (PSALM 139:17).

God is closer to us than our last breath. He made us, knows us, and loves us, and He's ever worthy of our worship and praise.

JAMES BANKS

For what aspect of God's care would you like to praise Him this moment? How can you encourage someone with the thought that He cares for them today?

You're amazing, God! Thank You for holding me up and getting me through every moment of the day.

We were eyewitnesses of his majesty. [2 PETER 1:16]

LIVE WIRE

"I felt like I had touched a live wire," said Professor Holly Ordway, describing her reaction to John Donne's majestic poem "Holy Sonnet 14." *There's something happening in this poetry,* she thought. *I wonder what it is.* Ordway recalls it as the moment her previously atheistic worldview allowed for the possibility of the supernatural. Eventually she would believe in the transforming reality of the resurrected Christ.

Touching a live wire—that must have been how Peter, James, and John felt on the day Jesus took them to a mountaintop, where they witnessed a dramatic transformation. Christ's "clothes became dazzling white" (MARK 9:3) and Elijah and Moses appeared— an event we know today as the transfiguration.

Descending from the mountain, Jesus told the disciples not to tell anyone what they'd seen until He'd risen (V. 9). But they didn't even know what He *meant* by "rising from the dead" (V. 10).

The disciples' understanding of Jesus was woefully incomplete, because they couldn't conceive of a destiny that included His death and resurrection. But eventually their experiences with their resurrected Lord would utterly transform their lives. Late in his life, Peter described his encounter with Christ's transfiguration as the time when the disciples were first "eyewitnesses of his majesty" (2 PETER 1:16).

As Professor Ordway and the disciples learned, when we encounter the power of Jesus we touch a "live wire." There's something happening here. The living Christ beckons us.   *TIM GUSTAFSON*

What are some of your "live wire" experiences: moments when you encountered God in a radically new way? How has your knowledge of Him changed over time?

Father, when we approach You in prayer, forgive us for taking for granted the majesty of Your presence.

Many are the plans in a person's heart, but it is the
LORD's purpose that prevails. [PROVERBS 19:21]

PLANS DISRUPTED

J ane's plans to become a speech therapist ended when an
internship revealed the job was too emotionally challenging
for her. Then she was given the opportunity to write for a
magazine. She'd never seen herself as an author, but years later
she found herself advocating for needy families through her writing. "Looking back, I can see why God changed my plans," she
says. "He had a bigger plan for me."

The Bible has many stories of disrupted plans. On his second
missionary journey, Paul had sought to bring the gospel into
Bithynia, but the Spirit of Jesus stopped him (ACTS 16:6–7). This
must have seemed mystifying: Why was Jesus disrupting plans
that were in line with a God-given mission? The answer came in
a dream one night: Macedonia needed him even more. There,
Paul would plant the first church in Europe. Solomon also
observed, "Many are the plans in a person's heart, but it is the
LORD's purpose that prevails" (PROVERBS 19:21).

It's sensible to make plans. A well-known adage goes, "Fail to
plan, and you plan to fail." But God may disrupt our plans with
His own. Our challenge is to listen and obey, knowing we can
trust God. If we submit to His will, we'll find ourselves fitting into
His purpose for our lives.

As we continue to make plans, we can add a new twist: Plan
to listen. Listen to God's plan.   *LESLIE KOH*

How can you submit your plans to God today?
How can you listen to His plans?

All-knowing God, give me the faith to listen to You when my plans are
disrupted, knowing that You have a greater purpose for my life.

All Scripture is God-breathed.
[2 TIMOTHY 3:16]

CURLING UP WITH THE GOOD BOOK

The small country of Iceland is a nation of readers. In fact, it's reported that each year this nation publishes and reads more books per person than any other country. On Christmas Eve, it's a tradition for Icelanders to give books to family and friends and then read long into the night. This tradition dates back to World War II, when imports were restricted but paper was cheap. Icelandic publishers began flooding the market with new titles in late fall. Now a catalog of the country's new releases is sent to every Icelandic home in mid-November. This tradition is known as the Christmas Book Flood.

We can be thankful God blessed so many with the ability to craft a good story and to educate, inspire, or motivate others through their words. There's nothing like a good book! The best-selling book of all, the Bible, was composed by many authors who wrote in poetry and prose—some great stories, some not so—but all of it inspired. As the apostle Paul reminded Timothy, "All Scripture is God-breathed and is useful for teaching, rebuking, correcting and training in righteousness" and equipping God's people "for every good work" (2 TIMOTHY 3:16–17). Reading the Bible convicts, inspires, and helps us to live for Him—and guides us into the truth (2:15).

In our reading, let's not forget to find time to curl up with the greatest book of all, the Bible.   *ALYSON KIEDA*

What have you read lately that helped you learn more about or draw closer to God? What helps you to spend time in Scripture?

God, thank You for inspiring creativity in the authors of "many books." I'm especially thankful for Your Book.

Now you are the body of Christ, and each one of you
is a part of it. [1 CORINTHIANS 12:27]

MORE THAN MEETS THE EYE

Attend any rodeo with riding and roping competition and you'll see them—competitors with four fingers on one hand and a nub where their thumb should be. It's a common injury in the sport—a thumb gets caught between a rope on one end and a decent-sized steer pulling on the other, and the thumb is usually the loser. It's not a career-ending injury, but the absence of a thumb changes things. Without using your thumb, try to brush your teeth or button a shirt or comb your hair or tie your shoes or even eat. That little overlooked member of your body plays a significant role.

The apostle Paul indicates a similar scenario in the church. Those often less visible and frequently less vocal members sometimes experience an "I don't need you" response from the others (1 CORINTHIANS 12:21). Usually this is unspoken, but there are times when it's said aloud.

God calls us to have equal concern and respect for one other (V. 25). Each and every one of us is a part of Christ's body (V. 27), regardless of the gifting we've received, and we need each other. Some of us are eyes and ears, so to speak, and some of us are thumbs. But each of us plays a vital role in the body of Christ, sometimes more than meets the eye.   *JOHN BLASE*

**If you're an "eye," what's one way you could encourage a
"thumb"? And if you think you're a lesser member, why not
memorize 1 Corinthians 12:27, an important scriptural truth.**

*Father, forgive us for our failure to remember that each of us is a
member of the body of Christ. We're the members, and You and You
alone are the Head.*

Your praise reaches to the ends of the earth.
[PSALM 48:10]

★ *MARCH TOPIC: EVANGELISM*

RAISE PRAISE

You can generally tell where a map was drawn by what lies in its middle. We tend to think our home is the center of the world, so we put a dot in the middle and sketch out from there. Nearby towns might be fifty miles to the north or half a day's drive to the south, but all are described in relation to where we are. The Psalms draw their "map" from God's earthly home in the Old Testament, so the center of biblical geography is Jerusalem.

Psalm 48 is one of many psalms that praise Jerusalem. This "city of our God, his holy mountain" is "beautiful in its loftiness, the joy of the whole earth" (VV. 1–2). Because "God is in her citadels," He "makes her secure forever" (VV. 3, 8). God's fame begins in Jerusalem's temple and spreads outward to "the ends of the earth" (VV. 9–10).

Unless you're reading this in Jerusalem, your home is not in the center of the biblical world. Yet your region matters immensely, because God will not rest until His praise reaches "to the ends of the earth" (V. 10). Would you like to be part of the way God reaches His goal? Worship each week with God's people, and openly live each day for His glory. God's fame extends "to the ends of the earth" when we devote all that we are and have to Him.

MIKE WITTMER

How have you spread God's fame this week?
What else might you do?

Father, use me to spread Your fame to the ends of the earth.

The LORD watches over you.
[PSALM 121:5]

WATCHED BY GOD

Our little grandson waved goodbye, then turned back with a question. "Grandma, why do you stand on the porch and watch until we leave?" I smiled at him, finding his question "cute" because he's so young. Seeing his concern, however, I tried to give a good answer. "Well, it's a courtesy," I told him. "If you're my guest, watching until you leave shows I care." He weighed my answer, but still looked perplexed. So, I told him the simple truth. "I watch," I said, "because I love you. When I see your car drive away, I know you're safely heading home." He smiled, giving me a tender hug. Finally, he understood.

His childlike understanding reminded me what all of us should remember—that our heavenly Father is constantly watching over each of us, His precious children. As Psalm 121 says, "The LORD watches over you—the LORD is your shade at your right hand" (V. 5).

What assurance for Israel's pilgrims as they climbed dangerous roads to Jerusalem to worship. "The sun will not harm you by day, nor the moon at night. The LORD keeps you from all harm—he will watch over your life" (VV. 6-7). Likewise, as we each climb our life's road, sometimes facing spiritual threat or harm, "The LORD will watch over [our] coming and going." Why? His love. When? "Now and forevermore" (V. 8).   *PATRICIA RAYBON*

What "mountain" are you climbing today? What assurance do you find in knowing God is watching over you?

Our loving Father, as we travel the road of life, thank You for watching over us, keeping us safe.

You give them something to eat.
[LUKE 9:13]

BROKEN TO BE SHARED

We met every Thursday after he lost his wife in a car accident. Sometimes he came with questions to which no answers exist; sometimes he came with memories he wanted to relive. Over time, he accepted that even though the accident was a result of the brokenness in our world, God could work in the midst of it. A few years later, he taught a class at our church about grief and how to lament well. Soon, he became our go-to guide for people experiencing loss. Sometimes it's when we don't feel like we have anything to offer that God takes our "not enough" and makes it "more than enough."

Jesus told His disciples to give the people something to eat. They'd protested that there was nothing to give; Jesus multiplied their meager supplies and then turned back to the disciples and gave them the bread, as if to say, "I meant it: You give them something to eat!" (LUKE 9:13–16). Christ will do the miraculous, but He often chooses to involve us.

Jesus says to us, "Place who you are and what you have in My hands. Your broken life. Your story. Your frailty and your failure, your pain and your suffering. Put it in My hands. You'll be surprised what I can do with it." Jesus knows that out of our emptiness, He can bring fullness. Out of our weakness, He can reveal His strength.

GLENN PACKIAM

What brokenness have you experienced? What would it look like to offer that experience to Jesus and ask Him to bring life to others from it?

Dear Jesus, take my "not enough" and make it "more than enough." Take my pain, my failure, and my frailty, and make it something more.

His understanding has no limit.
[PSALM 147:5]

HE KNOWS ALL ABOUT IT

Finn, a Siamese fighting fish, lived at our house for two years. My young daughter would often bend down to talk with him after dropping food into his tank. When the topic of pets came up in kindergarten, she proudly claimed him as her own. Eventually, Finn passed away, and my daughter was heartbroken.

My mother advised me to listen closely to my daughter's feelings and tell her, "God knows all about it." I agreed that God knows everything, yet wondered, *How will that be comforting?* Then it occurred to me that God isn't simply aware of the events in our lives—He compassionately sees into our souls and knows how they affect us. He understands that "little things" can feel like big things depending on our age, past wounds, or lack of resources.

Jesus saw the real size of a widow's gift—and heart—as she dropped two coins into a temple collection box. He described what it meant for her as He said, "This poor widow has put more into the treasury than all the others. . . . [She put in] all she had to live on" (MARK 12:43–44).

The widow kept quiet about her situation but Jesus recognized that what others considered a tiny donation was a sacrifice to her. He sees our lives in the same way. May we find comfort in His limitless understanding.   *JENNIFER BENSON SCHULDT*

How might you show compassion to someone who is upset about a "small" problem? How does God respond when you tell Him about your problems?

God, thank You for knowing me completely and loving me. Help me to feel Your comfort when I consider Your infinite knowledge of my life.

My only aim is to finish the race and complete the
task the Lord Jesus has given me. [ACTS 20:24]

A GOAL AND A PURPOSE

I n 2018, endurance athlete Colin O'Brady took a walk that had
never been taken before. Pulling a supply sled behind him,
O'Brady trekked across Antarctica entirely alone—a total of
932 miles in 54 days. It was a momentous journey of dedication
and courage.

Commenting on his time alone with the ice, the cold, and the
daunting distance, O'Brady said, "I was locked in a deep flow
state [fully immersed in the endeavor] the entire time, equally
focused on the end goal, while allowing my mind to recount the
profound lessons of this journey."

For those of us who have put our faith in Jesus, that statement
might strike a familiar chord. It sounds a lot like our calling as
believers: focused on the goal of walking through life in a way
that glorifies (honors) God and reveals Him to others. In Acts
20:24, Paul, no stranger to dangerous journeys, said, "I consider
my life worth nothing to me; my only aim is to finish the race and
complete the task the Lord Jesus has given me—the task of testi-
fying to the good news of God's grace."

As we walk on in our relationship with Jesus, may we recognize what we know about the purpose for our journey and press
on to the day we'll see our Savior face to face.   *DAVE BRANON*

**How does your relationship with Jesus affect your walk in life?
What can you do today to reveal to others your love for Him?**

*Dear heavenly Father, as we walk through life, help us to honor You
in all we do. And may we encourage others to journey with You.*

Godliness with contentment is great gain.
[1 TIMOTHY 6:6]

WHACK-A-MOLE

You might know what it's like. The bills keep arriving after a medical procedure—from the anesthesiologist, the surgeon, the lab, the facility. Jason experienced this after an emergency surgery. He complained, "We owe thousands of dollars after insurance. If only we can get these bills paid, then life will be good and I'll be content! I feel like I'm playing the arcade game Whack-a-Mole"—where plastic moles pop up from their holes, and the player hits them wildly with a mallet.

Life comes at us like that at times. The apostle Paul certainly could relate. He said, "I know what it is to be in need," yet he'd "learned the secret of being content in any and every situation" (PHILIPPIANS 4:12). His secret? "I can do all this through him who gives me strength" (V. 13). When I was going through a particularly discontented time, I read this on a greeting card: "If it isn't here, where is it?" That was a powerful reminder that if I'm not content here and now, what makes me think I'd be *if only* I were in another situation?

How do we learn to rest in Jesus? Maybe it's a matter of focus. Of enjoying and being thankful for the good. Of learning more about a faithful Father. Of growing in trust and patience. Of recognizing that life is about God and not me. Of asking Him to teach me contentment in Him.   *ANNE CETAS*

In what areas of your life do you need to grow in contentment? How might you change your focus?

God, You are good and all You do is good. Teach me contentment in You. I want to learn.

Because your love is better than life,
my lips will glorify you. [PSALM 63:3]

BETTER THAN LIFE

T hough Mary loved Jesus—life was hard, real hard. Two sons
preceded her in death as did two grandsons, both victims
of shootings. And Mary herself suffered a crippling stroke
that left her paralyzed on one side. Yet, as soon as she was able
she made her way to church services where it wasn't uncommon
for her—with fractured speech—to express praise to the Lord
with words like, "My soul loves Jesus; bless His name!"

Long before Mary expressed her praise to God, David penned
the words of Psalm 63. The heading of the psalm notes that David
wrote it "when he was in the Desert of Judah." Though in a less
than desirable—even desperate—situation, he didn't despair
because he hoped in God. "You, God, are my God, earnestly I seek
you; I thirst for you...in a dry and parched land where there is no
water" (V. 1).

Perhaps you've found yourself in a place of difficulty, without
clear direction or adequate resources. Uncomfortable situations
can confuse us, but they need not derail us when we cling to the
One who loves us (V. 3), satisfies us (V. 5), helps us (V. 7), and whose
right hand upholds us (V. 8). Because God's love is better than life,
like Mary and David, we can express our satisfaction with lips
that praise and honor God (VV. 3–5).   *ARTHUR JACKSON*

**How would you describe your attitude when you find yourself in
a "desert season" of life? How can Psalm 63 help you to better
prepare for such seasons?**

*Jesus, I'm so grateful that I can praise You in the dry, desperate times
of my life because Your love is better than life!*

Let your light shine before others,
that they may see your good deeds
and glorify your Father in heaven. [MATTHEW 5:16]

★ *MARCH TOPIC: EVANGELISM*
SHINING LIGHT

I felt nervous about a five-week prayer class I agreed to teach at a local church. *Would the students like it? Would they like me?* My anxiety was ill-focused, leading me to over-prepare lesson plans, presentation slides, and class handouts. Yet with a week to go, I still hadn't encouraged many people to attend.

In prayer, however, I was reminded that the class was a service that shined light on God. Because the Holy Spirit would use the class to point people to our heavenly Father, I could set aside my nervousness about public speaking. When Jesus taught His disciples in His Sermon on the Mount, He told them, "You are the light of the world. A town built on a hill cannot be hidden. Neither do people light a lamp and put it under a bowl. Instead they put it on its stand, and it gives light to everyone in the house" (MATTHEW 5:14–15).

Reading those words, I finally sent out a class announcement on social media. Almost immediately, people started registering—expressing gratitude and excitement. Seeing their reactions, I reflected more on Jesus' teaching: "Let your light shine before others, that they may see your good deeds and glorify your Father in heaven" (V. 16).

With that perspective, I taught the class with joy. I pray that my simple deed becomes a beacon and encourages others to shine their light for God as well.   *PATRICIA RAYBON*

When have you felt nervous or self-conscious about sharing your deeds and gifts for God? How can your deeds and gifts help others, and what are ways you can share them?

Jesus, empower me to let my God-given light shine so others can see and glorify You.

Great is the LORD and
most worthy of praise. [PSALM 96:4]

THE MAN WHO COULDN'T TALK

S itting in his wheelchair at a senior citizens home in Belize, a
man joyfully listened as a group of American high school
teenagers sang about Jesus. Later, as some of the teens
tried to communicate with him, they discovered he couldn't talk.
A stroke had robbed him of his ability to speak.

Since they couldn't carry on a conversation with the man, the
teens decided to sing to him. As they began to sing, something
amazing happened. The man who couldn't talk began to sing. With
enthusiasm, he belted out "How Great Thou Art" right along with
his new friends.

It was a remarkable moment for everyone. This man's love for
God broke through the barriers and poured out in audible worship—heartfelt, joyous worship.

We all have worship barriers from time to time. Maybe it's a
relationship conflict or a money problem. Or it could be a heart
that's grown a bit cold in its relationship to God.

Our non-talking friend reminds us that the greatness and majesty of our almighty God can overcome any barrier. "O Lord, my
God—when I in awesome wonder, consider all the worlds Thy
hands have made!"

Struggling in your worship? Reflect on how great our God is by
reading a passage such as Psalm 96, and you too may find your
obstacles and objections replaced by praise.   *DAVE BRANON*

**As you read Psalm 96, what stands out about our great God? What
barriers to worship sometimes halt you? How can you grow from
silence to praise?**

*Our great God, I do hold You in awesome wonder.
How great Thou art!*

Before they call I will answer; while they are still speaking I will hear. [ISAIAH 65:24]

BEFORE YOU EVEN ASK

My friends Robert and Colleen have experienced a healthy marriage for decades, and I love watching them interact. One will pass the butter to the other at dinner before being asked for it. The other will refill a glass at the perfect moment. When they tell stories, they finish each other's sentences. Sometimes it seems they can read each other's mind.

It's comforting that God knows and cares for us even more than any person we know and love. When the prophet Isaiah describes the relationship between God and His people in the coming kingdom, he describes a tender, intimate relationship. God says about His people, "Before they call I will answer; while they are still speaking I will hear" (ISAIAH 65:24).

But how can this be true? There are things I've prayed about for years without receiving a response. I believe that as we grow in intimacy with God, aligning our hearts with His, we can learn to trust in His timing and care. We can begin to desire what God desires. When we pray, we ask for—among other things—the things that are part of God's kingdom as described in Isaiah 65: An end to sorrow (V. 19). Safe homes and full bellies and meaningful work for all people (VV. 21–23). Peace in the natural world (V. 25). When God's kingdom comes in its fullness, God will answer these prayers completely. *AMY PETERSON*

How might you participate in bringing God's kingdom to earth? What will you ask God for today?

God, thank You for always hearing my prayers. I trust that You love me and are working all things together for good for those whom You've called. Please transform my desires so that I want what You want.

Though you do not see him now, you believe in him
and are filled with an inexpressible and glorious joy.
[1 PETER 1:8]

DEATH ROW JOY

I n 1985 Anthony Ray Hinton was charged with the murders of
two restaurant managers. It was a set up—he'd been miles
away when the crimes happened—but he was found guilty and
sentenced to death. At the trial, Ray forgave those who lied about
him, adding that he still had joy despite this injustice. "After my
death, I'm going to heaven," he said. "Where are you going?"

Life on death row was hard for Ray. Prison lights flickered
whenever the electric chair was used for others, a grim reminder
of what lay ahead. Ray passed a lie detector test but the results
were ignored, one of many injustices he faced getting his case
reheard.

Finally, on Good Friday 2015, Ray's conviction was overturned
by the US Supreme Court. He'd been on death row for nearly thirty
years. His life is a testament to the reality of God. Because of his
faith in Jesus, Ray had a hope beyond his trials (1 PETER 1:3–5) and
experienced supernatural joy in the face of injustice (V. 8). "This joy
that I have," Ray said after his release, "they couldn't ever take that
away in prison." Such joy proved his faith to be genuine (VV. 7–8).

Death row joy? That's hard to fabricate. It points us to a God
who exists even though He's unseen and who's ready to sustain
us in our own ordeals.   *SHERIDAN VOYSEY*

**Reflect on others who've experienced God's joy in their ordeals.
What have been the qualities of their faith? How can you bring
God's joy to someone facing injustice right now?**

*God of all hope, fill us with Your joy and peace as we trust in You
despite our circumstances. We love You!*

Keep this Book of the Law always on your lips;
meditate on it day and night. [JOSHUA 1:8]

DELIGHT IN THE BOOK

Tsundoku. It's the word I've always needed! A Japanese
term, it refers to the stack of books on a bedside table waiting to be read. Books offer the potential for learning or an
escape to a different time or place, and I long for the delights and
insights found within their pages. So, the stack remains.

The idea that we can find enjoyment and help in a book is
even more true for the book of books—the Bible. I see the
encouragement to immerse oneself in Scripture in God's instructions to Joshua, the newly appointed leader of Israel, commis-
sioned to lead them into the land promised to the Israelites
(JOSHUA 1:8).

Knowing the difficulty ahead, God assured Joshua, "I will be
with you" (V. 5). His help would come, in part, through Joshua's
obedience to God's commands. So God instructed him to "Keep
this Book of the Law always on your lips; meditate on it day and
night, so that you may be careful to do everything written in it"
(V. 8). Although Joshua had the Book of the Law, he needed to
regularly search it to gain insight and understanding into who
God is and His will for His people.

Do you need instruction, truth, or encouragement for your
day? As we take time to read, obey, and find nourishment
through Scripture, we can savor all that's contained in its pages
(2 TIMOTHY 3:16).   *LISA M. SAMRA*

**What are the most common issues that keep you from opening
Scripture? How might you commit to reading more this week?**

*Heavenly Father, thank You for Your guidance through Scripture.
Help us to desire more and more to hear from You
in all the ways You speak.*

You are a forgiving God, gracious and compassionate, slow to anger and abounding in love. [NEHEMIAH 9:17]

SLOW FOR A REASON

In the BBC video series *The Life of Mammals,* host David Attenborough climbs a tree to take a humorous look at a three-toed sloth. Getting face to face with the world's slowest moving mammal, he greets it with a "boo!" Failing to get a reaction, he explains that going slow is what you do if you are a three-toed sloth living primarily on leaves that are not easily digested and not very nutritious.

In a rehearsal of Israel's history, Nehemiah reminds us of another example and explanation for going slow (9:9–21), but this one isn't comical. According to Nehemiah, our God is the ultimate example of going slow—when it comes to anger. Nehemiah recounted how God cared for His people, instructing them with life-giving laws, sustaining them on their journey out of Egypt and providing them with the Promised Land (VV. 9–15). Although Israel constantly rebelled (V. 16), God never stopped loving them. Nehemiah's explanation? Our Creator is by nature "gracious and compassionate, slow to anger and abounding in love" (V. 17). Why else would He have borne so patiently His people's complaints, disbelief, and distrust for forty years? (V. 21). It was because of God's "great compassion" (V. 19).

What about us? A hot temper signals a cold heart. But the greatness of God's heart gives us room to patiently live and love with Him.　　　　　　　　　　　　　　　*MART DEHAAN*

In what areas of your life do you need to practice being slow to anger? How does it make you feel that God is slow to anger with you?

Father in heaven, fill us with the Spirit of Your graciousness, compassion, mercy, and love so that others can see not just our restraint, but our love because of You.

The ravens brought him bread and meat in the morning and bread and meat in the evening, and he drank from the brook. [1 KINGS 17:6]

CHIRPY

For twelve years, Chirpy, a seagull, has made daily visits to a man who'd helped him heal from a broken leg. John wooed Chirpy to himself with dog biscuits and was then able to nurse him back to health. Though Chirpy only resides in Instow Beach in Devon, England, between September and March, he and John Sumner find each other easily—Chirpy flies straight to him when he arrives at the beach each day, though he doesn't approach any other human. It's an uncommon relationship, to be sure.

John and Chirpy's bond reminds me of another uncommon relationship between man and bird. When Elijah, one of God's prophets, was sent into the wilderness to "hide in the Kerith Ravine" during a time of drought, God said he was to drink from the brook, and He'd send ravens to supply him with food (1 KINGS 17:3–4). Despite the difficult circumstances and surroundings, Elijah would have his needs for food and water met. Ravens were unlikely caterers—naturally feeding on unseemly meals themselves—yet they brought Elijah wholesome food.

It may not surprise us that a man would help a bird, but when birds provide for a man with "bread and meat in the morning and bread and meat in the evening," it can only be explained by God's power and care (V. 6). Like Elijah, we too can trust in His provision for us. *KIRSTEN HOLMBERG*

How has God provided for your needs in surprising ways? How has this deepened your trust in Him?

Loving God, please help me to trust in You to meet my needs no matter what my circumstances might be.

Preach the word; be prepared in season
and out of season. [2 TIMOTHY 4:2]

★ *MARCH TOPIC: EVANGELISM*

A RISKY DETOUR

What a waste of time, thought Harley. Her insurance agent was insisting they meet again. Harley knew it would be yet another boring sales pitch, but she decided to make the most of it by looking for an opportunity to talk about her faith.

Noticing that the agent's eyebrows were tattooed, she hesitantly asked why and discovered that the woman did it because she felt it would bring her luck. Harley's question was a risky detour from a routine chat about finances, but it opened the door to a conversation about luck and faith, which gave her an opportunity to talk about why she relied on Jesus. That "wasted" hour turned out to be a divine appointment.

Jesus also took a risky detour. While traveling from Judea to Galilee, He went out of His way to speak to a Samaritan, something unthinkable for a Jew. Worse, she was an adulterous woman avoided even by other Samaritans. Yet He ended up having a conversation that led to the salvation of many (JOHN 4:1–26, 39–42).

Are you meeting someone you don't really want to see? Do you keep bumping into a neighbor you normally avoid? The Bible reminds us to be always ready—"in season and out of season"—to share the good news (2 TIMOTHY 4:2). Consider taking a "risky detour." Who knows, God may be giving you a divine opportunity to talk to someone about Him today!   *LESLIE KOH*

Whom might you meet today? How might there be an opportunity to talk about Jesus? How can you go out of your way to share the good news in a bold but loving, sensitive way?

Jesus, teach me to see the doors You've opened for me to share Your love, and give me the courage to tell others about You.

Look! God's dwelling place is now
among the people. [REVELATION 21:3]

REUNION

The little boy excitedly ripped open a big box from his ser-
viceman daddy, whom he believed wouldn't be home to
celebrate his birthday. Inside that box was yet another
giftwrapped box, and inside that box was another that simply
held a piece of paper saying, "Surprise!" Confused, the boy
looked up—just as his dad entered the room. Tearfully the son
leapt into his father's arms, exclaiming, "Daddy, I missed you"
and "I love you!"

That tearful yet joyful reunion captures for me the heart of
Revelation 21's description of the glorious moment when God's
children see their loving Father face to face—in the fully renewed
and restored creation. There, "[God] will wipe every tear from
[our] eyes." No longer will we experience pain or sorrow, because
we'll be with our heavenly Father. As the "loud voice" in
Revelation 21 declares, "Look! God's dwelling place is now
among the people, and he will dwell with them" (VV. 3–4).

There's a tender love and joy that followers of Jesus already
enjoy with God, as 1 Peter 1:8 describes: "Though you have not
seen him, you love him; and even though you do not see him
now, you believe in him and are filled with an inexpressible and
glorious joy." Yet imagine our incredible, overflowing joy when
we see the one we've loved and longed for welcoming us into His
open arms!   *ALYSON KIEDA*

**What do you most look forward to about life in God's presence
in the restored creation? How do you experience glimpses of that
joy now?**

*Loving God, we anticipate with joy the day when we will be with You.
Until then, help us to happily serve You as we wait.*

I tell you that you are Peter, and on this rock I will build
my church, and the gates of Hades will not overcome it.
[MATTHEW 16:18]

THE BELL

J ackson dreamed of becoming a US Navy Seal from early
  childhood—an ambition that led to years of physical discipline and self-sacrifice. He eventually faced grueling tests of
strength and endurance including what's referred to by trainees
as "hell week."

Jackson was physically unable to complete the exhaustive
training, and reluctantly rang a bell to inform the commander
and other trainees of his choice to leave the program. For most,
this would feel like failure. But in spite of the extreme disappointment, Jackson was later able to see his military failure as preparation for his life's work.

The apostle Peter experienced his own form of failure. He boldly
proclaimed that he would remain loyal to Jesus even to prison or
death (LUKE 22:33). Yet later he wept bitterly after he denied that he
knew Jesus (VV. 60–62). But God had plans beyond his failure. Prior
to Peter's denial, Jesus informed him, "I tell you that you are Peter,
and on this rock I will build my church, and the gates of Hades will
not overcome it" (MATTHEW 16:18; SEE ALSO LUKE 22:31–32).

Are you struggling with a failure causing you to feel unworthy
or unqualified to move on? Don't let the ringing bell of failure
cause you to miss God's greater purposes for you.   *EVAN MORGAN*

**What did you view as a failure in your life that God used to help
you grow in Him? Why is it vital for us to find our identity in how
God views us?**

*God, help me to use every circumstance, even my failures,
for Your glory and honor!*

Pray in the Spirit on all occasions with all kinds of
prayers and requests. [EPHESIANS 6:18]

IT'S TIME TO PRAY . . . AGAIN

I pulled into my driveway, waving at my neighbor Myriam and her little girl Elizabeth. Over the years, Elizabeth had grown accustomed to our spontaneous chats lasting longer than the promised "few minutes" and morphing into prayer meetings. She climbed the tree planted in the center of their front yard, dangled her legs over a branch, and busied herself while her mother and I spoke. After a while, Elizabeth hopped down from her roost and ran to where we stood. Grabbing our hands, she smiled and almost sang, "It's time to pray . . . *again*." Even at an early age, Elizabeth seemed to understand how important prayer was in our friendship.

After encouraging believers to "be strong in the Lord and in his mighty power" (EPHESIANS 6:10), the apostle Paul offered special insight on the crucial role of continual prayer. He described the necessary armor God's people would need during their spiritual walk with the Lord, who provides protection, discernment, and confidence in His truth (VV. 11–17). However, the apostle emphasized this God-given strength grew from deliberate immersion in the life-giving gift of prayer (VV. 18–20).

God hears and cares about our concerns, whether they're spoken boldly, sobbed silently, or secured deep in a hurting heart. He's always ready to make us strong in His power, as He invites us to pray again and again and again.　　*XOCHITL DIXON*

How can ongoing prayer change our perspective, relationships, and day-to-day living? What would it mean for you to consider your time in prayer to be as vital as breathing?

Heavenly Father, thank You for the privilege of coming to You in prayer.

All people will see God's salvation.
[LUKE 3:6]

SEEING SALVATION

At fifty-three, the last thing Sonia expected to do was abandon her business and her country to join a group of asylum seekers journeying to a new land. After gangs murdered her nephew and tried to force her seventeen-year-old son into their ranks, Sonia felt escape was her only option. "I pray to God. . . .I will do whatever is necessary," Sonia explained. "I will do anything so [my son and I] don't die of hunger. . .I prefer to see him suffer here than end up in a bag or canal."

Does the Bible have anything to say to Sonia and her son—or to so many who have suffered injustice and devastation? When John the Baptist proclaimed the arrival of Jesus, he announced good news to Sonia, to us, to the world. "Prepare the way for the Lord," John proclaimed (LUKE 3:4). He insisted that when Jesus arrived, God would enact a powerful, comprehensive rescue. The biblical word for this rescue is *salvation*.

Salvation encompasses both the healing of our sinful hearts and—one day—the healing of all the world's evils. God's transforming work is for every story, every human system, and is available to everyone. "All people will see God's salvation," John said (V. 6).

Whatever evil we face, Christ's cross and resurrection assure us we'll see God's salvation. One day we'll experience His final liberation.   *WINN COLLIER*

Where do you need to see God's salvation in your life? How has God called you to be part of His transforming work on earth?

God, You promise that all people will see Your salvation. I claim this promise. Show me Your rescue and healing.

Precious in the sight of the LORD is
the death of his faithful servants. [PSALM 116:15]

PRECIOUS DEPARTURE

Sculptor Liz Shepherd's 2018 exhibition *The Wait* was described by a *Boston Globe* correspondent as "evok[ing] the precious, exposed, and transcendent in life." Inspired by the time Shepherd spent at her dying father's bedside, the exhibition attempts to convey yearning, the emptiness of loss, and the fragile sense that loved ones are just out of reach.

The idea that death is precious might seem counterintuitive; however, the psalmist declares, "Precious in the sight of the LORD is the death of his faithful servants" (PSALM 116:15). God treasures the death of His people, for in their passing He welcomes them home.

Who are these faithful servants ("saints" NKJV) of God? According to the psalmist, they are those who serve God in gratitude for His deliverance, who call on His name, and who honor the words they speak before Him (PSALM 116:16–18). Such actions represent deliberate choices to walk with God, accept the freedom He offers, and cultivate a relationship with Him.

In so doing, we find ourselves in the company of Jesus, who is "chosen by God and precious to him . . . . For in Scripture it says: 'See, I lay a stone in Zion, a chosen and precious cornerstone, and the one who trusts in him will never be put to shame' " (1 PETER 2:4–6). When our trust is in God, our departure from this life is precious in His sight.   *REMI OYEDELE*

**How does your perception of death compare with God's view
of the passing of His people? To what extent is your perception
influenced by what the Bible says about death?**

*Dear God, help me to trust You even in the challenges
and losses of life.*

Cast all your anxiety on him because he cares for you. [1 PETER 5:7]

THE WOULD-BE WOODCUTTER

One year when I was in college, I cut, stacked, sold, and delivered firewood. It was a hard job, so I have empathy for the hapless logger in the 2 Kings 6 story.

Elisha's school for prophets had prospered, and their meeting place had become too small. Someone suggested they go into the woods, cut logs, and enlarge their facilities. Elisha agreed and accompanied the workers. Things were going remarkably well until someone's axhead fell into the water (V. 5).

Some have suggested that Elisha simply probed in the water with his stick until he located the axhead and dragged it into sight. That would hardly be worth mentioning, however. No, it was a miracle: The axhead was set in motion by God's hand and began to float so the man could retrieve it (VV. 6–7).

The simple miracle enshrines a profound truth: God cares about the small stuff of life—lost axheads, lost keys, lost glasses, lost phones—the little things that cause us to fret. He doesn't always restore what's lost, but He understands and comforts us in our distress.

Next to the assurance of our salvation, the assurance of God's care is essential. Without it we would feel alone in the world, exposed to innumerable worries. It's good to know He cares and is moved by our losses—small as they may be. Our concerns are His concerns.　　　　　　　　　　　　　　　　　*DAVID H. ROPER*

What "little" things are troubling you that you can cast on God right now? How does it encourage you to know that you can be assured of His daily care for you?

Loving God, here are my concerns. Please take them, provide as You see best, and give me Your peace.

From [Christ] the whole body, joined and held together by every supporting ligament, grows and builds itself up in love, as each part does its work. [EPHESIANS 4:16]

PREACH OR PLOW?

According to the family legend, two brothers, one named Billy and the other Melvin, were standing on the family's dairy farm one day when they saw an airplane doing some skywriting. The boys watched as the plane sketched out the letters "GP" overhead.

Both brothers decided that what they saw had meaning for them. One thought it meant "Go preach." The other read it as "Go plow." Later, one of the boys, Billy Graham, dedicated himself to preaching the gospel, becoming an icon of evangelism. His brother Melvin went on to faithfully run the family dairy farm for many years.

Skywriting signs aside, if God did call Billy to preach and Melvin to plow, as seems to be the case, they both honored God through their vocations. While Billy had a long preaching career, his success doesn't mean that his brother's obedience to his calling to plow was any less important.

While God does assign some to be in what we call full-time ministry (EPHESIANS 4:11–12), that doesn't mean those in other jobs and roles aren't doing something just as important. In either case, as Paul said, "each part [should do] its work" (V. 16). That means honoring Jesus by faithfully using the gifts He's given us. When we do, whether we "go preach" or "go plow," we can make a difference for Jesus wherever we serve or work.   *DAVE BRANON*

How can you use your gifts to honor God in your vocation? How can you encourage others you know so they too can use their calling as a way to serve Jesus?

Help me, God, to be used right where You put me. Help me to see that my words, actions, and work ethic can profoundly affect others.

Jesus took some bread and blessed it.
[MATTHEW 26:26 NLT]

BLESSED BREAD

When our oldest child became a teenager, my wife and I gave her a journal that we'd been writing in since her birth. We'd recorded her likes and dislikes, quirks and memorable one-liners. At some point the entries became more like letters, describing what we see in her and how we see God at work in her. When we gave it to her on her thirteenth birthday, she was mesmerized. She'd been given the gift of knowing a crucial part of the origins of her identity.

In blessing something as common as bread, Jesus was revealing its identity. What it—along with all creation—was made to reflect: God's glory. I believe Jesus was also pointing to the future of the material world. All creation will one day be filled with the glory of God. So in blessing bread (MATTHEW 26:26), Jesus was pointing to the *origin* and the *destiny* of creation (ROMANS 8:21–22).

Maybe the "beginning" of your story feels messed up. Maybe you don't think there's much of a future. But there's a bigger story. It's a story of a God who made you on purpose and for a purpose, who took pleasure in you. It's a story of God who came to rescue you (MATTHEW 26:28); a God who put His Spirit in you to renew you and recover your identity. It's a story of a God who wants to *bless* you.   *GLENN PACKIAM*

**How does seeing your true origin story as being made on purpose
and for a purpose change the way you see yourself? What's the
bigger story than simply your situation right now?**

*Dear Jesus, I place my life like bread in Your hands.
Only You can return me to my origin. Only You can carry me to my
destiny. Jesus, You are the author and the
finisher of my faith.*

He predestined us for adoption to sonship through
Jesus Christ, in accordance with his pleasure and will.
[EPHESIANS 1:5]

INHERITANCE ISN'T EARNED

"**T**hanks for dinner, Dad," I said as I set my napkin on the restaurant table. I was home on a break from college and, after being gone for a while, it felt strange to have my parents pay for me. "You're welcome, Julie," my dad replied, "but you don't have to thank me for everything all the time. I know you've been off on your own, but you're still my daughter and a part of the family." I smiled. "Thanks, Dad."

In my family, I haven't done anything to earn my parents' love or what they do for me. But my dad's comment reminds me that I haven't done anything to deserve to be a part of God's family either.

In the book of Ephesians, Paul tells his readers that God chose them "to be holy and blameless in his sight" (1:4), or to stand without blemish before Him (5:25–27). But this is only possible through Jesus, in whom "we have redemption through his blood, the forgiveness of sins, in accordance with the riches of God's grace" (1:7). We don't have to earn God's grace, forgiveness, or entrance into His family. We simply accept His free gift.

When we turn our lives over to Jesus, we become children of God, which means we receive eternal life and have an inheritance waiting for us in heaven. Praise God for offering such a wonderful gift!   *JULIE SCHWAB*

In what ways do you feel or act as if you have to earn God's love? How can you practice living in the freedom of His love?

Faithful God, thank You for freely giving Your Son so I can be a part of Your family. Help me to honor You in all You've done for me.

CITIZENS OF TWO WORLDS

But our citizenship is in heaven. And we eagerly await a Savior from there, the Lord Jesus Christ. PHILIPPIANS 3:20

Followers of Jesus live in two worlds with two citizenships. We have, as Paul said, citizenship in heaven but now we have our citizenships in this world. Some even refer to our current status as that of "resident aliens" because our primary citizenship is not of this world.

However, having citizenship in heaven doesn't preclude us from having responsibilities in this world. How we can live out our heavenly citizenship here?

Pray for leaders: "I urge, then, first of all, that petitions, prayers, intercession and thanksgiving be made for all people—for kings and all those in authority, that we may live peaceful and quiet lives in all godliness and holiness" (1 TIMOTHY 2:1–2).

Submit to government authority: "Let everyone be subject to the governing authorities, for there is no authority except that which God has established" (ROMANS 13:1).

Render to Caesar: "Give back to Caesar what is Caesar's, and to God what is God's" (MATTHEW 22:21).

Live an honorable life: "Show proper respect to everyone, love the family of believers, fear God, honor the emperor" (1 PETER 2:17).

We also have the challenge of living like Jesus in our countries of citizenship. This involves the things that represent His heart—care for the poor, help for the weak, and justice for the oppressed.

All of this, however, exists with a significant qualifier. When threatened by the leaders of the religious government of Israel, Peter wisely responded: "We must obey God rather than human beings!" (ACTS 5:29). Our first allegiance is always to our Savior and His kingdom.

BILL CROWDER, OUR DAILY BREAD *AUTHOR*

Whatever you do, do it all for the glory of God.
[1 CORINTHIANS 10:31]

★ *APRIL TOPIC: CITIZENSHIP*

DOES WHAT WE DO MATTER?

I dropped my forehead to my hand with a sigh, "I don't know how I'm going to get it all done." My friend's voice crackled through the phone: "You have to give yourself some credit. You're doing a lot." He then listed the things I was trying to do—maintain a healthy lifestyle, work, do well in graduate school, write, and attend a Bible study. I wanted to do all these things for God, but instead I was more focused on what I was doing than how I was doing it—or that perhaps I was trying to do too much.

Paul reminded the church in Colossae that they were to live in a way that glorified God. Ultimately, what they specifically did on a day-to-day basis was not as important as *how* they did it. They were to do their work with "compassion, kindness, humility, gentleness and patience" (COLOSSIANS 3:12), to be forgiving, and above all to love (VV. 13–14) and to "do it all in the name of the Lord Jesus" (V. 17). Their work wasn't to be separated from Christlike living.

What we do matters, but *how* we do it, *why*, and *who* we do it for matters more. Each day we can choose to work in a stressed-out way or in a way that honors God and seeks out the meaning Jesus adds to our work. When we pursue the latter, we find satisfaction.　　　　　　　　　　　*JULIE SCHWAB*

In what ways do you do things out of need or obligation rather than for God's glory? How do you think meaning is found in Christ rather than accomplishments?

Jesus, forgive me for the times I stress over what I'm trying to accomplish. Help me to instead seek to accomplish things for Your glory.

God loves a cheerful giver.
[2 CORINTHIANS 9:7]

CHEERFUL GIVERS

Years ago, my wife received a small rebate from something she'd purchased. It wasn't something she'd expected, it just showed up in the mail. About the same time, a good friend shared with her the immense needs of women in another country, entrepreneurial-minded women trying to better themselves by way of education and business. As is often the case, however, their first barrier was financial.

My wife took that rebate and made a micro-loan to a ministry devoted to helping these women. When the loan was repaid, she simply loaned again, and again, and so far has made twenty-seven such investments. My wife enjoys many things, but there's rarely a smile as big on her face as when she receives an update on the flourishing taking place in the lives of women she's never met.

We often hear emphasis on the last word in this phrase—"God loves a cheerful *giver*" (2 CORINTHIANS 9:7)—and rightly so. But our giving has a specific quality about it—it shouldn't be done "reluctantly or under compulsion," and we're called not to sow "*sparingly*" (VV. 6–7). In a word, our giving is to be "cheerful." And while each of us will give a little differently, our faces are places for telling evidence of our cheer. 　　　*JOHN BLASE*

When did you last "cheerfully" give?
Why do you believe God loves a cheerful giver?

Generous Father God, thank You for the joy that comes in giving from a cheer-filled heart. And thank You for the ways in which You provide abundantly for our needs.

There is in store for me the crown of righteousness,
which the Lord ... will award to me on that day.
[2 TIMOTHY 4:8]

WHAT COMES NEXT?

On the night of April 3, 1968, Dr. Martin Luther King gave his final speech, "I've Been to the Mountaintop." In it, he hints that he believed he might not live long. He said, "We've got some difficult days ahead. But it doesn't matter with me now. Because I've been to the mountaintop. And I've looked over. And I've seen the promised land. I may not get there with you.... [But] I'm happy tonight. I'm not worried about anything. I'm not fearing any man. Mine eyes have seen the glory of the coming of the Lord." The next day, he was assassinated.

The apostle Paul, shortly before his death, wrote to his protégé Timothy: "I am already being poured out like a drink offering, and the time for my departure is near....Now there is in store for me the crown of righteousness, which the Lord, the righteous Judge, will award to me on that day" (2 TIMOTHY 4:6, 8). Paul knew his time on earth was drawing to a close, as did Dr. King. Both men realized lives of incredible significance, yet never lost sight of the true life ahead. Both men welcomed what came next.

Like them, may we "fix our eyes not on what is seen, but on what is unseen, since what is seen is temporary, but what is unseen is eternal" (2 CORINTHIANS 4:18).   *REMI OYEDELE*

What is your understanding of this life's temporary nature? How do you think it plays into the life that comes next?

Heavenly Father, help us to keep our eyes on You and not on the troubles and trials of this life.

Whoever loves wealth is never satisfied.
[ECCLESIASTES 5:10]

OUR DEEPEST LONGINGS

As a young man, Duncan had been afraid of not having enough money, so in his early twenties, he began ambitiously building his future. Climbing the ladder at a prestigious Silicon Valley company, Duncan achieved vast wealth. He had a bulging bank account, a luxury sports car, and a million-dollar California home. He had everything he desired; yet he was profoundly unhappy. "I felt anxious and dissatisfied," Duncan said. "In fact, wealth can actually make life worse." Piles of cash didn't provide friendship, community, or joy—and often brought him only more heartache.

Some people will expend immense energy attempting to amass wealth in an effort to secure their lives. It's a fool's game. "Whoever loves money never has enough," Scripture insists (ECCLESIASTES 5:10). Some will work themselves to the bone. They'll strive and push, comparing their possessions with others and straining to achieve some economic status. And yet even if they gain supposed financial freedom, they'll still be unsatisfied. It's not enough. As the writer of Ecclesiastes states, "This too is meaningless" (V. 10).

The truth is, striving to find fulfillment apart from God will prove futile. While Scripture calls us to work hard and use our gifts for the good of the world, we can never accumulate enough to satisfy our deepest longings. Jesus alone offers a real and satisfying life (JOHN 10:10)—one based on a loving relationship that's truly enough!   *WINN COLLIER*

What brings you true satisfaction and fulfillment? How can you more fully live out the fact that only God is enough?

Gracious God, allow me to find my true fulfillment and joy in You. Keep me from a wrong view of work and material things.

When your words came, I ate them; they were
my joy and my heart's delight. [JEREMIAH 15:16]

HUNGRY FOR GOD

A new believer in Jesus was desperate to read the Bible. However, he'd lost his eyesight and both hands in an explosion. When he heard about a woman who read Braille with her lips, he tried to do the same—only to discover that the nerve endings of his lips had also been destroyed. Later, he was filled with joy when he discovered that he could feel the Braille characters with his tongue! He had found a way to read and enjoy the Scriptures.

Joy and delight were the emotions the prophet Jeremiah experienced when he received God's words. "When your words came, I ate them," he said, "they were my joy and my heart's delight" (JEREMIAH 15:16). Unlike the people of Judah who despised His words (8:9), Jeremiah had been obedient and rejoiced in them. His obedience, however, also led to the prophet being rejected by his own people and persecuted unfairly (15:17).

Some of us may have experienced something similar. We once read the Bible with joy, but obedience to God led to suffering and rejection from others. Like Jeremiah, we can bring our confusion to God. He answered Jeremiah by repeating the promise He gave him when He first called him to be a prophet (VV. 19-21; SEE 1:18–19). God reminded him that He never lets His people down. We can have this same confidence too. He's faithful and will never abandon us.

POH FANG CHIA

**When have you experienced joy in reading the Scriptures?
What can help you regain your hunger and thirst for God?**

Faithful God, thank You for speaking to me through the words of the Bible. Help me to seek You earnestly and to obey You faithfully.

Blessed are those who are persecuted because of
righteousness. [MATTHEW 5:10]

STRENGTH IN SUFFERING

In 1948, Haralan Popov, the pastor of an underground church,
was taken from his home for a "little questioning." Two weeks
later, he received around-the-clock interrogation and no food
for ten days. Each time he denied being a spy, he was beaten.
Popov not only survived his harsh treatment but also led fellow
prisoners to Jesus. Finally, eleven years later, he was released and
continued to share his faith until, two years later, he was able to
leave the country and be reunited with his family. He spent the
following years preaching and raising money to distribute Bibles
in closed countries.

Like countless believers in Jesus throughout the ages, Popov
was persecuted because of his faith. Christ, long before His own
torture and death and the subsequent persecution of His followers, said, "Blessed are those who are persecuted because of
righteousness, for theirs is the kingdom of heaven" (MATTHEW 5:10).
He continued, "Blessed are you when people . . . persecute you
and falsely say all kinds of evil against you because of me" (V. 11).

"Blessed"? What could Jesus have meant? He was referring to
the wholeness, joy, and comfort found in a relationship with
Him (VV. 4, 8–10). Popov persevered because he felt the presence
of God infusing strength into him, even in suffering. When we
walk with God, no matter our circumstances, we too can experience His peace. He is with us.   *ALYSON KIEDA*

With which of the Beatitudes do you most identify, and why?
When have you felt God's peace and presence in a trial?

*Loving Father, we thank You for never leaving or forsaking us in our
darkest times.*

Immediately he spoke to them and said,
"Take courage! It is I. Don't be afraid." [MARK 6:50]

THE FULL REVEAL

Moviegoers heard the beautiful voice of Emily Blunt as the starring role in *Mary Poppins Returns.* Amazingly, it was four years into their marriage before her husband discovered her vocal talent. In an interview, he revealed his surprise the first time he heard her sing, thinking, "When were you going to tell me this?"

In relationships we often learn new, sometimes unexpected, details that surprise us. In Mark's gospel, Christ's disciples initially started with an incomplete picture of Jesus and struggled to grasp all of who He is. In an encounter on the Sea of Galilee, however, Jesus revealed more of Himself—this time the extent of His power over the forces of nature.

After feeding a crowd numbering more than 5,000 people, Jesus sent His disciples out on the Sea of Galilee, where they were caught in a fierce storm. Just before dawn, the disciples were terrified to see someone walking on the water. Christ's familiar voice spoke words of comfort, saying, "Take courage! It is I. Don't be afraid" (MARK 6:50). Then He calmed the raging sea. Upon seeing such great power, the disciples were "completely amazed" (6:51) even as they struggled to fully comprehend this experience of Christ's power.

As we experience Jesus and His power over the storms of our lives, we gain a more complete picture of who He is. And we're amazed.   *LISA M. SAMRA*

How does learning of Christ's power help develop a fuller picture of who He is? What other stories in the Bible reveal His power?

Jesus, You amaze us with Your power. Open our eyes and reveal to us more of who You are so that we might worship You.

Don't harm yourself! We are all here!
[ACTS 16:28]

★ APRIL TOPIC: CITIZENSHIP

NOT TAKING ADVANTAGE

Several inmates were collecting roadside garbage to reduce their jail time when their supervisor, James, collapsed. They rushed to his aid and realized he was having a medical emergency. One inmate borrowed James' phone to call for help. The sheriff's department later thanked the inmates for helping get their supervisor prompt medical attention, especially because they could have instead neglected him—to his great detriment as he was having a stroke—or used the situation to their own advantage to escape.

The kindness of the inmates' actions is not unlike those of Paul and Silas when they were imprisoned. After they'd been stripped, beaten, and thrown into prison, an earthquake struck so violently that it loosed their chains and shook the prison doors off their hinges (ACTS 16:23–26). When the jailer awoke, he naturally assumed the prisoners had fled, so he prepared to take his own life (to preempt what would've been his punishment for their escape). When Paul shouted, "We are all here!" (V. 28) the jailer was so moved by their actions—uncharacteristic of prisoners—that he became curious about the God they worshiped, ultimately coming to believe in Him too (VV. 29–34).

The way we treat others reveals what we believe and value. When we choose to do good instead of harm, our actions might just prompt them to wonder about the God we know and love.

KIRSTEN HOLMBERG

In what situation can you choose to not take advantage for your own gain? How might that decision benefit someone else?

Loving God, help me to make choices that will draw others to You.

Gracious words are a honeycomb, sweet to
the soul and healing to the bones. [PROVERBS 16:24]

HEALING WORDS

A recent study has shown that encouraging words from a health-care provider can help patients recuperate faster from their ailments. A simple experiment exposed volunteer study participants to a skin allergen to make them itch and then compared the reactions between those who received assurance from their physician and those who didn't. Patients who received encouragement from their doctors had less discomfort and itching than their counterparts.

The writer of Proverbs knew how important encouraging words are. "Gracious words" bring "healing to the bones," he wrote (PROVERBS 16:24). The positive effect of words isn't limited to our health: when we heed the wisdom of instruction, we're also more likely to prosper in our efforts (V. 20). So too encouragement buoys us for the challenges we face now and may encounter in the future.

We may not yet fully understand why or even how much wisdom and encouragement bring strength and healing to our daily lives. Yet the cheers and guidance of our parents, coaches, and colleagues seem to help us endure difficulty and steer us toward success. Similarly, the Bible brings us encouragement when we face trials, equipping us to bear up under even the most unthinkable circumstances. Help us, God, to be strengthened by Your wisdom and to, in turn, offer the healing and hope of "gracious words" to those You've placed in our lives.   KIRSTEN HOLMBERG

Who has spoken "gracious words" into your life? Why is it vital for you to share words of encouragement with others?

Dear Father, thank You for Your words of healing and hope.

They took palm branches and went out to meet him,
shouting, "Hosanna!" [JOHN 12:13]

THE ONE WHO SAVES

He was called "one of the bravest persons alive," but he wasn't what others expected. Desmond was a soldier who declined to carry a gun. As a medic, he single-handedly rescued seventy-five injured soldiers from harm in one battle, including some who once called him a coward and ridiculed him for his faith. Running into heavy gunfire, Desmond prayed continually, "Lord, please help me get one more." He was awarded the Medal of Honor for his heroism.

Scripture tells us that Jesus was greatly misunderstood. On a day foretold by the prophet Zechariah (9:9), Jesus entered Jerusalem on a donkey and the crowd waved branches, shouting "Hosanna!" (an exclamation of praise meaning "Save!"). Quoting Psalm 118:26, they cried: "Blessed is he who comes in the name of the Lord!" (JOHN 12:13). But the very next verse in that psalm refers to *bringing a sacrifice* "with boughs in hand" (PSALM 118:27). While the crowd in John 12 anticipated an earthly king to save them from Rome, Jesus was much more. He was King of Kings *and our sacrifice*—God in the flesh, willingly embracing the cross to save us from our sins—a purpose prophesied centuries earlier.

"At first his disciples did not understand all this," John writes. Only later "did they realize that these things had been written about him" (JOHN 12:16). Illumined by His Word, God's eternal purposes became clear. He loves us enough to send a mighty Savior!

JAMES BANKS

How has Jesus saved you? How can you express your grateful praise to Him today?

Risen Savior, I praise You for Your sacrifice for us at the cross. Help me to live serving and praising You, my eternal King!

Because he himself suffered when he was tempted,
he is able to help those who are being tempted.
[HEBREWS 2:18]

ABLE TO HELP

Joe's eight-week "break" from his job as a crisis care worker at a New York City church was not a vacation. In his words, it was "to live again among the homeless, to become one of them, to remember what hungry, tired, and forgotten feel like." Joe's first stint on the streets had come nine years earlier when he arrived from Pittsburgh without a job or a place to stay. For thirteen days he lived on the streets with little food or sleep. That's how God had prepared him for decades of ministry to needy people.

When Jesus came to earth, He also chose to share the experiences of those He came to save. "Since the children have flesh and blood, he too shared in their humanity so that by his death he might break the power of him who holds the power of death—that is, the devil" (HEBREWS 2:14). From birth to death, nothing was missing from Christ's human experience—except sin (4:15). Because He conquered sin, He can help us when we're tempted to sin.

And Jesus doesn't need to reacquaint Himself with our earthly cares. The One who saves us remains connected to us and is deeply interested in us. Whatever life brings, we can be assured that the One who rescued us from our greatest foe, the devil (2:14), stands ready to help us in our times of greatest need. *ARTHUR JACKSON*

How does it encourage you to know that Jesus became one of us to identify with us and help us? What difference does knowing that He "walked in our shoes" make during this season in your life?

Father, help me to remember that You're ready to help me in all areas of my life.

They turned aside after dishonest gain and
accepted bribes and perverted justice. [1 SAMUEL 8:3]

IN THE FATHER'S WAYS

I n the 1960s, the bustling community of North Lawndale, on Chicago's West Side, was a pilot community for interracial living. A handful of middle-class African Americans bought homes there on "contract"—that combined the responsibilities of home ownership with the disadvantages of renting. In a contract sale, the buyer accrued no equity, and if he missed a single payment, he would immediately lose his down payment, all his monthly payments, and the property itself. Unscrupulous sellers sold at inflated prices, then the families were evicted when they missed a payment. Another family would buy on contract, and the cycle fueled by greed just kept going.

Samuel appointed his sons judges over Israel, and they were driven by greed. His sons "did not follow his ways" (1 SAMUEL 8:3). In contrast to Samuel's integrity, his sons "turned aside after dishonest gain" and used their position to their own advantage. This unjust behavior displeased the elders of Israel and God, putting in motion a cycle of kings that fills the pages of the Old Testament (VV. 4–5).

To refuse to walk in God's ways allows room for the perversion of those values, and as a result injustice flourishes. To walk in His ways means honesty and justice are clearly seen not only in our words but in our deeds as well. Those good deeds are never an end in themselves but always that others may see and honor our Father in heaven.   *JOHN BLASE*

What current example of injustice are you aware of? What is one way you can work toward justice in that example?

God, injustice surrounds us on every side, often overwhelming our hearts. Help me to stand with those who suffer and commit my life to walking in Your ways.

You, God, are my God, earnestly I seek you.
[PSALM 63:1]

SEEKING GOD

I t's inspiring to watch people's passion and dedication in pursuing their dreams. A young woman I know recently graduated from college in just three years—a task that took total commitment. A friend wanted a particular car, so he worked diligently baking and selling cakes until he reached his goal. Another person who's in sales seeks to meet one hundred new people every week.

While it can be good to earnestly seek something of earthly value, there's a more important kind of seeking that we must consider.

In desperation, struggling in a desert, King David wrote, "You, God, are my God, earnestly I seek you" (PSALM 63:1). As David cried out to Him, God drew close to the weary king. David's deep spiritual thirst for God could only be satisfied in His presence.

The king remembered meeting with God in His "sanctuary" (V. 2), experiencing His all-conquering love (V. 3), and praising Him day after day—finding true satisfaction in Him that's not unlike enjoying a full and satisfying meal (VV. 4–5). Even during the night he contemplated God's greatness, recognizing His help and protection (VV. 6–7).

Today the Holy Spirit convicts us to earnestly seek after God. As we cling to Him, in power and love God holds us up with His strong right hand. By the leading of the Spirit, may we draw close to the Maker of all good things.   *DAVE BRANON*

How has the Holy Spirit been prompting you to seek God? What are some things you can do this week to grow closer to Him?

Thank You, God, for drawing me to seek after You. To know You better. To love You more. To recognize Your greatness. I'm so grateful for Your presence in my life.

Lord, we don't know where you are going, so how can
we know the way? [JOHN 14:5]

STAY ON THE WAY

Dusk fell as I followed Li Bao along the tops of terraced walls cut into the mountains of central China. I had never been this way before, and I couldn't see more than one step ahead or how steep the ground dropped off to our left. I gulped and stuck close to Li. I didn't know where we were going or how long it would take, but I trusted my friend.

I was in the same position as Thomas, the disciple who always seemed to need reassurance. Jesus told His disciples that He must leave to prepare a place for them and that they knew "the way to the place where [He was] going" (JOHN 14:4). Thomas asked a logical follow-up question: "Lord, we don't know where you are going, so how can we know the way?" (V. 5).

Jesus didn't quench Thomas's doubt by explaining where He was taking them. He simply assured His disciple that He was the way there. And that was enough.

We too have questions about our future. None of us know the details of what lies ahead. Life is full of twists we don't see coming. That's okay. It's enough to know Jesus, who is "the way and the truth and the life" (V. 6).

Jesus knows what's next. He only asks that we walk close to Him. *MIKE WITTMER*

**What's your biggest fear about your future?
Why is it enough to follow Jesus into that future?**

*Father, help us see that the journey is the destination,
and the way is Your Son.*

Stand firm. Let nothing move you.
[1 CORINTHIANS 15:58]

★ *APRIL TOPIC: CITIZENSHIP*
STANDING FIRM

I n the country where they live, Adrian and his family suffer persecution for their faith in Jesus. Yet, through it all, they demonstrate Christ's love. Standing in his church courtyard, which was pummeled by bullets when terrorists used it as training ground, he said, "Today is Good Friday. We remember that Jesus suffered for us on the cross." And suffering, he continued, is something that believers there understand. But his family chooses to remain: "We're still here, still standing."

These believers follow the example of the women who stood watching as Jesus died on the cross (MARK 15:40). They—including Mary Magdalene, Mary the mother of James and Joseph, and Salome—were brave to remain, for friends and family members of an enemy of the state could be ridiculed and punished. Yet the women showed their love for Jesus by their very presence with Him. Even as they "followed him and cared for his needs" in Galilee (V. 41), they stood with Him at His hour of deepest need.

On this day when we remember the greatest gift of our Savior, His death on a cross, take a moment to consider how we can stand for Jesus as we face trials of many kinds (SEE JAMES 1:2–4). Think too about fellow believers around the world who suffer for their faith. As Adrian asked, "Can you please stand with us in your prayers?"   *AMY BOUCHER PYE*

What does standing for Christ look like in your neighborhood? How can you support persecuted believers around the world?

Loving Savior, You willingly died to save us from our sins. On this day of remembrance, give us a deeper sense of gratitude for this amazing gift.

Since we have confidence to enter the
Most Holy Place … by a new and living way …
let us draw near to God. [HEBREWS 10:19–22]

CURTAINED OFF

As my flight reached cruising speed, the flight attendant pulled back the curtain that cordoned off first class, and I was given a startling reminder of the stark differences between areas on airplanes. Some travelers get to board first, enjoying premium seating with extra legroom and personalized service. The curtain was a humbling reminder of my separation from those perks.

Exclusionary distinctions between groups of people can be found throughout history, including, in a way, even God's temple in Jerusalem, though not due to one's ability to pay more. Non-Jewish people were only allowed to worship in the outer court. Next came the women's court, and even closer, an area designated for men. Finally, the holy of holies, seen as the place where God uniquely revealed Himself, was concealed behind a curtain and only accessible to one consecrated priest each year (HEBREWS 9:1–10).

But, wonderfully, this separation no longer exists. Jesus has completely eliminated any barriers that might hinder anyone seeking access to God—even our sin (10:17). Just as the temple curtain was torn in two at the moment of Christ's death (MATTHEW 27:50–51), His crucified body has torn away all obstructions to God's presence. There's no barrier that need separate any believer from experiencing the glory and love of the living God. *LISA M. SAMRA*

How does the truth that Christ's death provides access to God give you confidence when you worship and pray? What else does His death provide believers?

Jesus, thank You for being willing to die to open up full access to God to all who long for it.

I have seen the Lord!
[JOHN 20:18]

GRIEF OVERTURNED

According to Jim and Jamie Dutcher, filmmakers known for their knowledge of wolves, when happy, wolves wag their tails and romp about. But after the death of a pack member, they grieve for weeks. They visit the place where the pack member died, showing grief by their drooping tails and mournful howls.

Grief is a powerful emotion that we've all experienced, particularly at the death of a loved one or a treasured hope. Mary Magdalene experienced it. She had belonged to Christ's supporters and traveled with Him and His disciples (LUKE 8:1–3). But His cruel death on a cross separated them now. The only thing left for Mary to do for Jesus was to finish anointing His body for burial—a task the Sabbath had interrupted. But imagine how Mary felt upon arriving at the tomb and finding not a lifeless, broken body but a living Savior! Though she hadn't at first recognized the man standing before her, the sound of her name spoken by Him told her who He was—Jesus! Instantly, grief turned to joy. Mary now had joyful news to share: "I have seen the Lord!" (JOHN 20:18).

Jesus entered our dark world to bring freedom and life. His resurrection is a celebration of the fact that He accomplished what He set out to do. Like Mary, we can celebrate Christ's resurrection and share the good news that He's alive! *Alleluia!*   LINDA WASHINGTON

When have you experienced a time when your sadness turned to joy? How will you share the news of Christ's resurrection this week?

Jesus, I celebrate Your resurrection and the new life I can experience in You.

The LORD Almighty is with us.
[PSALM 46:11]

BEING CARED FOR

Debbie, the owner of a housecleaning service, was always searching for more clients to build up her business. On one call she talked with a woman whose response was, "I won't be able to afford that now; I'm undergoing cancer treatment." Right then Debbie decided that "no woman undergoing cancer treatment would ever be turned away. They would even be offered a free housecleaning service." So in 2005 she started a nonprofit organization where companies donated their cleaning services to women battling cancer. One such woman felt a rush of confidence when she came home to a clean house. She said, "For the first time, I actually believed I could beat cancer."

A feeling of being cared for and supported can help sustain us when we're facing a challenge. An awareness of God's presence and support can especially bring hope to encourage our spirit. Psalm 46, a favorite of many people going through trials, reminds us: "God is our refuge and strength, an ever-present help in trouble" and "Be still, and know that I am God; ...I will be exalted in the earth. The LORD Almighty is with us" (VV. 1, 10–11).

Reminding ourselves of God's promises and His presence with us can be a means to help renew our hearts and give us the courage and confidence to go through hard times. *ANNE CETAS*

For what trials are you depending on God for strength?
What Bible verses help you?

I'm grateful, God, for Your presence and Your promises. May I live out an attitude of confidence in You and Your ability to sustain me.

Let the one who has my word
speak it faithfully. [JEREMIAH 23:28]

THE FORECASTER'S MISTAKE

At noon on September 21, 1938, a young meteorologist warned the U.S. Weather Bureau of two fronts forcing a hurricane northward toward New England. But the chief of forecasting scoffed at Charles Pierce's prediction. Surely a tropical storm wouldn't strike so far north.

Two hours later, the 1938 New England Hurricane made landfall on Long Island. By 4:00 p.m. it had reached New England, tossing ships onto land as homes crumbled into the sea. More than six hundred people died. Had the victims received Pierce's warning—based on solid data and his detailed maps—they likely would have survived.

The concept of knowing whose word to heed has precedent in Scripture. In Jeremiah's day, God warned His people against false prophets. "Do not listen [to them]," He said. "They fill you with false hopes. They speak visions from their own minds, not from the mouth of the LORD" (JEREMIAH 23:16). God said of them, "If they had stood in my council, they would have proclaimed my words to my people" (V. 22).

"False prophets" are still with us. "Experts" dispense advice while ignoring God altogether or twisting His words to suit their purposes. But through His Word and Spirit, God has given us what we need to begin to discern the false from the true. As we gauge everything by the truth of His Word, our own words and lives will increasingly reflect that truth to others.   *TIM GUSTAFSON*

What's the standard I use when I decide whether something is true? What in my attitude needs to change toward those who disagree with me?

God, so many claim to speak for You these days. Help us learn what You really have to say. Make us sensitive to Your Spirit, not the spirit of this world.

Why, my soul, are you downcast? Why so disturbed within me? Put your hope in God, for I will yet praise him, my Savior and my God. [PSALM 42:5]

THE SINGING REVOLUTION

What does it take to ignite a revolution? Guns? Bombs? Guerrilla warfare? In late-1980s Estonia, it took songs. After the people had lived under the burden of Soviet occupation for decades, a movement began with the singing of a series of patriotic songs. These songs birthed the "Singing Revolution," which played a key role in restoring Estonian independence in 1991.

"This was a non-violent revolution that overthrew a very violent occupation," says a website describing the movement. "But singing had always been a major unifying force for Estonians while they endured fifty years of Soviet rule."

Music can also play a significant part in helping us through our own hard times. I wonder if that's why we so readily identify with the psalms. It was in a dark night of the soul that the psalmist sang, "Why, my soul, are you downcast? Why so disturbed within me? Put your hope in God, for I will yet praise him, my Savior and my God" (PSALM 42:5). It was in a season of deep disillusionment that Asaph, the worship leader, reminded himself, "Surely God is good to Israel, to those who are pure in heart" (73:1).

In our own challenging times, may we join the psalmists with a singing revolution for our hearts. Such a revolution overwhelms the personal tyranny of despair and confusion with faith-fueled confidence in God's great love and faithfulness.   *BILL CROWDER*

How do you respond when life is overwhelming?
What songs bring you the most comfort and why?

Father, I thank You that Your mercies are new every morning and Your faithfulness is great. Empower me to sing the song of Your great love—even when I must sing it through my tears.

How much more, having been reconciled,
shall we be saved through his life! [ROMANS 5:10]

FRIENDS AGAIN

A mother and her young daughter are sitting in church one day. During the service, opportunity is given for people to publicly receive God's forgiveness. Every time someone walks forward to do so, the little girl begins to clap. "I'm so sorry," the mother later tells the church leader. "I explained to my daughter that repentance makes us friends with God again, and she just wanted to cheer for everyone."

Simplified for a child's mind, the mother's words were a good explanation of the gospel. Once God's enemies, we have been reconciled to Him through Christ's death and resurrection (ROMANS 5:9–10). Now we're indeed God's friends. Since we were the ones to break the friendship (V. 8), repentance is our part in completing the restoration process. And the little girl's response couldn't have been more appropriate. Since all heaven claps when just one person repents (LUKE 15:10), she was unknowingly echoing its applause.

Jesus described His reconciling work in similar terms. "Greater love has no one than this: to lay down one's life for one's friends" (JOHN 15:13). As a result of this sacrificial act of friendship *toward* us, we can now be friends *with* Him. "I no longer call you servants.... Instead, I have called you friends" (15:15).

Once God's enemies, we are now God's friends. It's an over-whelming thought. And one worth clapping about.   *SHERIDAN VOYSEY*

How often do you describe your relationship with God as one of friendship? In practical terms, how is your friendship with Him going today?

God, thank You for loving me when I was still Your enemy. I repent of everything that disappoints You and celebrate being Your friend.

He holds success in store for the upright.
[PROVERBS 2:7]

★ *APRIL TOPIC: CITIZENSHIP*
NOW, THEN NEXT

I recently attended a high school graduation during which the speaker provided a needed challenge for the young adults awaiting their diplomas. He mentioned that this was a time in their lives when everyone was asking them, "What's next?" What career would they be pursuing next? Where would they be going to school or working next? Then he said that the more important question was what were they doing now?

In the context of their faith journey, what daily decisions would they be making that would guide them to live for Jesus and not for themselves?

His words reminded me of the book of Proverbs, which makes many pointed statements about how to live—now. For instance: practicing honesty, now (11:1); choosing the right friends, now (12:26); living with integrity, now (13:6); having good judgment, now (13:15); speaking wisely, now (14:3).

Living for God now, by the leading of the Holy Spirit, makes the decisions about what is next much easier. "The LORD gives wisdom; …He holds success in store for the upright, …he guards the course of the just and protects the way of his faithful ones" (2:6–8). May God supply what we need for us to live by His guidelines now, and may He guide us into what's next for His honor.   *DAVE BRANON*

What changes in direction do you need to make now to honor God? How can you seek God's guidance and empowerment in doing so?

Thank You, heavenly Father, for Your guidance in my life today. Protect me and give me wisdom to live in a way that both pleases You and reveals who You are.

Though one may be overpowered,
two can defend themselves. A cord of three strands
is not quickly broken. [ECCLESIASTES 4:12]

THE SADDEST GOOSE

Why is there a football in the parking lot? I wondered. But as I got closer, I realized the greyish lump wasn't a football: it was a *goose*—the saddest Canada goose I'd ever seen.

Geese often congregate on the lawn near my workplace in the spring and fall. But today there was only one, its neck arced back and its head tucked beneath a wing. *Where are your buddies?* I thought. Poor thing was all alone. It looked so lonely, I wanted to give it a hug. (Note: don't try this.)

I've rarely seen a goose completely alone like my lonesome feathered friend. Geese are notably communal, flying in a V-formation to deflect the wind. They're made to be together.

As human beings, we were created for community too (SEE GENESIS 2:18). And in Ecclesiastes 4:10, Solomon describes how vulnerable we are when we're alone: "Pity anyone who falls and has no one to help them up." There's strength in numbers, he added, for "though one may be overpowered, two can defend themselves. A cord of three strands is not quickly broken" (V. 12).

This is just as true for us spiritually as it is physically. God never intended for us to "fly" alone, vulnerably isolated. We need relationships with each other for encouragement, refreshment, and growth (SEE ALSO 1 CORINTHIANS 12:21).

Together, we can stand firm when life's headwinds gust our way. *Together.*   ADAM R. HOLZ

What kinds of circumstances tempt you to go it alone? Who do you know who could use a word of encouragement from you?

Loving God, help us to remember that You never meant us to fly solo, but together with our brothers and sisters in Christ. Today, help us to see and support someone in need of encouragement.

Oh, the depth of the riches of the wisdom and
knowledge of God! How unsearchable his judgments,
and his paths beyond tracing out! [ROMANS 11:33]

DIVINELY ALIGNED

I was deeply troubled and woke in the night to pace the floor
and pray. Frankly, my attitude was not one of prayerful sub-
mission to God, but one of questioning and anger. Finding no
release, I sat and stared out a large window at the night sky. I was
unexpectedly drawn to focus on Orion's Belt—those three perfectly arranged stars often visible on clear nights. I knew just
enough about astronomy to understand that those three stars
were hundreds of light years apart.

I realized the closer I could be to those stars, the less they
would appear to be aligned. Yet from my distant perspective,
they looked carefully configured in the heavens. At that moment,
I realized I was too close to my life to see what God sees. In His
big picture, everything is in perfect alignment.

The apostle Paul, as he completes a summary of the ultimate
purposes of God, breaks into a hymn of praise (ROMANS 11:33–36).
His words lift our gaze to our sovereign God, whose ways are
beyond our limited ability to understand or trace (V. 33). Yet the
One who holds all things together in the heavens and on earth is
intimately and lovingly involved with every detail of our lives
(MATTHEW 6:25–34; COLOSSIANS 1:16).

Even when things seem confusing, God's divine plans are unfold-
ing for our good and for God's honor and glory.　　*EVAN MORGAN*

**What questions do you long for God to answer? How can you
find rest and release through faith that His perspective of
our lives is in perfect alignment with His ultimate purposes?**

*Dear God, remind me that Your purposes and plans for my life are
beyond my understanding, and help me rest in You.*

He looked and saw the hills full of horses and chariots
of fire all around Elisha. [2 KINGS 6:17]

RUN TOWARD CHALLENGE

Tom chased the young men who were stealing his poor friend's bike. He didn't have a plan. He only knew he needed to get it back. To his surprise, the three thieves looked his way, dropped the bike and backed away. Tom was both relieved and impressed with himself as he picked up the bike and turned around. That's when he saw Jeff, his muscular friend who had been trailing close behind.

Elisha's servant panicked when he saw his town surrounded by an enemy army. He ran to Elisha, "Oh no, my lord! What shall we do?" Elisha told him to relax. "Those who are with us are more than those who are with them." Then God opened the servant's eyes, and he "saw the hills full of horses and chariots of fire all round Elisha" (VV. 15–17).

If you strive to follow Jesus, you may find yourself in some dicey situations. You may risk your reputation, and perhaps even your security, because you're determined to do what's right. You may lose sleep wondering how it will all turn out. Remember, you're not alone. You don't have to be stronger or smarter than the challenge before you. Jesus is with you, and His power is greater than all rivals. Ask yourself Paul's question, "If God is for us, who can be against us?" (ROMANS 8:31). Really, *who*? No one. Run toward your challenge, with God.   *MIKE WITTMER*

What wakes you up at night?
How can you give your worries to God?

Help me, Jesus, to truly see that You're bigger than any problem
facing me today. Thank You for Your everlasting presence!

He ... will rejoice over you with singing.
[ZEPHANIAH 3:17]

OUR FATHER SINGS

Dandy loves encouraging people by singing to them. One day we were having lunch at his favorite restaurant, and he noticed the waitress was having a hard day. He asked her a few questions and then started quietly singing a catchy, upbeat song to cheer her up. "Well, kind sir, you just made my day. Thank you so much," she said with a big smile, as she wrote down our food order.

When we open the book of Zephaniah, we find that God loves to sing. The prophet masterfully drew a picture with his words in which he described God as a musician who loves to sing for and with His children. He wrote that God "will take great delight in you; in his love he will no longer rebuke you, but will rejoice over you with singing" (3:17). God promised to be present forever with those who have been transformed by His mercy. But it doesn't stop there! He invites and joins in with His people to "be glad and rejoice with all your heart" (V. 14).

We can only imagine the day when we'll be together with God and with all those who've put their trust in Jesus as their Savior. How amazing it will be to hear our heavenly Father sing songs for and with us and experience His love, approval, and acceptance.

ESTERA PIROSCA ESCOBAR

How can you celebrate God's love for you? What song is He singing over you and with you today?

Heavenly Father, we know that because of our allegiance to Jesus, You not only accept us but celebrate with us and delight in us as Your children. Thank You for Your love.

When you pass through the waters,
I will be with you. [ISAIAH 43:2]

THROUGH THE WATERS

The movie *The Free State of Jones* tells the US Civil War story of Newton Knight and some Confederate deserters and slaves who aided the Union Army and then resisted slave-holders after the war. Many herald Knight as the hero, but two slaves first saved *his* life after his desertion. They carried him deep into a secluded swampland and tended a leg wound he suffered while fleeing Confederate forces. If they'd abandoned him, he would have died.

The people of Judah were wounded and desperate, facing enemies and feeling helpless. Israel had been overtaken by Assyria, and Isaiah prophesied that one day they (Judah) would also be overcome by an enemy—Babylonia. Judah needed a God who would help, who would rescue and not forsake them. Imagine, then, the surging hope when the people heard God's assurance: "Do not be afraid, for I am with you" (ISAIAH 43:5). Whatever calamity they faced or trouble they would endure, He would be with them. He would "pass through the waters" with them, leading them to safety (V. 2). He would "walk through the fire" with them, helping them through the scorching flames (V. 2).

Throughout Scripture, God promises to be with His people, to care for us, guide us, and never abandon us—whether in life or death. Even when you find yourself in difficult places, God is with you. He'll help you pass through the waters.   *WINN COLLIER*

What deep waters are you facing? How does God's promise to pass through them with you strengthen your heart today?

God, the water is deep, and I don't see how I'm going to make it through. Thank You for promising to be with me and to carry me through!

Paul did not think it wise to take him,
because he had deserted them. [ACTS 15:38]

A FRIEND IN FAILURE

O n November 27, 1939, three treasure hunters accompanied by film crews dug through the asphalt outside of the Hollywood Bowl amphitheater in Southern California. They were looking for the Cahuenga Pass treasure, consisting of gold, diamonds, and pearls rumored to have been buried there seventy-five years earlier.

They never found it. After twenty-four days of digging, they struck a boulder and stopped. All they accomplished was a nine-foot-wide, forty-two-foot-deep hole in the ground. They walked away dejected.

To err is human—we all fail sometimes. Scripture tells us that young Mark walked away from Paul and Barnabas on a missionary trip "and had not continued with them in the work." Because of this, "Paul did not think it wise to take him" on his next trip (ACTS 15:38), which resulted in a strong disagreement with Barnabas. But in spite of his initial failings, Mark shows up years later in surprising ways. When Paul was lonely and in prison toward the end of his life, he asked for Mark and called him "helpful to me in my ministry" (2 TIMOTHY 4:11). God even inspired Mark to write the gospel that bears his name.

Mark's life shows us that God won't leave us to face our errors and failures alone. We have a Friend who's greater than every mistake. As we follow our Savior, He'll provide the help and strength we need. *JAMES BANKS*

**What mistakes or failures have you faced recently?
In what ways have you discovered God's strength
as you shared them with Him in prayer?**

*Jesus, thank You for being there whenever I want to talk to You.
I praise You for the comfort and hope only You can give!*

The LORD our God is near us whenever
we pray to him. [DEUTERONOMY 4:7]

RIGHT BESIDE YOU

Each day at a post office in Jerusalem, workers sort through piles of undeliverable letters in an attempt to guide each to its recipient. Many end up in a specially marked box labeled "Letters to God."

About a thousand such letters reach Jerusalem each year, addressed simply to God or Jesus. Puzzled by what to do with them, one worker began taking the letters to Jerusalem's Western Wall to have them placed between its stone blocks with other written prayers. Most of the letters ask for a job, a spouse, or good health. Some request forgiveness, others just offer thanks. One man asked God if his deceased wife could appear in his dreams because he longed to see her again. Each sender believed God would listen, if only He could be reached.

The Israelites learned much as they journeyed through the wilderness. One lesson was that their God wasn't like the other gods known at the time—distant, deaf, geographically bound, reached only by lengthy pilgrimage or international mail. No, "the LORD our God is near us whenever we pray to him" (DEUTERONOMY 4:7). What other people could claim that? This was revolutionary news!

God doesn't live in Jerusalem. He's close by us, wherever we are. Some still need to discover this radical truth. If only each of those letters could be sent the reply: God is right beside you. Just talk to Him.   *SHERIDAN VOYSEY*

God's accessibility to us is a profound gift. How can you avoid taking it for granted? Who in your life needs to know of God's readiness to hear their prayer?

God, You are bigger than the universe yet closer than a breath. Thank You for being so interested in us, attending to every prayer.

If the Son sets you free,
you will be free indeed. [JOHN 8:36]

FREE INDEED

The film *Amistad* tells the story of West African slaves in 1839 taking over the boat that was transporting them and killing the captain and some of the crew. Eventually they were recaptured, imprisoned, and taken to trial. An unforgettable courtroom scene features Cinqué, leader of the slaves, passionately pleading for freedom. Three simple words—repeated with increasing force by a shackled man with broken English—eventually silenced the courtroom, "Give us free!" Justice was served and the men were freed.

Most people today aren't in danger of being physically bound, yet true liberation from the spiritual bondage of sin remains elusive. The words of Jesus in John 8:36 offer sweet relief: "So if the Son sets you free, you will be free indeed." Jesus pointed to Himself as the source of true emancipation because He offers forgiveness to anyone who believes in Him. Though some in Christ's audience claimed freedom (V. 33), their words, attitudes, and actions regarding Jesus betrayed their claim.

Jesus longs to hear those who would echo Cinqué's plea and say, "Give me freedom!" With compassion He awaits the cries of those who are shackled by unbelief or fear or failure. Freedom is a matter of the heart. Such liberty is reserved for those who believe that Jesus is God's Son who was sent into the world to break the power of sin's hold on us through His death and resurrection.

ARTHUR JACKSON

How has Jesus set you free? What can you share with others about God's liberating power?

Jesus, help me to believe that You can set me free.

REVEALED THROUGH CREATION

In the 1901 hymn "This is My Father's World," pastor and poet Maltbie Babcock wrote of the delight he felt on his frequent walks where he was captivated by breathtaking panoramic vistas. Writing of his fascination with the skies, seas, and creatures, he described sensing God's presence and concluded, "He speaks to me everywhere."

Although creation doesn't have an audible voice, as His handiwork it's one important way we learn about the One who "made the heavens and the earth and the sea and everything in them" (ACTS 14:15). In creation we see evidence of God's glory (PSALM 19:1), as well as aspects of who God is, such as His eternal nature (ROMANS 1:20).

> **Creation is a way that God restores our souls.**

When we observe the strength of the wind or the roar of rushing water, creation showcases God's power. Described in the poetry of Job 38, His power is evident in ordering the seasons (VV. 12–13), directing the weather (VV. 22–30), overseeing the cosmos (VV. 31–33), and sustaining living creatures (VV. 39–41).

Creation is also the means by which we experience many of God's blessings. Through creation, God blesses us with food and drink (GENESIS 1:29–30), as well as many other necessities that sustain us (MATTHEW 6:25–33). More than simply a physical blessing, creation is a way that God restores our souls as we experience the peace of gentle pastures and quiet streams (PSALM 23: 1–3).

In all these ways and more, creation is visible and tangible evidence of who our Creator God is, revealing His character, love, and constant care of us.

LISA M. SAMRA, OUR DAILY BREAD *AUTHOR*

[The LORD said,] "I will be their God
and they will be my people." [JEREMIAH 31:33]

★ *MAY TOPIC: CREATION*

THE MAKER OF THE MOON

After astronauts set the *Eagle* down in the Sea of Tranquility, Neil Armstrong said, "That's one small step for man, one giant leap for mankind." He was the first human to walk on the surface of the moon. Other space travelers followed, including the commander of the last Apollo mission, Gene Cernan. "There I was, and there you are, the Earth—dynamic, overwhelming, and I felt . . . it was just too beautiful to happen by accident," Cernan said, "There has to be somebody bigger than you and bigger than me." Even from their unique view in deep space, these men understood their smallness in comparison to the vastness of the universe.

The prophet Jeremiah also considered the immensity of God as Creator and Sustainer of the earth and beyond. The Maker of all promised to reveal Himself intimately as He offered His people love, forgiveness, and hope (JEREMIAH 31:33–34). Jeremiah affirms God's enormity as He who "appoints the sun to shine by day, who decrees the moon and stars to shine by night" (V. 35). Our Creator and Lord Almighty will reign above all as He works to redeem all of His people (VV. 36–37).

We'll never finish exploring the immeasurable vastness of the heavens and depths of the earth's foundations. But we can stand in awe at the complexity of the universe and trust the maker of the moon—and everything else.   XOCHITL DIXON

How does imagining God's bigness as Creator and Sustainer of the universe help you trust Him with the obstacles that come your way? How does the complexity of the universe help you trust God with the details of your life?

Creator and Sustainer of all, thanks for inviting us to know You and trust You today and forever.

He took bread, gave thanks and broke it,
and gave it to them, saying, "This is my body
given for you." [LUKE 22:19]

COMMUNITY MEMORY

I n his book *Restless Faith*, theologian Richard Mouw talks about
the importance of remembering the lessons of the past. He
quotes sociologist Robert Bellah, who said that "healthy nations
must be 'communities of memory.' " Bellah extended that principle to other societal bonds such as families. Remembering is an
important part of living in community.

The Scriptures teach the value of community memory as well.
The Israelites were given the Passover feast to remind them of
what God had done to rescue them from slavery in Egypt
(SEE EXODUS 12:1–30). Still today, Jewish people around the world
revisit that rich community memory every spring.

Passover holds great meaning for followers of Christ too, for
Passover has always pointed to the work of the Messiah on the
cross. It was during Passover, the night before the cross, that Jesus
established His own memorial table. Luke 22:19 records, "He took
bread, gave thanks and broke it, and gave it to them, saying, 'This
is my body given for you; do this in remembrance of me.'"

Every time we gather at the Lord's Table to celebrate Communion,
we remember that Christ rescued us from slavery to sin and provided us with eternal life. May the rescuing love of Jesus remind us
that His cross is worth remembering—together.   *BILL CROWDER*

**Why is it valuable to take Communion with other believers
in Jesus? How does the shared event remind you of Jesus'
sacrificial love?**

*Thank You, Father, for the gift of Your Son. Thank You also that He
has given us a tangible way to remember His sacrifice whenever we
gather at the Table.*

You may be sure that your sin
will find you out. [NUMBERS 32:23]

THE ONE WHO SEES

"**O**h no!" My wife's voice rang out when she stepped into the kitchen. The moment she did, our ninety-pound Labrador retriever "Max" bolted from the room.

Gone was the leg of lamb that had been sitting too close to the edge of the counter. Max had consumed it, leaving only an empty pan. He tried to hide under a bed. But only his head and shoulders fit. His uncovered rump and tail betrayed his whereabouts when I went to track him down.

"Oh, Max," I murmured, "Your 'sin' will find you out." The phrase was borrowed from Moses, when he admonished two tribes of Israel to be obedient to God and keep their promises. He told them: "But if you fail to do this, you will be sinning against the LORD; and you may be sure that your sin will find you out" (NUMBERS 32:23).

Sin may feel good for a moment, but it causes the ultimate pain of separation from God. Moses was reminding his people that God misses nothing. As one biblical writer put it, "Everything is uncovered and laid bare before the eyes of him to whom we must give account" (HEBREWS 4:13).

Though seeing all, our holy God lovingly draws us to confess our sin, repent of it (turn from it), and walk rightly with Him (1 JOHN 1:9). May we follow Him in love today.   *JAMES BANKS*

How does the truth that God sees everything we do and still loves us encourage you to turn from sin? In what practical ways can you respond to His love today?

Thank You for being "the God who sees me" (GENESIS 16:13). I praise You that though You see both good and bad, You sent Your Son to save and set me free. Help me to walk in loving obedience.

I will restore David's fallen shelter—I will repair its broken walls and restore its ruins—and will rebuild it as it used to be. [AMOS 9:11]

ECLIPSE

I was prepared with eye protection, an ideal viewing location, and homemade moon pie desserts. Along with millions of people in the US, my family watched the rare occurrence of a total solar eclipse—the moon covering the entire disk of the sun.

The eclipse caused an unusual darkness to come over the typically bright summer afternoon. Although for us this eclipse was a fun celebration and a reminder of God's incredible power over creation (PSALM 135:6–7), throughout history darkness during the day has been seen as abnormal and foreboding (EXODUS 10:21; MATTHEW 27:45), a sign that everything is not as it should be.

This is what darkness signified for Amos, a prophet during the time of the divided monarchy in ancient Israel. Amos warned the Northern Kingdom that destruction would come if they continued to turn away from God. As a sign, God would "make the sun go down at noon and darken the earth in broad daylight" (AMOS 8:9).

But God's ultimate desire and purpose was—and is—to make all things right. Even when the people were taken into exile, God promised to one day bring a remnant back to Jerusalem and "repair its broken walls and restore its ruins" (9:11).

Even when life is at its darkest, like Israel, we can find comfort in knowing God is at work to bring light and hope back—to *all* people (ACTS 15:14–18).   *LISA M. SAMRA*

When was a time you chose to reject or disobey God? How did God provide rescue and bring light into your dark situation?

Jesus, as we read in Revelation 21:23, thank You that You shine brighter than the sun and turn back the darkness.

All at once an angel touched him and said,
"Get up and eat." [1 KINGS 19:5]

STRENGTH FOR THE JOURNEY

One summer, I faced what seemed an impossible task—a big writing project with a looming deadline. Having spent day after day on my own, endeavoring to get the words onto the page, I felt exhausted and discouraged, and I wanted to give up. A wise friend asked me, "When's the last time you felt refreshed? Maybe you need to allow yourself to rest and to enjoy a good meal."

I knew immediately that she was right. Her advice made me think of Elijah and the terrifying message he received from Jezebel (1 KINGS 19:2)—although, of course, my writing project wasn't anywhere near the cosmic scale of the prophet's experience. After Elijah triumphed over the false prophets on Mount Carmel, Jezebel sent word that she would capture and kill him, and he despaired, longing to die. But then he enjoyed a good sleep and was twice visited by an angel who gave him food to eat. After God renewed his physical strength, he was able to continue with his journey.

When the "journey is too much" for us (V. 7), we might need to rest and enjoy a healthy and satisfying meal. For when we are exhausted or hungry, we can easily succumb to disappointment or fear. But when God meets our physical needs through His resources, as much as possible in this fallen world, we can take the next step in serving Him.　　　　　　　　　　　　　*AMY BOUCHER PYE*

Looking back, when have you needed to slow down and receive sustenance before pressing on? How can you look for signs of burnout as you serve God?

Creator God, You formed us as Your people. Thank You for our limitations, which remind us that You're God and we're not. Help us to serve You with gladness and joy.

Father, forgive them.
[LUKE 23:34]

IMPOSSIBLE FORGIVENESS

Liberators found the following prayer crumpled among the remains of the Ravensbruck concentration camp where Nazis exterminated nearly 50,000 women: *O Lord, remember not only the men and women of goodwill, but also those of ill will. But do not remember the suffering they have inflicted upon us. Remember the fruits we brought thanks to this suffering—our comradeship, our loyalty, our humility, the courage, the generosity, the greatness of heart which has grown out of this. And when they come to judgment, let all the fruits that we have borne be their forgiveness.*

I can't imagine the fear and pain inflicted on the terrorized woman who wrote this prayer. I can't imagine what kind of inexplicable grace these words required of her. She did the unthinkable: she sought God's forgiveness for her oppressors.

This prayer echoes Christ's prayer. After being wrongly accused, mocked, beaten, and humiliated before the people, Jesus was "crucified . . . along with [two] criminals" (LUKE 23:33). Hanging, with mutilated body and gasping for breath, from a rough-hewn cross, I would expect Jesus to pronounce judgment on His tormentors, to seek retribution or divine justice. However, Jesus uttered a prayer contradicting every human impulse: "Father, forgive them, for they do not know what they are doing" (V. 34).

The forgiveness Jesus offers seems impossible, but He offers it to us. In His divine grace, impossible forgiveness spills free.

WINN COLLIER

How has God's impossible forgiveness changed you? How can we help others experience true forgiveness in Him?

God, Your forgiveness is a strange, impossible thing. In our pain, it's hard to imagine this possibility. Help us. Teach us Your love.

BIBLE IN A YEAR | 1 KINGS 21–22; LUKE 23:26–56

The Spirit intercedes for God's people.
[ROMANS 8:27]

GO-BETWEEN PRAYER

Late one Saturday afternoon, my family and I stopped at a local restaurant for lunch. As the waiter set crispy fries and thick burgers on our table, my husband glanced up and asked his name. Then he said, "We pray as a family before we eat. Is there something we can pray for you today?" Allen, whose name we now knew, looked at us with a mixture of surprise and anxiety. A short silence followed before he told us that he was sleeping on his friend's couch each night, his car had just quit working, and he was broke.

As my husband quietly asked God to provide for Allen and show him His love, I thought about how our go-between prayer was similar to what happens when the Holy Spirit takes up our cause and connects us with God. In our moments of greatest need—when we realize we're no match to handle life on our own, when we don't know what to say to God, "The Spirit intercedes for God's people" (ROMANS 8:27). What the Spirit says is a mystery, but we're assured that it always fits with God's will for our lives.

The next time you pray for God's guidance, provision, and protection in someone else's life, let that act of kindness remind you that your spiritual needs are also being lifted to God who knows your name and cares about your problems.

JENNIFER BENSON SCHULDT

Is there anyone you can pray for today? How might you respond to temptation differently if you knew that the Holy Spirit was praying for you during the struggle?

Jesus, I thank You that temptation has no power to separate me from You. Please give me victory today through the power of Your resurrection from the dead.

I praise you because I am fearfully
and wonderfully made; your works are wonderful,
I know that full well. [PSALM 139:14]

★ *MAY TOPIC: CREATION*

AMAZING SKILL

The leader of our college singing group directed the group *and* accompanied us on the piano at the same time, skillfully balancing those responsibilities. At the close of one concert, he looked particularly weary, so I asked him if he was okay. He responded, "I've never had to do that before." Then he explained. "The piano was so out of tune that I had to play the whole concert in two different keys—my left hand playing in one key and my right hand in another!" I was blown away by the startling skill he displayed, and I was amazed at the One who creates humans to be capable of such things.

King David expressed an even greater sense of wonder when he wrote, "Thank you for making me so wonderfully complex! Your workmanship is marvelous—how well I know it" (PSALM 139:14 NLT). Whether in people's abilities or nature's marvels, the wonders of creation point us to the majesty of our Creator.

One day, when we're in God's presence, people from every generation will worship Him with the words, "You are worthy, our Lord and God, to receive glory and honor and power, for you created all things, and by your will they were created and have their being" (REVELATION 4:11). The amazing skills God gives us and the great beauty God has created are ample reason to worship Him.

BILL CROWDER

What parts of God's creation cause you to respond in worship? Why is it important for you to thank and praise God for the skills He's given you?

How wonderful You are, God! I see Your fingerprints everywhere. Thank You for all that You've made.

BIBLE IN A YEAR | 2 KINGS 4–6; LUKE 24:36–53   135

The LORD gave and the LORD has taken away;
may the name of the LORD be praised. [JOB 1:21]

DOUBT AND FAITH

MingTeck woke up with a severe headache and thought it was another migraine. But when he got out of bed, he collapsed onto the floor. He was admitted to the hospital where the doctors informed him he'd had a stroke. After four months of rehabilitation, he recovered his ability to think and talk but still walks with a painful limp. He often struggles with despair, but he finds great comfort from the book of Job.

Job lost all his wealth and his children overnight. Despite the harrowing news, he at first looked to God in hope and praised Him for being the source of everything. He acknowledged God's sovereign hand even in times of calamity (JOB 1:21). We marvel at his strong faith, but Job also struggled with despair. After he lost his health too (2:7), he cursed the day he was born (3:1). He was honest with his friends and God about his pain. Eventually, however, he came to accept that both good and bad come from God's hand (13:15; 19:25–27).

In our sufferings, we too may find ourselves vacillating between despair and hope, doubt and faith. God doesn't require us to be dauntless in the face of adversity but instead invites us to come to Him with our questions. Though our faith may fail at times, we can trust God to always be faithful.   *POH FANG CHIA*

What doubts and questions do you need to bring before God today? How can you use Job 1:21 to guide you in your prayers?

Dear Father, when doubts and fears overwhelm me, help me remember I'm precious in Your sight. You're always in control, and You care for me.

And so we know and rely on the love
God has for us. God is love. [1 JOHN 4:16]

FOREVER LOVE

Years ago, my four-year-old son gave me a framed wooden heart mounted on a metal plate with the word *forever* painted in its center. "I love you forever, Mommy," he said. I thanked him with a hug. "I love you more."

That priceless gift still assures me of my son's never-ending love. On tough days, God uses that sweet present to comfort and encourage me as He affirms I'm deeply loved.

The frame also reminds me of the gift of God's everlasting love, as expressed throughout His Word and confirmed by His Spirit. We can trust God's unchanging goodness and sing grateful praises that confirm His enduring love, as the psalmist does (PSALM 136:1). We can exalt the Lord as greater than and above all (VV. 2–3), as we reflect on His endless wonders and unlimited understanding (VV. 4–5). The God who loves us forever is the conscious and caring Maker of the heavens and earth, who maintains control of time itself (VV. 6–9).

We can rejoice because the everlasting love the psalmist sang about is the same continuing love our all-powerful Creator and Sustainer pours into the lives of His children today. No matter what we're facing, the One who made us and remains with us strengthens us by asserting He loves us unconditionally and completely. Thank You, God, for the countless reminders of Your endless and life-transforming love!   *XOCHITL DIXON*

**How has God assured you of His love? How has He strengthened
your faith?**

*God, please help us to love You and others, as we become more
confident in Your never-ending love for us.*

From the lips of children and infants you, Lord, have called forth your praise. [MATTHEW 21:16]

LEARNING FROM LITTLE ONES

When a friend and I rode into one of the slums in Nairobi, Kenya, our hearts were deeply humbled by the poverty we witnessed. In that same setting, however, different emotions—like fresh waters—were stirred in us as we witnessed young children running and shouting, *"Mchungaji, Mchungaji!"* (Swahili for "pastor"). Such was their joy-filled response upon seeing their spiritual leader in the vehicle with us. With these tender shouts, the little ones welcomed the one known for his care and concern for them.

As Jesus arrived in Jerusalem riding on a donkey, joyful children were among those who celebrated Him. "Blessed is he who comes in the name of the Lord! . . . Hosanna to the Son of David" (MATTHEW 21:9, 15). But praises for Jesus were not the only sounds in the air. One can imagine the noisiness of scurrying, money-making merchants who were put to flight by Jesus (VV. 12–13). Furthermore, religious leaders who had witnessed His kindness in action "were indignant" (VV. 14–15). They voiced their displeasure with the children's praises (V. 16) and thereby exposed the poverty of their own hearts.

We can learn from the faith of children of God of all ages and places who recognize Jesus as the Savior of the world. He's the One who hears our praises and cries, and He cares for and rescues us when we come to Him with childlike trust.   *ARTHUR JACKSON*

How have your views of Jesus changed over the years? What things get in the way of seeing Him as the Son of God who has come to save you?

Jesus, help me to see You for who You are—my Lord and Savior.

In my distress I called to the LORD ....
My cry came to his ears. [2 SAMUEL 22:7]

OPEN ARMS

Saydee and his family have an "open arms and open home" philosophy. People are always welcome in their home, "especially those who are in distress," he says. That's the kind of household he had growing up in Liberia with his nine siblings. Their parents always welcomed others into their family. He says, "We grew up as a community. We loved one another. Everybody was responsible for everybody. My dad taught us to love each other, care for each other, protect each other."

When King David was in need, he found this type of loving care in God. Second Samuel 22 (and Psalm 18) records his song of praise to God for the ways He had been a refuge for him throughout his life. He recalled, "In my distress I called to the LORD; I called out to my God. From his temple he heard my voice; my cry came to his ears" (2 SAMUEL 22:7). God had delivered him from his enemies, including King Saul, many times. He praised God for being his fortress and deliverer in whom he took refuge (VV. 2–3).

While our distresses may be small in comparison to David's, God welcomes us to run to Him to find the shelter we long for. His arms are always open. Therefore we "sing the praises of [His] name" (V. 50). *ANNE CETAS*

**When has God been your refuge?
How can you help someone else run to Him?**

God, I'm grateful You've always been and will always be my secure place to land.

He must become greater;
I must become less. [JOHN 3:30]

PHOTOBOMBING JESUS

When my pastor asked our class a difficult question about the life of Jesus, my hand shot up. I had just read the story, so I knew this one. And I wanted the others in the room to know that I knew it too. After all, I'm a Bible teacher. How embarrassing it would be to be stumped in front of them! Now I was embarrassed by my fear of embarrassment. So I lowered my hand. *Am I this insecure?*

John the Baptist shows a better way. When his disciples complained that people were beginning to leave him and follow Jesus, John said he was glad to hear it. He was merely the messenger. "I am not the Messiah but am sent ahead of him. . . . He must become greater; I must become less" (3:28–30). John realized the point of his existence was Jesus. He is "the one who comes from heaven" and "is above all" (V. 31)—the divine Son who gave His life for us. He must receive all the glory and fame.

Any attention drawn to ourselves distracts from God. And since He is our only Savior and the only hope for the world, any credit we steal from Him ends up hurting us.

Let's resolve to step out of the picture—to stop photobombing Jesus. It's best for Him, for the world, and for us.　　*MIKE WITTMER*

**When are you tempted to share the spotlight with Jesus?
How can you turn the attention to where it belongs?**

Heavenly Father, help us understand that our task is to direct everyone's attention to Your Son, so that He increasingly fills up the frame. Help us see that we must decrease and He must increase.

For by one sacrifice he has made perfect forever those
who are being made holy. [HEBREWS 10:14]

UNDER CONSTRUCTION

hey just repaved this road, I thought to myself as the traffic
slowed. *Now they're tearing it up again!* Then I wondered,
*Why is road construction never done? I mean, I've never
seen a sign proclaiming, "The paving company is finished. Please
enjoy this perfect road."*

But something similar is true in my spiritual life. Early in my
faith, I imagined reaching a moment of maturity when I'd have it
all figured out, when I'd be "smoothly paved." Thirty years later,
I confess I'm still "under construction." Just like the perpetually
potholed roads I drive, I never seem to be "finished" either.
Sometimes that can feel equally frustrating.

But Hebrews 10 contains an amazing promise. Verse 14 says,
"For by one sacrifice he has made perfect forever those who are
being made holy." Jesus' work on the cross has *already* saved us.
Completely. Perfectly. In God's eyes, we are whole and finished.
But paradoxically, that process isn't done yet while we're still on
earth. We're still being shaped into His likeness, still "being
made holy."

One day, we'll see Him face-to-face, and we shall be like him
(1 JOHN 3:2). But until then, we're still "under construction," people who anxiously await the glorious day when the work in us is
truly complete. *ADAM R. HOLZ*

**Do you ever get frustrated that spiritual progress seems slower
than you expected? How does this passage from Hebrews
encourage you to think about your spiritual growth?**

*Faithful God, sometimes I get frustrated that my spiritual progress
seems slow. Help me to remember that You're still at work in my life,
shaping me and helping me to become more and more like You.*

There will be no night there.
[REVELATION 21:25]

★ *MAY TOPIC: CREATION*

LOOK UP!

When filmmaker Wylie Overstreet showed strangers a live picture of the moon as seen through his powerful telescope, they were stunned at the up-close view, reacting with whispers and awe. To see such a glorious sight, Overstreet explained, "fills us with a sense of wonder that there's something much bigger than ourselves."

The psalmist David also marveled at God's heavenly light. "When I consider your heavens, the work of your fingers, the moon and the stars, which you have set in place, what is mankind that you are mindful of them, human beings that you care for them?" (PSALM 8:3–4).

David's humbling question puts our awe in perspective when we learn that, after God creates His new heaven and earth, we'll no longer need the moon or the sun. Instead, said John the apostle, God's shimmering glory will provide all necessary light. "The city does not need the sun or the moon to shine on it, for the glory of God gives it light, and the Lamb is its lamp. . . . There will be no night there" (REVELATION 21:23–25).

What an amazing thought! Yet we can experience His heavenly light now—simply by seeking Christ, the Light of the world. In Overstreet's view, "We should look up more often." As we do, may we see God.   *PATRICIA RAYBON*

What does God's heavenly light teach you about God?
When you praise the glory of God, what do you experience?

Our wondrous God, I'm awed by Your holy glory,
and I praise You for Your marvelous Light.

He did not say anything to them
without using a parable. [MARK 4:34]

TELL ME A STORY

Once upon a time. Those four words just might be among the most powerful in the entire world. Some of my earliest memories as a boy contain a variation on that potent phrase. My mother came home one day with a large, hardcover illustrated edition of biblical stories—*My Good Shepherd Bible Story Book.* Every evening before lights-out, my brother and I would sit expectantly as she read to us of a time long ago filled with interesting people and the God who loved them. Those stories became a lens for how we looked at the great big world.

The undisputed greatest storyteller ever? Jesus of Nazareth. He knew we all carry inside us an innate love for stories, so that was the medium He consistently used to communicate His good news: *Once upon a time* there was a man who scattered "seed on the ground" (MARK 4:26). *Once upon a time* there was "a mustard seed" (V. 31), and on and on. Mark's gospel clearly indicates that Jesus used stories in His interactions with everyday people (V. 34) as a way to help them see the world more clearly and understand more thoroughly the God who loved them.

That's wise to remember as we desire to share with others God's good news of mercy and grace. The use of story is almost impossible to resist.　　　　　　　　　　　　　　*JOHN BLASE*

How could you weave a story or parable into your conversations this week? Maybe something like, "Once upon a time, God answered my prayer in a surprising way . . . ."

Jesus, You're the Wonderful Counselor and the Great and Mighty God. Give us creativity in the ways in which we share Your love with a world that still slows down to hear a story.

[Jesus] was the son, so it was thought, of Joseph.
[LUKE 3:23]

WHAT'S IN A NAME?

In God's timing, our son Kofi was born on a Friday, which is exactly what his name means—boy born on Friday. We named him after a Ghanaian friend of ours, a pastor whose only son died. He prays for our Kofi constantly. We're deeply honored.

It's easy to miss the significance in a name if you don't know the story behind it. In Luke 3, we find a fascinating detail about a name in the ancestry of Joseph. The genealogy traces Joseph's line backward all the way to Adam and even to God (V. 38). In verse 31 we read: "the son of Nathan, the son of David." Nathan? That's interesting. In 1 Chronicles 3:5 we learn that Nathan was born to Bathsheba.

Is it coincidence that David named Bathsheba's child Nathan? Recall the backstory. Bathsheba was never supposed to be David's wife. Another Nathan—the prophet—bravely confronted the king for abusing his authority to exploit Bathsheba and murder her husband (SEE 2 SAMUEL 12).

David accepted the prophet's point-blank rebuke and repented of his horrific offenses. With the healing passage of time, he would name his son Nathan. How appropriate that this was Bathsheba's son, and that he would be one of the ancestors of Joseph, Jesus' earthly dad (LUKE 3:23).

In the Bible, we keep finding God's grace woven into everything—even into an obscure name in a seldom-read genealogy. God's grace is everywhere.   *TIM GUSTAFSON*

What unlikely places have you seen God's grace showing up in your life? How can focusing on God's big story help you find the grace in your part of that story?

Dear God, help us to find Your grace everywhere we look.

You may now dismiss your servant in peace. For my
eyes have seen your salvation. [LUKE 2:29–30]

THE GIFT OF PEACE

"I believe in Jesus and He is my Savior, and I have no fear of
death," said Barbara Bush, the wife of former US President
George H. W. Bush, to her son before she died. This incredible and confident statement suggests a strong and deep-rooted
faith. She experienced God's gift of peace that comes from
knowing Jesus, even when faced with death.

Simeon, a resident of Jerusalem during the first century, also
experienced profound peace because of Jesus. Moved by the Holy
Spirit, Simeon went to the temple where Mary and Joseph brought
baby Jesus "to present him to the Lord" (LUKE 2:22). Although not
much is known about Simeon, from Luke's description one can tell
he was a special man of God, just and devout, waiting faithfully for
the coming Messiah, and "the Holy Spirit was on him" (V. 25). Yet
Simeon did not experience *shalom* (peace), a deep sense of completeness, until he saw Jesus.

While holding Jesus in his arms, Simeon broke into a song of
praise, expressing full satisfaction in God: "You may now dismiss
your servant in peace. For my eyes have seen your salvation, which
you have prepared in the sight of all nations" (VV. 29–31). He had
peace because he foresaw the future hope of the whole world.

As we celebrate the life, death, and resurrection of Jesus, the
promised Savior, may we rejoice in God's gift of peace.

ESTERA PIROSCA ESCOBAR

**Have you experienced this deep sense of satisfaction and
completeness that comes from knowing Jesus? How can you
celebrate God's gift of peace today?**

Dear Father, thank You for Jesus, Your gift of peace.

The LORD watches over the way of the righteous.
[PSALM 1:6]

WHERE CHOICES LEAD

With no cell service and no trail map, we had just our memory of a fixed map at the trailhead to guide us. More than an hour later, we finally emerged from the woods into the parking lot. Having missed the turn-off that would have made for a half-mile hike, we took a *much* longer trek.

Life can be like that: we have to ask not simply if something is right or wrong, but where it will lead. Psalm 1 compares two ways of living—that of the righteous (those who love God) and that of the wicked (the enemies of those who love God). The righteous flourish like a tree, but the wicked blow away like chaff (VV. 3–4). This psalm reveals what flourishing really looks like. The person who lives it out is dependent on God for renewal and life.

So how do we become that kind of person? Among other things, Psalm 1 urges us to disengage from destructive relationships and unhealthy habits and to delight in God's instruction (V. 2). Ultimately, the reason for our flourishing is God's attentiveness to us: "The LORD watches over the way of the righteous" (V. 6).

Commit your way to God, let Him redirect you from old patterns that lead to nowhere, and allow the Scriptures to be the river that nourishes the root system of your heart.   *GLENN PACKIAM*

**What friendships or habits do you need to make a break from?
How can you create more time in your schedule to read the Bible?**

Dear Jesus, give me the grace to turn away from the things leading me down the wrong path. Lead me to the river of Your presence, and nourish me with the Scriptures. Make my life faithful and fruitful for Your honor.

God ... has set you above your companions by
anointing you with the oil of joy. [HEBREWS 1:9]

THE SMILING JESUS

I f you were to play the part of Jesus in a movie, how would you
approach the role? That was the challenge faced by Bruce
Marchiano, who played Jesus in the 1993 Visual Bible movie
Matthew. Knowing that millions of viewers would draw conclu-
sions about Jesus based on his work, the weight of getting Christ
"right" felt overwhelming. He fell to his knees in prayer and
begged Jesus for—well, for *Jesus*.

Bruce gained insight from the first chapter of Hebrews, where
the writer tells us how God the Father set the Son apart by
anointing Him "with the oil of joy" (1:9). This kind of joy is one of
celebration—a gladness of connection to the Father expressed
wholeheartedly. Such joy ruled in Jesus' heart throughout His
life. As Hebrews 12:2 describes it, "For the joy set before him he
endured the cross, scorning its shame, and sat down at the right
hand of the throne of God."

Taking his cue from this scriptural expression, Bruce offered a
uniquely joy-filled portrayal of his Savior. As a result, he became
known as "the smiling Jesus." We too can dare to fall to our knees
and "beg Jesus for Jesus." May He so fill us with His character
that people around us see the expression of His love in us!

ELISA MORGAN

**What are your perceptions of Jesus and how might they need
to change? How can you represent Him as you show His heart to
the world?**

*Dear Jesus, we beg You for You. May Your heart be what others see in
us today. May we radiate Your joy in all we say and do.*

Nation will not take up sword against nation, nor will
they train for war anymore. [ISAIAH 2:4]

THE KNIFE ANGEL

When knife crime rose across the United Kingdom, the British Ironwork Centre came up with an idea. Working with local police forces, the Centre built and placed two hundred deposit boxes around the country and ran an amnesty campaign. One hundred thousand knives were anonymously surrendered, some still with blood on their blades. These were then shipped to artist Alfie Bradley, who blunted them, inscribed some with the names of young knife-crime victims, plus messages of regret from ex-offenders. All 100,000 weapons were then welded together to create the *Knife Angel*—a twenty-seven-foot-high angelic sculpture with shimmering steel wings.

When I stood before the *Knife Angel,* I wondered how many thousands of wounds had been prevented by its existence. I thought too of Isaiah's vision of the new heavens and earth (ISAIAH 65:17), a place where children won't die young (V. 20) or grow up in crime-breeding poverty (VV. 22–23), a place where knife crime is no more because all swords have been reshaped and given more creative purposes (2:4).

That new world isn't yet here, but we are to pray and serve until its arrival (MATTHEW 6:10). In its own way, the *Knife Angel* gives us a glimpse of God's promised future. Swords become plow shares. Weapons become artworks. What other redemptive projects can we conjure up to glimpse that future a little more?

SHERIDAN VOYSEY

What inspires you to combat evil? How can you work for peace in your community?

Jesus, we can't wait until the world is at peace under Your reign. Move us by Your Spirit to help see Your kingdom come in our communities.

The LORD God took the man and put him in
the Garden of Eden to work it and take care of it.
[GENESIS 2:15]

★ *MAY TOPIC: CREATION*

CULTIVATING GOD'S WORLD

"**D**ad, why do you have to go to work?" The question from my young daughter was motivated by her desire to play with me. I would have preferred to skip work and spend time with her, but there was a growing list of things at work that required my attention. The question, nevertheless, is a good one. Why *do* we work? Is it simply to provide for ourselves and for the people we love? What about labor that's unpaid—why do we do that?

Genesis 2 tells us that God placed the first human in the garden to "work it and take care of it" (V. 15). My father-in-law is a farmer, and he often tells me he farms for the sheer love of land and live-stock. That's beautiful, but it leaves lingering questions for those who don't love their work. Why did God put us in a particular place with a particular assignment?

Genesis 1 gives us the answer. We're made in God's image to carefully steward the world He made (V. 26). Pagan stories of the way the world began reveal "gods" making humans to be their slaves. Genesis declares that the one true God made humans to be His representatives—to steward what He'd made on His behalf. May we reflect His wise and loving order into the world. Work is a call to cultivate God's world for His glory.   *GLENN PACKIAM*

**What's the work God has given you to do? How could you cultivate
this "field" by bringing order into it and bringing good from it,
by His grace?**

*Dear God, thank You for the honor of joining You in Your work in the
world. Help me to reflect Your love, wisdom, and order in my life and
in the place where I work.*

For God . . . made his light shine in our hearts.
[2 CORINTHIANS 4:6]

KEEPERS OF THE LIGHT

They call them "Keepers of the Light."

At the lighthouse on the cape of Hatteras Island just off the North Carolina coast of the United States, there's a memorial to those who've tended the light stations there since 1803. Shortly after the existing structure was moved inland because of shoreline erosion, the names of the keepers were etched on the old foundation stones and arranged into an amphitheater shape facing the new site. That way—as a placard explains—today's visitors can follow in the historical keepers' footsteps and "watch over" the lighthouse as well.

Jesus is the ultimate light-giver. He said, "I am the light of the world. Whoever follows me will never walk in darkness, but will have the light of life" (JOHN 8:12). That's a radical thing for anyone to claim. But Jesus said it to affirm His relationship with His heavenly Father, the Creator of light and life who sent Him.

When we look to Jesus for salvation and follow His teaching, we're restored in relationship with God, and He gives us new power and purpose. His transforming life and love—"the light of all mankind" (1:4)—shines in us and through us and out to a dark and sometimes dangerous world.

As believers in Jesus, we become "keepers of the light." May others see His light shine from us and discover the life and hope He alone can give! *JAMES BANKS*

In what practical ways can you shine Jesus' light? Where is God calling you to be obedient to Him today?

Jesus, I praise You for Your light and love.
Help me to shine for You.

Every day they continued to meet together in the
temple courts. [ACTS 2:46]

TALKING TABLES

oneliness is one of the greatest threats to our sense of well-
being, affecting our health through our behaviors on social
media, food consumption, and the like. One study suggests
that nearly two-thirds of all people—regardless of age or gen-
der—feel lonely at least some of the time. One British supermar-
ket has created "talking tables" in their store cafés as a way to
foster connection between people. Those looking for human
interaction simply seat themselves at a table designated for that
purpose, joining others or indicating a desire to be joined.
Conversation ensues, providing a sense of connection and community.

The people of the early church were committed to shared
connection too. Without each other, they would likely have felt
very alone in the practice of their faith, which was still new to the
world. Not only did they "[devote] themselves to the apostles'
teaching" to learn what following Jesus meant, they also "[met]
together in the temple courts" and "broke bread in their homes"
for mutual encouragement and fellowship (ACTS 2:42, 46).

We need human connection; God designed us that way!
Painful seasons of loneliness point to that need. Like the people
of the early church, it's important for us to engage in the human
companionship our well-being requires and to offer it to those
around us who also need it.   *KIRSTEN HOLMBERG*

**How can you intentionally connect with someone today?
How might you be overlooking opportunities for friendship?**

*Help us, God, to seek connection for our sake
and that of others!*

Greater love has no one than this: to lay down one's
life for one's friends. [JOHN 15:13]

REMEMBERING

O n Memorial Day, I think of many military veterans but especially my dad and uncles, who served in the military during
World War II. They made it home, but in that war hundreds
of thousands of families tragically lost loved ones in service to
their country. Yet, when asked, my dad and most soldiers from
that era would say they were willing to give up their lives to protect their loved ones and stand for what they believed to be right.

When someone dies in defense of their country, John 15:13
—"Greater love has no one than this: to lay down one's life for
one's friends"—is often recited during the funeral service to
honor their sacrifice. But what were the circumstances behind
this verse?

When Jesus spoke those words to His disciples during the
Last Supper, He was about to die. And, in fact, one of His small
group of disciples, Judas, had already left to betray Him (13:18–30).
Yet Christ knew all of this and still chose to sacrifice His life for
His friends *and* enemies.

Jesus was willing and ready to die for those who'd one day
believe in Him, even for those who were still His enemies
(ROMANS 5:10). In return, He asks His disciples (then and now) to
"love each other" as He has loved them (JOHN 15:12). His great love
compels us to sacrificially love others—friend and foe alike.

ALYSON KIEDA

**Before we believed in Jesus, we were His enemies. Yet Jesus died
for us. How can you honor and remember Jesus for His death on
the cross for you? How can you sacrificially love others?**

Jesus, we're so thankful that You were willing to die for us!

Gracious words are a honeycomb, sweet to the soul
and healing to the bones. [PROVERBS 16:24]

SWEETER THAN HONEY

His topic was racial tension. Yet the speaker remained calm and collected. Standing on stage before a large audience, he spoke boldly—but with grace, humility, kindness, and even humor. Soon the tense audience visibly relaxed, laughing along with the speaker about the dilemma they all faced: how to resolve their hot issue, but cool down their feelings and words. Yes, how to tackle a sour topic with sweet grace.

King Solomon advised this same approach for all of us: "Gracious words are a honeycomb, sweet to the soul and healing to the bones" (PROVERBS 16:24). In this way, "The hearts of the wise make ...their lips promote instruction" (V. 23).

Why would a powerful king like Solomon devote time to addressing how we speak? Because words can destroy. During Solomon's time, kings relied on messengers for information about their nations, and calm and reliable messengers were highly valued. They used prudent words and reasoned tongues, not over-reacting or speaking harshly, no matter the issue.

We all can benefit by gracing our opinions and thoughts with godly and prudent sweetness. In Solomon's words, "To humans belong the plans of the heart, but from the LORD comes the proper answer of the tongue" (V. 1).   *PATRICIA RAYBON*

What is your way of speaking when talking about a hot and divisive topic? When you allow God's Spirit to sweeten your tongue, what changes in your words?

Our holy God, when we speak on hard topics, soften our hearts and words with Your sweet Spirit.

Why have you made me your target?
Have I become a burden to you? [JOB 7:20]

WHY ME?

The *Book of Odds* says that one in a million people are struck by lightning. It also says that one in 25,000 experiences a medical condition called "broken heart syndrome" in the face of overwhelming shock or loss. In page after page the odds of experiencing specific problems pile up without answering: What if we're the one?

Job defied all odds. God said of him, "There is no one on earth like him; he is blameless and upright, a man who fears God and shuns evil" (JOB 1:8). Yet Job was chosen to suffer a series of losses that defied all odds. Of all people on earth, Job had reason to beg for an answer. It's all there for us to read in chapter after chapter of his desperate struggle to understand, "Why me?"

Job's story gives us a way of responding to the mystery of unexplained pain and evil. By describing the suffering and confusion of one of God's best examples of goodness and mercy (CH. 25), we gain an alternative to the inflexible rule of sowing and reaping (4:7–8). By providing a backstory of satanic mayhem (CH. 1) and an afterword (42:7–17) from the God who would one day allow His Son to bear our sins, the story of Job gives us reason to live by faith rather than sight.   *MART DEHAAN*

How do you feel about a God who sometimes allows suffering without explanation? How does the story of Job help you understand this?

God of creation, Giver of life, Father of our Lord Jesus Christ, please help us to trust You more than our own eyes and hearts.

Give, and it will be given to you.
[LUKE 6:38]

GOOD MEASURE

At a gas station one day, Staci encountered a woman who had left home without her bank card. Stranded with her baby, she was asking passersby for help. Although unemployed at the time, Staci spent $15 to put gas in the stranger's tank. Days later, Staci came home to find a gift basket of children's toys and other presents waiting on her porch. Friends of the stranger had reciprocated Staci's kindness and converted her $15 blessing into a memorable Christmas for her family.

This heartwarming story illustrates the point Jesus made when he said, "Give, and it will be given to you. A good measure, pressed down, shaken together and running over, will be poured into your lap. For with the measure you use, it will be measured to you" (LUKE 6:38).

It can be tempting to hear this and focus on what we get out of giving, but doing so would miss the point. Jesus preceded that statement with this one: "Love your enemies, do good to them, and lend to them without expecting to get anything back. Then your reward will be great, and you will be children of the Most High, because he is kind to the ungrateful and wicked" (V. 35).

We don't give to get things; we give because God delights in our generosity. Our love for others reflects His loving heart toward us.   *REMI OYEDELE*

In what ways have you experienced God's generosity in your life? How can you extend generosity to others?

Gracious Father, help me to give generously to others because You've been so generous to me.

Christ will make his home in your hearts as you
trust in him. Your roots will grow down into God's
love and keep you strong. [EPHESIANS 3:17 NLT]

LIVING IN THE BRANCHES

As I shared with my counselor my roller-coaster of emotions
after a stress-filled week, she listened thoughtfully. Then she
invited me to look out the window at the trees, lush with
autumnal oranges and golds, the branches swaying in the wind.

Pointing out that the *trunks* weren't moving at all in the wind,
my counselor explained, "We're a bit like that. When life is blowing
at us from every direction, of course our emotions will go up and
down and all around. But sometimes we live as if we only have
branches. Our goal is to help you find your own *trunk*. That way,
even when life is pulling from all sides, you won't be *living* in your
branches. You'll still be secure and stable."

It's an image that's stuck with me; and it's similar to the image
Paul offered new believers in Ephesians. Reminding them of God's
incredible gift—a new life of tremendous purpose and value
(EPHESIANS 2:6–10), Paul shared his longing that they'd become
deeply "rooted and established" in Christ's love (3:17), no longer
"blown here and there by every wind of teaching" (4:14).

On our own, it's easy to feel insecure and fragile, pummeled
by our fears and insecurities. But as we grow in our true identity
in Christ (VV. 22–24), we can experience deep peace with God and
each other (V. 3), nourished and sustained by Christ's power and
beauty (VV. 15–16).   *MONICA LA ROSE*

**When do you feel most "blown here and there" by life's
challenges? How might remembering your identity in Jesus
encourage and strengthen you?**

*Jesus, thank You for the overwhelmingly good news that the strength
needed to withstand life's challenges isn't our own. Help us to grow
ever-deeper roots in Your love and our place in Your family.*

For without him, who can eat or
find enjoyment? [ECCLESIASTES 2:25]

DO WHATEVER

I n a recent film, a self-proclaimed "genius" rants to the camera
about the world's "horror, corruption, ignorance, and poverty,"
declaring life to be godless and absurd. While such thinking isn't
unusual in many modern film scripts, what's interesting is where it
leads. In the end, the lead character turns to the audience and
implores us to do whatever it takes to find a little happiness. For
him, this includes leaving traditional morality behind.

But will "do whatever" work? Facing his own despair at life's
horrors, the Old Testament writer of Ecclesiastes gave it a try long
ago, searching for happiness through pleasure (ECCLESIASTES 2:1, 10),
grand work projects (VV. 4–6), riches (VV. 7–9), and philosophical
inquiry (VV. 12–16). And his assessment? "All of it is meaningless, a
chasing after the wind" (V. 17). None of these things is immune to
death, disaster, or injustice (5:13–17).

Only one thing brings the writer of Ecclesiastes back from
despair. Despite life's trials, we can find fulfillment when God is
part of our living and working: "for without him, who can eat or
find enjoyment?" (2:25). Life will at times feel meaningless, but
"remember your Creator" (12:1). Don't exhaust yourself trying to
figure life out, but "fear God and keep his commandments" (V. 13).

Without God as our center, life's pleasures and sorrows lead
only to disillusionment.   *SHERIDAN VOYSEY*

**How much do you seek happiness through things that won't
last? Since the writer of Ecclesiastes didn't know the hope of
resurrection, how would you consider his search in light of
Romans 8:11, 18–25?**

*God, today I place You anew at the center of my living, working,
joys, and disappointments, for without You nothing will satisfy or
make sense.*

It is God who works in you to will and to act in order
to fulfill his good purpose. [PHILIPPIANS 2:13]

EASY DOES IT

My father and I used to fell trees and cut them to size with
a two-man crosscut saw. Being young and energetic, I
tried to force the saw into the cut. "Easy does it," my
father would say. "Let the saw do the work."

I think of Paul's words in Philippians: "It is God who works in
you" (2:13). Easy does it. Let Him do the work of changing us.

C. S. Lewis said that growth is much more than reading what
Christ said and carrying it out. He explained, "A real Person,
Christ, . . . is doing things to you . . . gradually turning you perma-
nently into . . . a new little Christ, a being which . . . shares in His
power, joy, knowledge and eternity."

God is at that process today. Sit at the feet of Jesus and take in
what He has to say. Pray. "Keep yourselves in God's love" (JUDE 1:21),
reminding yourself all day long that you are His. Rest in the assurance that He's gradually changing you.

"But shouldn't we hunger and thirst for righteousness?" you
ask. Picture a small child trying to get a gift high on a shelf, his
eyes glittering with desire. His father, sensing that desire, brings
the gift down to him.

The work is God's; the joy is ours. Easy does it. We shall get
there some day.　　　　　　　　　　　　　　　　　*DAVID H. ROPER*

**What does it mean to you that "It is God who works in you"?
What do you want Him to do in you?**

*God, I'm grateful that You're changing my heart and actions to make
me like Jesus. Please give me a humble attitude to learn from You.*

WILD GENEROSITY

For more than a year, sixty-nine-year-old Brenda Jones waited on the donor list for a new liver. As the calendar inched forward, she worried that her transplant might not occur in time. When Brenda received news that she was next in line for one, however, she was elated. But then she learned of another woman, only twenty-three, who was clinging to life and had only hours to live. Without knowing what the decision might cost her, Brenda surrendered her spot. "I wouldn't have been able to live with the liver," Brenda said, "if I had let this little girl die." Thankfully, the hospital found another donor for Brenda, and both women received what they needed.

> **We're called to love with generosity, like Jesus.**

Whenever we encounter someone offering a gift that flagrantly discards self-interest, a gift that appears reckless or foolish, we marvel. This is why the ultimate story of wild generosity—Jesus surrendering His life for the very people who murdered Him and pouring out abundant forgiveness over us though we had nothing to offer in return—stuns us. We can't fathom such uncalculated big-heartedness.

Even more bewildering, we hear Jesus repeatedly encourage us to follow Him, to live as He lived. Throughout Scripture, we're called to humbly surrender our life for others, like Jesus (PHILIPPIANS 2:1–11). We're called to love with generosity, like Jesus (JOHN 15:9–17). These invitations may require us to give time we don't have or money we can't spare. It may mean surrendering our reputation or our expectations for how our life should unfold. It may look impossible, but whenever we gather our courage and follow Jesus, we'll find ourselves stepping into a wild, generous life.

WINN COLLIER, OUR DAILY BREAD *AUTHOR*

Be generous and willing to share.
[1 TIMOTHY 6:18]

★ *JUNE TOPIC: GENEROSITY*

AN OPEN, GENEROUS HEART

After Vicki's old car broke down with no option for repair, she started scraping together money for another vehicle. Chris, a frequent customer of the restaurant where Vicki works at the drive-thru window, one day heard her mention she needed a car. "I couldn't stop thinking about it," Chris said. "I [had] to do something." So he bought his son's used car (his son had just put it up for sale), shined it up, and handed Vicki the keys. Vicki was shocked. "Who . . . does that?" she said in amazement and gratitude.

The Scriptures call us to live with open hands, giving freely as we can—providing what's truly best for those in need. As Paul says: "Command [those who are rich] to do good, to be rich in good deeds" (1 TIMOTHY 6:18). We don't merely perform a benevolent act here or there, but rather live out a cheerful spirit of giving. Big-heartedness is our normal way of life. "Be generous and willing to share," we're told (V. 18).

As we live with an open, generous heart, we don't need to fear running out of what we need. Rather, the Bible tells us that in our compassionate generosity, we're taking "hold of [true] life" (V. 19). With God, genuine living means loosening our grip on what we have and giving to others freely.   *WINN COLLIER*

When do you struggle the most with being generous? How does God's generous heart encourage you to give more freely?

I want to hold what I have loosely, God. I want to be generous, like You. Transform my heart and help me to give freely.

Father, forgive them, for they do not know
what they are doing. [LUKE 23:34]

CHOSEN TO FORGIVE

s a middle-schooler, Patrick Ireland first sensed God had
chosen him for something. But what? Later as a survivor of
the horrific Columbine (Colorado) High School massacre
where thirteen were killed and twenty-four wounded, including
Patrick, he began to understand an answer.

Through his long recovery, Patrick learned that clinging to bitterness causes further wounding. God showed Patrick that the key to
forgiveness is to stop focusing on what others have done *to* us and
to focus on what Jesus has done *for* us. Christ's words on the cross
toward His tormenters, "Father, forgive them, for they do not know
what they are doing" (LUKE 23:34), fulfilled Zechariah the priest's
prophecy of Jesus' forgiveness (1:77). Additionally, His example
revealed a purpose for Patrick, and twenty years after the tragedy,
Patrick shared, "Maybe I was chosen to forgive."

While most of us will not endure an unimaginable calamity
such as the one committed at Columbine, each of us has been
wronged in some way. A spouse betrays. A child rebels. An
employer abuses. How do we move forward? Perhaps we look to
the example of our Savior. In the face of rejection and cruelty, He
forgave. It is through Jesus' forgiveness of our sins that we, ourselves, find salvation, which includes the ability to forgive others.
And like Patrick, we can choose to let go of our bitterness to open
our hearts to forgiveness.   *ELISA MORGAN*

**Is your heart open to forgive? How might you experience more of
the salvation Jesus died to provide by choosing to move toward
forgiving someone who has wronged you?**

*Dear Father, show me who I'm chosen to forgive today,
and give me the strength to offer the forgiveness You died
to provide.*

[Jesus] had compassion on them and
healed their sick. [MATTHEW 14:14]

COMPASSION ON THE JOB

My friend Ellen calculates payroll for an accounting firm. This may sound like a straightforward job, but there are times when employers submit their information later than requested. Ellen often makes up for this by working long hours so employees can receive their money without delay. She does this out of consideration for the families that depend on those funds to buy groceries, purchase medicine, and pay for housing.

Ellen's compassionate approach to her job points me to Jesus. On earth, He sometimes ministered to people when it was inconvenient for Him. For instance, Christ wanted some alone time after He heard that John the Baptist had been killed, so He boarded a boat in search of an isolated place (MATTHEW 14:13). Perhaps He needed to grieve for His relative and pray through His sorrow.

There was just one problem. Crowds of people tagged along behind Him. This group had various physical needs. It would have been much easier to send the people away, but "when Jesus landed and saw [them], he had compassion on them and healed their sick" (V. 14).

Although it was part of Jesus' calling to teach people and cure their diseases as He ministered on earth, His empathy affected the way in which He carried out His responsibilities. May God help us to recognize His compassion in our lives and give us the strength to pass it on to others.   *JENNIFER BENSON SCHULDT*

**How have you experienced God's compassion and care?
What prevents you from showing God's love when you carry out
your daily responsibilities?**

*Dear Jesus, thank You for meeting my spiritual and physical needs.
Help my thankfulness to overflow in the world so that I can glorify
You through caring for other people.*

Anyone who has seen me has seen
the Father. [JOHN 14:9]

MY FATHER'S CHILD

They looked down at the faded photograph, then up at me,
then over at my father, then back at me, then back at my
father. Their eyes were as wide as the proverbial saucers.
"Dad, you look just like Papa when he was young!" My father and I
grinned because this was something we'd known for a long time,
but it wasn't until recently that my children came to the same realization. While my father and I are different people, in a very real
sense to see me is to see my father as a younger man: tall, lanky
frame; full head of dark hair; prominent nose; and rather large ears.
No, I am not my father, but I am most definitely my father's son.

A follower of Jesus named Philip once asked, "Lord, show us
the Father" (JOHN 14:8). And while it wasn't the first time Jesus had
indicated as much, His response was still cause for pause: "Anyone
who has seen me has seen the Father" (V. 9). Unlike the physical
resemblances between my father and me, what Jesus says here is
revolutionary: "Don't you believe that I am in the Father, and that
the Father is in me?" (V. 10). His very essence and character were
the same as His Father's.

In that moment Jesus was being straightforward with His
beloved disciples and us: *If you want to know what God is like,
look at Me.*　　　　　　　　　　　　　　　　　　*JOHN BLASE*

**What are some of the characteristics of Jesus (and the Father)
that resonate strongly with you, and why?
How has He been molding your character?**

*Jesus, when things seem overwhelming,
remind me that to see You is to see the Father.
Help me keep my eyes fixed on You.*

Humbly accept the word planted in you,
which can save you. [JAMES 1:21]

USEFUL TEMPTATION

Fifteenth-century monk Thomas à Kempis, in the beloved classic *The Imitation of Christ*, offers a perspective on temptation that might be a bit surprising. Instead of focusing on the pain and difficulties temptation can lead to, he writes, "[temptations] are useful because they can make us humble, they can cleanse us, and they can teach us." Kempis explains, "The key to victory is true humility and patience; in them we overcome the enemy."

Humility and patience. How different my walk with Christ would be if that were how I naturally responded to temptation! More often, I react with shame, frustration, and impatient attempts to get rid of the struggle.

But, as we learn from James 1, the temptations and trials we face don't have to be without purpose or merely a threat we endure. Although giving in to temptation can bring heartbreak and devastation (VV. 13–15), when we turn to God with humble hearts seeking His wisdom and grace, we find He "gives generously to all without finding fault" (V. 5). Through His power in us, our trials and struggles to resist sin build perseverance, "so that [we] may be mature and complete, not lacking anything" (V. 4).

As we trust in Jesus, there's no reason to live in fear. As God's dearly loved children, we can find peace as we rest in His loving arms even as we face temptation.   MONICA LA ROSE

How might an attitude of humility and patience change how you respond to a current temptation or struggle? How is it freeing?

Jesus, I'm saddened when I realize how often I try to face life's temptations and struggles on my own—as if I'm self-sufficient, as if I don't need You. Thank You for Your unending love and patience with me.

For the Son of Man came to seek and
to save the lost. [LUKE 19:10]

FOUND ON THE EDGES

In the middle of the crowd at a motorcycle demonstration
where riders performed breathtaking tricks, I found myself
needing to stand on my tiptoes to see. Glancing around, I
noticed three children perched in a nearby tree, apparently
because they also couldn't get to the front of the crowd to see
the action.

Watching the kids peer out from their lofty location, I couldn't
help but think of Zacchaeus, who Luke identifies as a wealthy tax
collector (LUKE 19:2). Jews often viewed tax collectors as traitors
for working for the Roman government collecting taxes from fellow Israelites, as well as frequently demanding additional money
to pad their personal bank accounts. So Zacchaeus was likely
shunned from his community.

As Jesus passed through Jericho, Zacchaeus longed to see Him
but was unable to see over the crowd. So, perhaps feeling both
desperate and lonely, he climbed into a sycamore tree to catch a
glimpse (VV. 3–4). And it was there, on the outskirts of the crowd,
that Jesus searched him out and announced His intention to be a
guest at his home (V. 5).

Zacchaeus' story reminds us that Jesus came to "seek and to
save the lost," offering His friendship and the gift of salvation
(VV. 9–10). Even if we feel on the edges of our communities,
pushed to the "back of the crowd," we can be assured that, even
there, Jesus finds us.   *LISA M. SAMRA*

**How have you experienced feelings of being pushed aside by
friends or family? In the midst of loneliness, how has Jesus found
you and invited you to spend time with Him?**

*Jesus, thank You for never simply walking by when I'm hurting but
stopping to invite me into friendship with You.*

A Samaritan, as he traveled, came where the man was; and when he saw him, he took pity on him.
[LUKE 10:33]

IN NEED OF RESCUE

A teenager named Aldi was working alone on a fishing hut anchored about 125 kilometers (about 78 miles) off Indonesia's Sulawesi Island when heavy winds knocked the hut off its mooring and sent it out to sea. For forty-nine days, Aldi drifted in the ocean. Every time he spotted a ship, he turned on his lamp to try and get the sailors' attention, only to be disappointed. About ten ships passed the malnourished teen before he was rescued.

Jesus told a parable to an "expert in the law" (LUKE 10:25) about someone who needed to be rescued. Two men—a priest and a Levite—saw an injured man as they were traveling. But rather than help him, both "passed by on the other side" (VV. 31–32). We aren't told why. Both were religious men and would have been familiar with God's law to love their neighbor (LEVITICUS 19:17–18). They may have thought it was too dangerous. Or perhaps they didn't want to break Jewish laws about touching dead bodies, making them ceremonially unclean and unable to serve in the temple. In contrast, a Samaritan—who was despised by the Jews—acted nobly. He saw the man in need and selflessly took care of him.

Jesus wrapped up His teaching with the command that His followers should "go and do likewise" (LUKE 10:37). May God give us the willingness to risk reaching out in love to help others.

POH FANG CHIA

Who has Jesus put in your path that needs your help? How can you put your love into action today?

God, open my eyes to the needs around me and give me Your heart of compassion for others.

Each of you should give what you have decided
in your heart to give. [2 CORINTHIANS 9:7]

★ *JUNE TOPIC: GENEROSITY*

GIVE IT ALL YOU'VE GOT

*S*caling. It's a term used in the world of fitness that allows room for anyone to participate. If the specific exercise is a push-up, for example, then maybe you can do ten in a row, but I can only do four. The instructor's encouragement to me would be to *scale* back the push-ups according to my fitness level at the time. We're not all at the same level, but we can all move in the same direction. In other words, she would say, "Do your four push-ups with all the strength you have. Don't compare yourself with anyone else. Scale the movement for now, keep doing what you can do, and you may be amazed in time you're doing seven, and even one day, ten."

When it comes to giving, the apostle Paul was clear: "God loves a cheerful giver" (2 CORINTHIANS 9:7). But his encouragement to the believers in Corinth, and to us, is a variation of scaling. "Each of you should give what you have decided in your heart" (V. 7). We each find ourselves at different giving levels, and sometimes those levels change over time. Comparison is not beneficial, but attitude is. Based on where you are, give generously (V. 6). Our God has promised that the disciplined practice of such cheerful giving brings enrichment in every way with a blessed life that results in "thanksgiving to God" (V. 11).   *JOHN BLASE*

**How would you describe your giving: Cheerful? Reluctant?
Under compulsion? Not comparing yourself to anyone else,
what might cheerful giving look like?**

*Generous God, I want to be a cheerful giver, to give it my best effort.
I know that discipline in this area is crucial. Give me the wisdom not
to compare, the strength to sow generously, and the faith to leave
the results in Your hands.*

BIBLE IN A YEAR | 2 CHRONICLES 30–31; JOHN 18:1–18

My house will be called a house of prayer.
[MARK 11:17]

PURE WORSHIP

J ose pastored a church known for its programs and theatrical productions. They were well done, yet he worried the church's busyness had slipped into a business. Was the church growing for the right reasons or because of its activities? Jose wanted to find out, so he canceled all extra church events for one year. His congregation would focus on being a living temple where people worshiped God.

Jose's decision seems extreme, until you notice what Jesus did when He entered the temple's outer courts. The holy space that should have been full of simple prayers had become a flurry of worship business. "Get your doves here! Lily white, as God requires!" Jesus overturned the merchant's tables and stopped those who bought their merchandise. Furious at what they were doing, He quoted Isaiah 56 and Jeremiah 7: " 'My house will be called a house of prayer for all nations.' But you have made it 'a den of robbers'" (MARK 11:17). The court of the gentiles, the place for outsiders to worship God, had been turned into a mundane marketplace for making money.

There's nothing wrong with business or staying busy. But that's not the point of church. We're the living temple of God, and our main task is to worship Jesus. We likely won't need to flip over any tables as Jesus did, but He may be calling us to do something equally drastic.   *MIKE WITTMER*

Why do you attend church and meet with believers? What expectations of yours might you need to let the Spirit change?

Father, show us where our expectations of worship fail to please You. Help us see that it's all about You.

Always be prepared to give an answer to everyone
who asks you to give the reason for the hope that you
have. [1 PETER 3:15]

"GOD STUFF"

Most of Mike's co-workers knew little about Christianity, nor did they seem to care. But they knew *he* cared. One day near the Easter season, someone casually mentioned that they'd heard Easter had something to do with Passover and wondered what the connection was. "Hey, Mike!" he said. "You know about this God stuff. What's Passover?"

So Mike explained how God brought the Israelites out of slavery in Egypt. He told them about the ten plagues, including the death of the firstborn in every household. He explained how the death angel "passed over" the houses whose doorframes were covered by the blood of a sacrificed lamb. Then he shared how Jesus was later crucified at the Passover season as the once-and-for-all sacrificial Lamb. Suddenly Mike realized, *Hey, I'm witnessing!*

Peter the disciple gave advice to a church in a culture that didn't know about God. He said, "Always be prepared to give an answer to everyone who asks you to give the reason for the hope that you have" (1 PETER 3:15).

Because Mike had been open about his faith, he got the chance to share that faith naturally, and he could do so with "gentleness and respect" (V. 15).

We can too. With the help of God's Holy Spirit, we can explain in simple terms what matters most in life—that "stuff" about God.

TIM GUSTAFSON

How have you felt when someone wants to discuss matters of faith with you? Why does Peter add that we are to share our faith "with gentleness and respect"?

*Father, help me be ready to explain the hope and purpose
You can bring to life.*

I will not yield my glory to another.
[ISAIAH 48:11]

PERSPECTIVES FROM ABOVE

When Peter Welch was a young boy in the 1970s, using a metal detector was only a hobby. But since 1990, he's been leading people from around the world on metal-detecting excursions. They've made thousands of discoveries—swords, ancient jewelry, coins. Using "Google Earth," a computer program based on satellite imagery, they look for patterns in the landscape on farmland in the United Kingdom. It shows them where roads, buildings, and other structures may have been centuries ago. Peter says, "To have a perspective from above opens a whole new world."

God's people in Isaiah's day needed "a perspective from above." They prided themselves on being His people yet were disobedient and refused to give up their idols. God had another perspective. Despite their rebellion, He would rescue them from captivity to Babylon. Why? "For my own sake, . . . I will not yield my glory to another" (ISAIAH 48:11). God's perspective from above is that life is for His glory and purpose—not ours. Our attention is to be given to Him and His plans and to pointing others to praise Him too.

Having God's glory as our own life's perspective opens a whole new world. Only He knows what we will discover about Him and what He has for us. God will teach us what is good for us and lead us along the paths we should follow (V. 17).   *ANNE CETAS*

What can you praise God for today? How might you go about having God increase in your life and you decrease?

God, I want my life to be about You and not myself.
Teach me and change me.

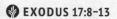
Two are better than one…: If either of them falls
down, one can help the other up. [ECCLESIASTES 4:9–10]

TOGETHER WE WIN

In the middle of the night, Pastor Samuel Baggaga received a call asking him to come to the home of a church member. When he arrived, he found a house engulfed by fire. The father, though burned himself, had reentered the home to rescue one of his children and emerged with an unconscious daughter. The hospital, in this rural Ugandan setting, was six miles (10 kilometers) away. With no transportation available, the pastor and the father started running to the hospital with the child. When one of them tired from carrying the injured girl, the other one took over. Together they made the journey; the father and his daughter were treated and then fully recovered.

In Exodus 17:8–13 the Lord orchestrated a great victory that included the efforts of Joshua, who led fighting men on the battlefield; and Moses, who kept his hands raised while holding the staff of God. When Moses' hands grew weary, Aaron and Hur assisted by each holding up one of his hands until the setting of the sun and the defeat of the enemy.

The value of interdependence can never be underestimated. God, in His kindness, graciously provides people as His agents for mutual good. Listening ears and helpful hands; wise, comforting, and correcting words—these and other resources come to us and through us to others. Together we win and God gets the glory!

ARTHUR JACKSON

At what times in your life have you benefited from the support of others? Who might you know who needs you to run with them in this season of their life?

Father, thank You for those You've graciously provided in my life and for those You've allowed me to share life with for our mutual good and Your glory.

BIBLE IN A YEAR | EZRA 3–5; JOHN 20

But if a wicked person . . . does what is just and right,
they will save their life. [EZEKIEL 18:27]

HE CHANGED ME

When John, who ran the biggest brothel in London, was sent to prison, he falsely believed, *I'm a good guy.* While there, he decided to attend the Bible study at the prison because there was cake and coffee, but he was struck by how happy the other inmates seemed to be. He started to cry during the first song and later received a Bible. Reading from the prophet Ezekiel changed him, hitting him "like a thunderbolt." He read, "But if a wicked person turns away from [their] wickedness . . . and does what is just and right, . . . that person will surely live; they will not die" (18:27–28). God's Word came alive to him and he realized, "I wasn't a good guy . . . I was wicked and I needed to change." While praying with the pastor, he said, "I found Jesus Christ and He changed me."

These words from Ezekiel were spoken to God's people when they were in exile. Although they had turned from God, He longed that they would rid themselves of their offenses and "get a new heart and a new spirit" (V. 31). Those words helped John to "Repent and live!" (V. 32) as he followed Jesus, the One who called sinners to repentance (LUKE 5:32).

May we respond to the Spirit's conviction of sin, that we too might enjoy forgiveness and freedom.   *AMY BOUCHER PYE*

How do you react to the question of whether or not you're a "good person"? In what areas of life could you "repent and live"?

Father God, thank You for making me aware of my sinful behavior through Your Holy Spirit. Soften my heart to repent and to receive Your forgiveness.

Let us not become weary in doing good.
[GALATIANS 6:9]

FAITHFUL UNTIL THE HARVEST

A woman I know planned an event at a local park and invited all the neighborhood children to participate. She was excited about the opportunity to share her faith with her neighbors.

She recruited her three grandchildren and two high school students to help her, gave the assignments, planned a number of games and other activities, prepared food, prepared a Bible story about Jesus to present to the children, and waited for them to gather.

Not a single child showed up the first day. Or the second day. Or the third day. Yet, each day my friend went through that day's activities with her grandchildren and helpers.

On the fourth day, she noticed a family picnicking nearby and invited the children to join in the games. One little girl came, entered into the fun, ate with them, and listened to the story about Jesus. Perhaps years from now she'll remember. Who knows what the outcome will be? God, through the book of Galatians, encourages us, "Let us not become weary in doing good, for at the proper time we will reap a harvest if we do not give up. Therefore, as we have opportunity, let us do good to all people" (6:9–10).

Don't worry about numbers or other visible measures of success. Our job is to be faithful to what He wants us to do and then leave the harvest to Him. God determines the outcomes.

DAVID H. ROPER

What best-laid plans of yours have gone wrong? How can you learn to trust God with the outcome despite disappointment?

God, I'm grateful that You're the one in charge of the results.
You're the one at work. Help me to do what You ask no matter what.

Be rich in good deeds, and [be] generous and
willing to share. [1 TIMOTHY 6:18]

★ *JUNE TOPIC: GENEROSITY*

THE MAN IN SEAT 2D

K elsey navigated the narrow airplane aisle with her eleven-
month-old daughter, Lucy, and Lucy's oxygen machine. They
were traveling to seek treatment for her baby's chronic lung
disease. Shortly after settling into their shared seat, a flight attendant approached Kelsey, saying a passenger in first class wanted to
switch seats with her. With tears of gratitude streaming down her
face, Kelsey made her way back up the aisle to the more spacious
seat, while the benevolent stranger made his way toward hers.

Kelsey's benefactor embodied the kind of generosity Paul
encourages in his letter to Timothy. Paul told Timothy to instruct
those in his care with the command to "do good, to be rich in good
deeds, and to be generous and willing to share" (1 TIMOTHY 6:18). It's
tempting, Paul says, to become arrogant and put our hope in the
riches of this world. Instead, he suggests that we focus on living a
life of generosity and service to others, becoming "rich" in good
deeds, like the man from seat 2D on Kelsey's flight.

Whether we find ourselves with plenty or in want, we all can
experience the richness of living generously by being willing to
share what we have with others. When we do, Paul says we will
"take hold of the life that is truly life" (V. 19).　　　*KIRSTEN HOLMBERG*

**Who has been "generous and willing to share" with you?
With whom can you share generously today?**

God, please give me a generous spirit as I renew my hope in You.

They have followed other gods to serve them.
[JEREMIAH 11:10]

JUST-IN-CASE IDOLS

Sam checks his retirement account twice each day. He saved for thirty years, and with the boost of a rising stock market, finally has enough to retire. As long as stocks don't plunge. This fear keeps Sam worrying about his balance.

Jeremiah warned about this: "You, Judah, have as many gods as you have towns; and the altars you have set up to burn incense to that shameful god Baal are as many as the streets of Jerusalem" (11:13).

Judah's idolatry is remarkable. They knew the Lord was God. How could they worship anyone else? They were hedging their bets. They needed the Lord for the afterlife, because only the true God could raise them from the dead. But what about now? Pagan gods promised health, wealth, and fertility, so why not pray to them too, just in case?

Can you see how Judah's idolatry is also our temptation? It's good to have talent, education, and money. But if we're not careful, we might shift our confidence to them. We know we'll need God when we die, and we'll ask Him to bless us now. But we'll also lean on these lesser gods, just in case.

Where is your trust? Back-up idols are still idols. Thank God for His many gifts, and tell Him you're not relying on any of them. Your faith is riding entirely on Him.   *MIKE WITTMER*

What good thing are you tempted to turn into an idol?
How might you use this gift while still depending fully on God?

Father, all my hope is in You. Help me trust in You alone,
not in my abilities and assets.

Some of those present were saying indignantly to one another, "Why this waste of perfume?" [MARK 14:4]

DANCING BEFORE THE LORD

A number of years ago, my wife and I visited a small church where during the worship service a woman began to dance in the aisle. She was soon joined by others. Carolyn and I looked at each other and an unspoken agreement passed between us: "Not me!" We come from church traditions that favor a serious liturgy, and this other form of worship was well beyond our comfort zone.

But if Mark's story of Mary's "waste" means anything at all, it suggests that our love for Jesus may express itself in ways that others find uncomfortable (MARK 14:1–9). A year's wages were involved in Mary's anointing. It was an "unwise" act that invited the disciples' scorn. The word Mark uses to describe their reaction means "to snort" and suggests disdain and mockery. Mary may have cringed, fearing Jesus' response. But He commended her for her act of devotion and defended her against His own disciples, for Jesus saw the love that prompted her action despite what some would consider the impractical nature of it. He said, "Why are you bothering her? She has done a beautiful thing to me" (V. 6).

Different forms of worship—informal, formal, quiet, exuberant—represent a sincere outpouring of love for Jesus. He's worthy of all worship that comes from a heart of love.   *DAVID H. ROPER*

Why do you think we're critical of unfamiliar forms of worship? How can we change our thoughts about a form of worship that's outside our comfort zone?

I bow before You, Almighty God, and worship You now. You're worthy of the highest praise and adoration.

He did what was right in the eyes of the LORD . . . ,
not turning aside to the right or to the left. [2 KINGS 22:2]

STRAIGHT AHEAD

It used to take the steady eye and the firm hand of a farmer to drive a tractor or combine down straight rows. But even the best eyes would overlap rows, and by end of day even the strongest hands would be fatigued. But now there's autosteer—a GPS-based technology that allows for accuracy to within one inch when planting, cultivating, and spraying. It's incredibly efficient and hands-free. Just imagine sitting in a mammoth combine and instead of gripping the wheel, you're gripping a roast beef sandwich. An amazing tool to keep you moving straight ahead.

You may recall the name Josiah. He was crowned king when he was only "eight years old" (2 KINGS 22:1). Years later, in his mid-twenties, Hilkiah the high priest found "the Book of the Law" in the temple (V. 8). It was then read to the young king, who tore his robes in sorrow due to his ancestors' disobedience to God. Josiah set about to do what was "right in the eyes of the LORD" (V. 2). The book became a tool to steer the people so there would be no turning to the right or left. God's instructions were there to set things straight.

Allowing the Scriptures to guide us day by day keeps our lives in line with knowing God and His will. The Bible is an amazing tool that, if followed, keeps us moving straight ahead.　　*JOHN BLASE*

**How is Bible reading a part of your daily routine?
What Scriptures has God been using to keep your life on track?**

*God, the Scriptures are a gift that brings truth and freedom to our lives.
Help me to hunger and thirst for Your words.*

[God] has made everything beautiful
in its time. [ECCLESIASTES 3:11]

TREASURE THE MOMENTS

S u Dongpo (also known as Su Shi) was one of China's greatest
poets and essayists. While in exile and gazing upon a full
moon, he wrote a poem to describe how much he missed
his brother. "We rejoice and grieve, gather and leave, while the
moon waxes and wanes. Since times of old, nothing remains
perfect," he writes. "May our loved ones live long, beholding this
beautiful scene together though thousands of miles apart."

His poem carries themes found in the book of Ecclesiastes. The
author, known as the Teacher (1:1), observed that there's "a time
to weep and a time to laugh . . . a time to embrace and a time to
refrain from embracing" (3:4–5). By pairing two contrasting activities, the Teacher, like Su Dongpo, seems to suggest that all good
things must inevitably come to an end.

As Su Dongpo saw the waxing and waning of the moon as
another sign that nothing remains perfect, the Teacher also saw
in creation God's providential ordering of the world He'd made.
God oversees the course of events, and "He has made everything
beautiful in its time" (V. 11).

Life may be unpredictable and sometimes filled with painful
separations, but we can take heart that everything takes place
under God's gaze. We can enjoy life and treasure the moments—
the good and the bad—for our loving God is with us.   *POH FANG CHIA*

**What are some things you're afraid to try because of life's
unpredictability? How can you lean on Jesus as you step forward in
courage to forge new friendships and deepen relationships?**

*Thank You, loving Father, for watching over all seasons of my life.
Help me to trust in You and enjoy the life You've given me.*

I will wait for the LORD....
I will put my trust in him. [ISAIAH 8:17]

IS GOD THERE?

Lela was dying of cancer, and her husband, Timothy, couldn't understand why a loving God would let his wife suffer. She had served Him faithfully as a Bible teacher and mentor to many. "Why did You let this happen?" he cried. Yet Timothy continued to be faithful in his walk with God.

"So why do you still believe in God?" I asked him frankly. "What keeps you from turning away from Him?"

"Because of what has happened before," Timothy replied. While he couldn't "see" God now, he recalled the times when God had helped and protected him. These were signs that God was still there caring for his family. "I know the God I believe in will come through in His own way," he said.

Timothy's words echo Isaiah's expression of trust in Isaiah 8:17. Even when he couldn't feel God's presence as his people braced for trouble from their enemies, he would "wait for the LORD." He trusted in God because of the signs He'd given of His continuing presence (V. 18).

There are times when we might feel as if God isn't with us in our troubles. That's when we depend on what we can see of His works in our lives, in the past and present. They're the visible reminder of an invisible God—a God who is always with us and will answer in His own time and way.   *LESLIE KOH*

**What signs can you see of God working in your life?
How can they remind you that you can still look to Him
for hope and comfort?**

*Father, thank You for always being there for me.
Give me the strength to trust in You even when I don't
understand what's going on.*

BIBLE IN A YEAR | ESTHER 1–2; ACTS 5:1–21   179

We fix our eyes not on what is seen,
but on what is unseen. [2 CORINTHIANS 4:18]

ETERNAL EYES

Eternal eyes, that's what my friend Madeline prays her children and grandchildren would have. Her family has gone through a tumultuous season that ended with the death of her daughter. As the family grieves from this horrific loss, Madeline longs for them to be less and less nearsighted—consumed by the pain of this world. And to be more and more farsighted—filled with hope in our loving God.

The apostle Paul and his co-workers experienced great suffering at the hands of persecutors and even from believers who tried to discredit them. Yet, they had their eyes fixed on eternity. Paul boldly acknowledged that "we fix our eyes not on what is seen, but on what is unseen, since what is seen is temporary, but what is unseen is eternal" (2 CORINTHIANS 4:18).

Although they were doing God's work, they lived with the reality of being "hard pressed on every side," "perplexed," "persecuted," and "struck down" (VV. 8–9). Shouldn't God have delivered them from these troubles? But instead of being disappointed, Paul built his hope on the "eternal glory" that supersedes momentary troubles (V. 17). He knew God's power was at work in him and had complete assurance that "the one who raised the Lord Jesus from the dead will also raise us with Jesus" (V. 14).

When our world around us feels shaky, may we turn our eyes to God—the eternal Rock that will never be destroyed.

ESTERA PIROSCA ESCOBAR

**In what do you choose to hope in spite of your difficulties?
How have you experienced God's faithfulness?**

*I lift my eyes to You today, O God. Give me a glimpse of
the security I have in You.*

You shall give it to the Levite, the foreigner, the fatherless and the widow. [DEUTERONOMY 26:12]

★ *JUNE TOPIC: GENEROSITY*

THE BILL IS PAID

"**W**hat happened to you?" asked Zeal, a Nigerian businessman, as he bent over a hospital bed in Lagos. "Someone shot me," replied the young man, his thigh bandaged. Although the injured man was well enough to return home, he wouldn't be released until he settled his bill—a policy that many government hospitals in the region follow. After consulting with a social worker, Zeal anonymously covered the bill through the charitable fund he'd earlier set up as a way to express his Christian faith. In return, he hopes that those receiving the gift of release will one day give to others too.

The theme of giving from God's bounty pulses throughout the Bible. For instance, when Moses instructed the Israelites on how to live in the Promised Land, he told them to give back to God first (SEE DEUTERONOMY 26:1–3) and to care for those in need—the foreigners, orphans, and widows (V. 12). Because they dwelled in a "land flowing with milk and honey" (V. 15), they were to express God's love to the needy.

We too can spread God's love through sharing our material goods, whether big or small. We might not have the opportunity to personally give exactly like Zeal did, but we can ask God to show us how to give or who needs our help.　　*AMY BOUCHER PYE*

How do you think the patients felt who were released because of Zeal? If you've experienced an unexpected gift of grace, how did you respond?

God, thank You for caring for those in need. Open my eyes to the material and spiritual needs of those near and far to me, and help me to know how to respond.

Samuel said, "Although you were once small in your own eyes, did you not become the head of the tribes of Israel? The LORD anointed you king over Israel." [1 SAMUEL 15:17]

UNDERESTIMATING OURSELVES

The young man became his team's captain. The professional sports squad was now led by a mild-mannered kid who barely needed to shave. His first press conference was underwhelming. He kept deferring to the coach and to his team-mates, and mumbled clichés about just trying to do his job. The team performed poorly that season, and by the end of it the young captain had been traded. He didn't grasp that he'd been entrusted with the authority to lead, or maybe he never believed he could.

Due to his failures, Saul was "small in [his] own eyes" (1 SAMUEL 15:17)—which is a funny thing to say about a guy who's described as being tall. He was literally head and shoulders above the rest (9:2). And yet that wasn't how he saw himself. In fact, his actions in the chapter show him trying to win the approval of the people. He hadn't fully grasped that God—not people—had chosen him and given him a mission.

But Saul's mistake is a picture of every human being's failure: we can miss that we were made in God's image to reflect His rule, and end up misusing our authority—spreading destruction in the world. To undo this, we need to return to God: to let the Father define us by His love, to let Him fill us with the Spirit, and to let Jesus send us out into the world.   *GLENN PACKIAM*

What assignment has God given you that you don't think you have the power to do? Why is it vital to have your identity based in what God says is true?

Dear Father, give me eyes to see myself as You see me, and grant me the grace to faithfully carry out the calling You've entrusted to me.

[Jesus Christ] loves us and has freed us from our sins
by his blood. [REVELATION 1:5]

DEBT ERASER

Stunned is just one word that describes the response of the crowd at the 2019 graduation ceremony at Morehouse College in Atlanta, Georgia. The commencement speaker announced that he and his family would be donating millions of dollars to erase the student debt of the entire graduating class. One student—with $100,000 in loans—was among the overwhelmed graduates who expressed their joys with tears and shouts.

Most of us have experienced indebtedness in some form—having to pay for homes, vehicles, education, medical expenses, or other things. But we've also known the amazing relief of a bill being stamped "PAID"!

After declaring Jesus as "the faithful witness, the firstborn from the dead, and the ruler of the kings of the earth," John worshipfully acknowledged His debt-erasing work: "To him who loves us and has freed us from our sins by his blood" (REVELATION 1:5). This statement is simple but its meaning is profound. Better than the surprise announcement the Morehouse graduating class heard is the good news that the death of Jesus (the shedding of His blood on the cross) frees us from the penalty that our sinful attitudes, desires, and deeds deserve. Because that debt has been satisfied, those who believe in Jesus are forgiven and become a part of God's kingdom family (V. 6). This good news is the best news of all!

ARTHUR JACKSON

If you haven't received forgiveness through faith in Christ, what's keeping you from accepting His free gift? When was the last time you worshiped and thanked God for the forgiveness and new life He's provided?

Jesus, thank You for Your death that erased my debt;
I'm eternally grateful!

BIBLE IN A YEAR | JOB 1–2; ACTS 7:22–43

The seed falling on good soil refers to someone who hears the word and understands it. [MATTHEW 13:23]

DEEP-ROOTED FAITH

The Holy Oak, towering next to Basking Ridge Presbyterian Church in New Jersey for more than three hundred years, had to be removed after more than six hundred years of life. At its prime, the twisting branches spanned high and wide. Cool breezes rustled its green leaves and acorns. The sun peeked through wind-blown gaps, creating dancing glimmers of light in the shade below its canopy. But beneath the ground's surface lay its true magnificence—its root system. An oak's main root grows vertically, securing a reliable supply of nourishment. From that taproot, a mass of roots spreads horizontally to supply the tree with a lifetime of moisture and nutrients. This intricate root system often grows more massive than the tree it supports and serves as a lifeline and an anchor for stabilizing the trunk.

Like the mighty oak, most of our life-giving growth occurs beneath the surface. When Jesus explained the parable of the sower to His disciples, He emphasized the importance of being firmly planted in a personal relationship with the Father. As we grow in the knowledge of God as revealed through the Scriptures, our faith roots are sustained by His Spirit. God helps His followers thrive through ever-changing circumstances, trials, persecution, and worry (MATTHEW 13:18–23).

Our loving Father nourishes our hearts with His Word. As His Spirit transforms our character, He makes sure the fruit of our deep-rooted faith becomes evident to people around us.

XOCHITL DIXON

What can you do this week to ensure your heart will be good soil nourished by God's Word? What fruit of deep-rooted faith have you seen become evident in your life over the last year?

Loving Father, please change me from the inside out and anchor me in faith rooted deep in the unchanging Scriptures.

March on, my soul; be strong!
[JUDGES 5:21]

BEAT AGAIN

In 2012, Phillips, Craig and Dean released their song "Tell Your Heart to Beat Again." It was inspired by the true story of a heart surgeon. After removing a patient's heart to repair it, the surgeon returned it to the chest and began gently massaging it back to life. But the heart wouldn't restart. More intense measures followed, but the heart still wouldn't beat. Finally, the surgeon knelt next to the unconscious patient and spoke to her: "Miss Johnson," he said, "this is your surgeon. The operation went perfectly. Your heart has been repaired. Now tell your heart to beat again." Her heart began to beat.

The idea that we could tell our physical heart to do something might seem strange, but it has spiritual parallels. "Why, my soul, are you downcast?" the psalmist says to himself. "Put your hope in God" (PSALM 42:5). "Return to your rest, my soul," says another, "for the LORD has been good to you" (116:7). After beating Israel's enemies in war, Deborah, a judge, revealed that she too had spoken to her heart during battle. "March on, my soul," she told it, "be strong!" (JUDGES 5:21), because the Lord had promised victory (4:6–7).

Our capable Surgeon has mended our heart (PSALM 103:3). So when fear, depression, or condemnation come, perhaps we too should address our souls and say: *March on! Be strong! Feeble heart, beat again.*   SHERIDAN VOYSEY

What was your first response to the surgeon's words to the patient? What words from Scripture do you need to speak to your soul today?

Master Physician, thank You for being with me in every trial and battle. Because of Your promised presence, I will direct my soul to act bravely.

If you remain in me and I in you,
you will bear much fruit. [JOHN 15:5]

A DIVINE DUET

At a children's music recital, I watched a teacher and student seat themselves in front of a piano. Before their duet began, the teacher leaned over and whispered some last-minute instructions. As music flowed from the instrument, I noticed that the student played a simple melody while the teacher's accompaniment added depth and richness to the song. Near the end of the piece, the teacher nodded his approval.

Our life in Jesus is much more like a duet than a solo performance. Sometimes, though, I forget that He's "sitting next to me," and it's only by His power and guidance that I can "play" at all. I try to hit all the right notes on my own—to obey God in my own strength, but this usually ends up seeming fake and hollow. I try to handle problems with my limited ability, but the result is often discord with others.

My Teacher's presence makes all the difference. When I rely on Jesus to help me, I find my life is more honoring to God. I serve joyfully, love freely, and am amazed as God blesses my relationships. It's like Jesus told His first disciples, "If you remain in me and I in you, you will bear much fruit; apart from me you can do nothing" (JOHN 15:5).

Each day we play a duet with our good Teacher—it's His grace and power that carry the melody of our spiritual lives.

JENNIFER BENSON SCHULDT

Why do you sometimes resist the help and encouragement God offers? How could reliance on Him change your outlook and your actions in certain situations?

Dear God, help me to remember that You're with me in every moment. I welcome Your influence and instruction today. Thank You for Your nearness.

Everyone who calls on the name of the Lord
will be saved. [ACTS 2:21]

REDEMPTION'S HOPE

The man seemed beyond redemption. His crimes included
eight shootings (killing six) and starting nearly 1,500 fires
that terrorized New York City in the 1970s. He left letters at
his crime scenes taunting the police, and he was eventually appre-
hended and given consecutive sentences of twenty-five years to
life for each murder.

Yet God reached down to this man. Today he is a believer in
Christ who spends time daily in the Scriptures, has expressed
deep regret to his victims' families, and continues to pray for
them. Although imprisoned for more than four decades, this man
who seemed beyond redemption finds hope in God and claims,
"My freedom is found in one word: Jesus."

Scripture tells of another unlikely conversion. Before he met the
risen Christ on the road to Damascus, Saul (who later became the
apostle Paul) was "breathing out murderous threats against the
Lord's disciples"(ACTS 9:1). Yet Paul's heart and life were transformed
by Jesus (VV. 17–18), and he became one of the most powerful wit-
nesses for Him in history. The man who once plotted the death of
Christians devoted his life to spreading the hope of the gospel.

Redemption is *always* a miraculous work of God. Some stories
are more dramatic, but the underlying truth remains the same:
None of us deserve His forgiveness, yet Jesus is a powerful Savior!
He "[saves] completely those who come to God through him"
(HEBREWS 7:25).   *JAMES BANKS*

**Do you know someone who seems like a "tough case"
for redemption? Nothing is too hard for God! Bring that person
before Him in prayer.**

*Dear Jesus, thank You for loving us so much You died to bring us
into a relationship with You.*

Before they call I will answer.
[ISAIAH 65:24]

SIMPLY ASK

Her doctor said her detached retinas couldn't be repaired. But after living without sight for fifteen years—learning Braille, and using a cane and service dog—a Montana woman's life changed when her husband asked another eye doctor a simple question: could she be helped? The answer was yes. As the doctor discovered, the woman had a common eye condition, cataracts, which the doctor removed from her right eye. When the eye patch came off the next day, her vision was 20/20. A second surgery for her left eye met with equal success.

A simple question also changed the life of Naaman, a powerful military man with leprosy. But Naaman raged arrogantly at the prophet Elisha's instructions to "wash yourself seven times in the Jordan, and your flesh will be restored" (2 KINGS 5:10). Naaman's servants, however, asked the military leader a simple question: "If the prophet had told you to do some great thing, would you not have done it?" (V. 13). Persuaded, Naaman washed "and his flesh was restored and became clean" (V. 14).

In our lives, sometimes we struggle with a problem because we won't ask God. *Will You help? Should I go? Will You lead?* He doesn't require complicated questions from us to help. "Before they call I will answer," God promised His people (ISAIAH 65:24). So today, simply ask Him.   PATRICIA RAYBON

How complex are your prayer requests?
What life problem can you offer to God in a simple prayer?

Dear heavenly Father, when life feels complicated and difficult, thank You for Your promise to hear even my simple prayers.

I will instruct you and teach you in the way you should
go; I will counsel you with my loving eye on you.
[PSALM 32:8]

NAVIGATING LIFE'S RAPIDS

"**E**verybody on the left, give me three strong forward
strokes!" our whitewater raft guide shouted. Those on the
left dug in, pulling our raft away from a churning vortex.
For several hours, we'd learned the importance of listening to our
guide's instructions. His steady voice enabled six people with little
rafting experience to work together to plot the safest course down
a raging river.

Life has its share of whitewater rapids, doesn't it? One moment,
it's smooth sailing. Then, in a flash, we're paddling like mad to
avoid suddenly swirling whirlpools. Those tense moments make us
keenly aware of our need for a skilled guide, a trusted voice to help
us navigate turbulent times.

In Psalm 32, God promises to be that voice: "I will instruct you
and teach you the way you should go" (V. 8). Backing up, we see that
confessing our sins (V. 5) and prayerfully seeking Him (V. 6) play a role
in hearing Him too. Still, I take comfort in the fact that God promises, "I will counsel you with my loving eye on you" (V. 8), a reminder
that His guidance flows from His love. Near the end of the chapter,
the psalmist concludes, "The LORD's unfailing love surrounds the
one who trusts him" (V. 10). And as we trust Him, we can rest in His
promise to guide us through life's rockiest passages.   ADAM R. HOLZ

**What circumstances in your life right now feel like whitewater
rapids? How might you seek God's guiding voice about
how to respond?**

*Father, thank You for Your promise to be my Guide. Help me to
seek You and listen to You as You direct the course of my life.*

CELEBRATION IN HIS PRESENCE

Many years ago, 100 high-pressured deodorant guns were installed at a large city dump, one of several hundred smelly landfill sites that had become the focus of growing public concern. To saturate the mounds of putrefying garbage, the cannons sprayed several gallons of fragrance a minute at a distance of more than 160 feet. But no matter how much deodorant was sprayed, the fragrance couldn't completely mask the problem.

Similar to the use of deodorant guns, King David attempted to mask the odor of his sin. After his adultery with Bathsheba and complicity in the murder of her husband (2 SAMUEL 11:1–17), David used the "deodorants" of silence, deceit, and outward piety to cover up his actions. But unable to withstand the guilt of his sin and the sting of God's conviction, David eventually cried out to Him for mercy and spiritual cleansing. He prayed, "Have mercy on me, O God.... Against you, you only, have I sinned" (PSALM 51:1, 4).

> *He'll restore the joy of our salvation.*

David uncovered his sins before God, and acknowledged, confessed, and repented of them (32:5). God forgave the king's disobedience and restored his joy (VV. 5, 7; 51:12–15). David, like a shaken bottle of carbonated water, burst forth with praise to teach others God's forgiveness. Celebration followed the king's confession and repentance.

When we sin, it's futile to try and cover it up. The odor of our disobedience can't be contained. But when we confess our sin and repent of it, He'll remove it and leave the fragrance of His grace and forgiveness. He'll restore the joy of our salvation, allowing us to once again celebrate in His presence.

MARVIN WILLIAMS, OUR DAILY BREAD *AUTHOR*

Let Israel rejoice in their Maker;
let the people of Zion be glad in their King.
[PSALM 149:2]

★ *JULY TOPIC: CELEBRATION*

OUR REASON FOR JOY

When the school year began, fourteen-year-old C.J. would hop off the bus every afternoon and dance down his driveway. His mom recorded and shared videos of C.J.'s after-school boogie time. He danced because he enjoyed life and "making people happy" with every move. One day, two garbage collectors took time out of their busy work schedule to stomp, spin, and sway with the young boy who inspires others to dance with him. This trio demonstrates the power of sincere and infectious joy.

The writer of Psalm 149 describes the original source of enduring and unconditional joy—God. The psalmist encourages God's people to join together and "sing to the LORD a new song" (V. 1). He invites Israel to "rejoice in their Maker" and "be glad in their King" (V. 2). He calls us to worship Him with dancing and music (VV. 1–3). Why? Because "the LORD takes delight in his people; he crowns the humble with victory" (V. 4).

Our adoring Father created us and sustains the universe. He delights in us just because we're His beloved children. He designed us, knows us, and invites us into a personal relationship with Him. What an honor! Our loving and living God is our reason for everlasting joy. We can rejoice in the gift of His constant presence and be grateful for every day our Maker has given us.   *XOCHITL DIXON*

> **Why does knowing God delights in us encourage joy in all circumstances? How can you express your joy in the Lord throughout the day?**
>
> *Thanks for loving us, delighting in us, and knowing us, God.*

The Lord's servant must not be quarrelsome.
[2 TIMOTHY 2:24]

GENTLE SPEECH

I was on Facebook, arguing. *Bad* move. What made me think I was obligated to "correct" a stranger on a hot topic—especially a divisive one? The results were heated words, hurt feelings (on my part anyway), and a broken opportunity to witness well for Jesus. That's the sum outcome of "internet anger." It's the term for the harsh words flung daily across the blogosphere. As one ethics expert explained, people wrongly conclude that rage "is how public ideas are talked about."

Paul's wise advice to Timothy gave the same caution. "Don't have anything to do with foolish and stupid arguments, because you know they produce quarrels. And the Lord's servant must not be quarrelsome but must be kind to everyone" (2 TIMOTHY 2:23–24).

Paul's good counsel, written to Timothy from a Roman prison, was sent to prepare the young pastor for teaching God's truth. Paul's advice is just as timely for us today, especially when the conversation turns to our faith. "Opponents must be gently instructed, in the hope that God will grant them repentance leading them to a knowledge of the truth" (V. 25).

Speaking kindly to others is part of this challenge, but not just for pastors. For all who love God and seek to tell others about Him, may we speak His truth in love. With every word, the Holy Spirit will help us.   PATRICIA RAYBON

Why is it vital as a believer in Jesus to avoid arguing with others on the internet (and in other contexts)? When you're led by the Holy Spirit, how does the tone of your comments—your heart—change?

Father God, when I'm speaking to others about Your truth—or other interests—indwell my heart and tongue with Your love.

The tongue is a small part of the body, but it makes great boasts. [JAMES 3:5]

JUST A SPARK

"We're in the library, and we can see the flames right outside!" She was scared. We could hear it in her voice. We know her voice—the voice of our daughter. At the same time we knew her college campus was the safest place for her and her almost 3,000 fellow students. The 2018 Woolsey Fire spread more quickly than anyone anticipated—most of all fire personnel. The record heat and dry conditions in the California canyon, along with the legendary Santa Ana winds, were all the rather small sparks needed to ultimately burn 97,000 acres, destroy more than 1,600 structures, and kill three people. In the photos taken after the fire was contained, the usual lush coastline resembled the barren surface of the moon.

In the book of James, the author names some small but powerful things: "bits [in] the mouths of horses" and the rudders of ships (3:3–4). And while familiar, these examples are somewhat removed from us. But then he names something a little closer to home, something small that every human being possesses—a tongue. And while this chapter is first directed specifically to teachers (V. 1), the application quickly spreads to each of us. The tongue, small as it is, can lead to disastrous results.

Our small tongues are powerful, but our big God is more powerful. His help on a daily basis provides the strength to rein in and guide our words.　　　　　　　　　　　　　　　*JOHN BLASE*

When was the last time your tongue got away from you? What will help you keep a tight rein on your words in God's strength?

Jesus, I've been on the receiving end of words that burn. And how many times have I said something that caused damage or pain? Help me to keep a tight rein on my tongue.

When the Lord saw her, his heart went out to her.
[LUKE 7:13]

THE KINDNESS MAN

Disillusioned and wanting a more meaningful life, Leon quit his job in finance. Then one day he saw a homeless man holding up this sign at a street corner: KINDNESS IS THE BEST MEDICINE. Leon says, "Those words rammed straight into me. It was an epiphany."

Leon decided to begin his new life by creating an international organization to promote kindness. He travels around the world, relying on strangers to provide him with food, gas, and a place to stay. Then he rewards them, through his organization, with good deeds such as feeding orphans or building on to a school for underprivileged children. He says, "It's sometimes seen as being soft. But kindness is a profound strength."

Christ's very essence as God is goodness, so kindness naturally flowed from Him. I love the story of what Jesus did when He came upon the funeral procession of a widow's only son (LUKE 7:11–17). The grieving woman most likely was dependent on her son for financial support. We don't read in the story that anyone asked Jesus to intervene. Purely from the goodness of His nature (V. 13), He was concerned and brought her son back to life. The people said of Christ, "God has come to help his people" (V. 16).　　*ANNE CETAS*

What kindnesses does Jesus pour out on you?
List them and thank Him.

You, God, are always showering me with Your gifts of love.
I praise You for caring for me.

Praise the LORD . . . who satisfies your desires with
good things. [PSALM 103:1, 5]

RENEWED STRENGTH

Psychiatrist Robert Coles once noticed a pattern in those who burn out while serving others. The first warning sign is weariness. Next comes cynicism about things ever improving, then bitterness, despair, depression, and finally burnout.

After writing a book about recovering from broken dreams, I once entered a busy season of conference speaking. Helping people find hope after disappointment was richly rewarding, but came at a cost. One day, about to step on stage, I thought I was going to faint. I hadn't slept well, a vacation hadn't fixed my weariness, and the thought of hearing another person's problems afterward filled me with dread. I was following Coles' pattern.

Scripture gives two strategies for beating burnout. In Isaiah 40, the weary soul is renewed when it hopes in the Lord (VV. 29–31). I needed to rest in God, trusting Him to work, rather than pushing on in my own dwindling strength. And Psalm 103 says God renews us by satisfying our desires with good things (V. 5). While this includes forgiveness and redemption (VV. 3–4), provisions of joy and play come from Him too. When I reworked my schedule to include more prayer, rest, and hobbies like photography, I began to feel healthy again.

Burnout begins with weariness. Let's stop it from going further. We serve others best when our lives include both worship and rest.

SHERIDAN VOYSEY

**What burdens do you need to offload to God right now?
How are you renewing your strength through prayer,
Scripture, and healthy play?**

*Loving God, I want to rise in strength like the eagle today.
I trust You to work in my exhausting situation, and receive
Your soul-filling gifts with gladness.*

Those who trust in their riches will fall, but the
righteous will thrive like a green leaf. [PROVERBS 11:28]

A FLOURISHING TREE

I've always had a collector's heart. As a kid, I collected stamps. Baseball cards. Comics. Now, as a parent, I see the same impulse in my kids. Sometimes I wonder, *Do you really need another teddy bear?*

Of course, it's not about *need*. It's about the allure of something new. Or sometimes the tantalizing draw of something old, something rare. Whatever captivates our imagination, we're tempted to believe that if we only had "X," our lives would be better. We'd be happy. Content.

Except those things never deliver the goods. Why? Because God created us to be filled by Him, not by the things that the world around us often insists will satisfy our longing hearts.

This tension is hardly new. Proverbs contrasts two ways of life: a life spent pursuing riches versus a life grounded in loving God and giving generously. In *The Message*, Eugene Peterson paraphrases Proverbs 11:28 like this: "A life devoted to things is a dead life, a stump; a God-shaped life is a flourishing tree."

What a picture! Two ways of life: one flourishing and fruitful, one hollow and barren. The world insists that material abundance equals "the good life." In contrast, God invites us to be rooted in Him, to experience His goodness, and to flourish fruitfully. And as we're shaped by our relationship with Him, God reshapes our hearts and desires, transforming us from the inside out.

ADAM R. HOLZ

When has an undue focus on material things become a major spiritual struggle for you? What helps you keep your desires in proper perspective?

Father, thank You for the good gifts You give. Help me to keep putting my trust in You rather than the stuff of this world.

Though it linger, wait for it; it will certainly come and will not delay. [HABAKKUK 2:3]

PRAYER EGGS

Just outside my kitchen window, a robin built her nest under the eaves of our patio roof. I loved watching her tuck grasses into a safe spot and then hunker down to incubate the eggs. Each morning I checked her progress; but each morning, there was nothing. Robin eggs take two weeks to hatch.

Such impatience isn't new for me. I've always strained against the work of waiting, especially in prayer. My husband and I waited nearly five years to adopt our first child. Decades ago, author Catherine Marshall wrote, "Prayers, like eggs, don't hatch as soon as we lay them."

The prophet Habakkuk wrestled with waiting in prayer. Frustrated at God's silence with Babylon's brutal mistreatment of the Southern Kingdom of Judah, Habakkuk commits to "stand at my watch and station myself on the ramparts," to "look to see what he will say to me" (HABAKKUK 2:1). God replies that Habakkuk is to wait for the "appointed time" (V. 3) and directs Habakkuk to "write down the revelation" so the word can be spread as soon as it's given (V. 2).

What God doesn't mention is that the "appointed time" when Babylon falls is six decades away, creating a long gap between promise and fulfillment. Like eggs, prayers often don't hatch immediately but rather incubate in God's overarching purposes for our world and our lives.　　　　*ELISA MORGAN*

How difficult do you find it to wait while God works? While you wait, how can you obey God in what He has already given you to do?

Dear God, help me to trust You to work while I'm waiting.

May the nations be glad and sing for joy.
[PSALM 67:4]

★ *JULY TOPIC: CELEBRATION*
LET US PRAISE!

When the alarm on Shelley's phone goes off every day at 3:16 in the afternoon, she takes a praise break. She thanks God and acknowledges His goodness. Although she communicates with God throughout the day, Shelley loves to take this break because it helps her celebrate her intimate relationship with Him.

Inspired by her joyful devotion, I decided to set a specific time each day to thank Christ for His sacrifice on the cross and to pray for those who have yet to be saved. I wonder what it would be like if all believers in Jesus stopped to praise Him in their own way and pray for others every day.

The image of a beautiful wave of worship rolling to the ends of the earth resounds in the words of Psalm 67. The psalmist pleads for God's grace, proclaiming his desire to make His name great in all the nations (VV. 1–2). He sings, "May the peoples praise you, God; may all the peoples praise you" (V. 3). He celebrates His sovereign rule and faithful guidance (V. 4). As a living testimony of God's great love and abundant blessings, the psalmist leads God's people into jubilant praise (VV. 5–6).

God's continued faithfulness toward His beloved children inspires us to acknowledge Him. As we do, others can join us in trusting Him, revering Him, following Him, and acclaiming Him as Lord.   *XOCHITL DIXON*

When can you take a few minutes today to praise God?
What do you have to be thankful for?

God, You are worthy of all our praise!

The message of the cross is foolishness to those who are perishing, but to us who are being saved it is the power of God. [1 CORINTHIANS 1:18]

THE FOOLISH WAY OF NEW LIFE

Some things just don't make sense until you experience them. When I was pregnant with my first child, I read multiple books about childbirth and listened to dozens of women tell their stories of labor and delivery. But I still couldn't really imagine what the experience would be like. What my body was going to do seemed impossible!

Paul writes in 1 Corinthians that birth into God's kingdom, the salvation that God offers us through Christ, seems equally incomprehensible to those who haven't experienced it. It sounds like "foolishness" to say that salvation could come through a cross—a death marked by weakness, defeat, and humiliation. Yet this "foolishness" was the salvation that Paul preached!

It wasn't what anyone could have imagined it would be like. Some people thought that salvation would come through a strong political leader or a miraculous sign. Others thought that their own academic or philosophical achievements would be their salvation (1 CORINTHIANS 1:22). But God surprised everyone by bringing salvation in a way that would only make sense to those who believed, to those who experienced it.

God took something shameful and weak—death on a cross—and made it the foundation of wisdom and power. God does the unimaginable. He chooses the weak and foolish things of the world to shame the wise (V. 27). And His surprising, confounding ways are always the best ways.

AMY PETERSON

How is God surprising you today? Why is it true that God's ways are better than your ways?

God, I pray, as high as the heavens are above the earth, so are Your ways higher than my ways, and Your thoughts higher than mine.

We have left everything to follow you!
[MARK 10:28]

GOD IS WORTH MORE

Having been hurt by believers in Jesus in the past, my mom responded in anger when I dedicated my life to Him. "So, now you're going to judge me? I don't think so." She hung up the phone and refused to talk to me for a whole year. I grieved, but eventually realized a relationship with God was even more important than one of my most valued relationships. I prayed for her every time she refused my calls and asked God to help me love her well.

Finally, we reconciled. A few months later, she said, "You've changed. I think I'm ready to hear more about Jesus." Soon after, she accepted Christ and lived the rest of her days loving God and others.

Like the man who ran up to Jesus asking how he could inherit eternal life but left in sorrow because he didn't want to part with his wealth (MARK 10:17–22), I struggled with the thought of giving up everything to follow Him.

It's not easy surrendering the things or people we think we can count on more than God (VV. 23–25). But the value of what we give up or lose in this world will never exceed the gift of eternal life with Jesus. Our loving God willingly sacrificed Himself to save all people. He wraps us in peace and woos us with priceless and persistent love.   *XOCHITL DIXON*

What was the hardest thing you gave up or lost when you started following Jesus? Why does it feel easier to trust worldly comforts, material wealth, and people more than Him?

God, thanks for loving us more than we deserve and reminding us You're worth more than anything or anyone in this world.

With your blood you purchased for God persons from
every tribe and language and people and nation.
[REVELATION 5:9]

A PARADE OF COLORS

For decades, London has been one of the most cosmopolitan cities in the world. In 1933, journalist Glyn Roberts wrote of England's great capital, "I still think the parade of peoples and colours and tongues is just about the best thing in London." That "parade" is still in evidence today with the blended smells, sounds, and sights of a global community. The beauty of diversity is part of the breathtaking appeal of one of the world's greatest cities.

As with any city inhabited by human beings, however, London is not without its problems. Change brings challenges. Cultures sometimes clash. And that is one of the reasons no city built by human hands can compare to the wonder of our eternal home.

When the apostle John was transported into the presence of God, diversity was one of the elements of heavenly worship, as the redeemed sang, "You are worthy to take the scroll and to open its seals, because you were slain, and with your blood you purchased for God persons from every tribe and language and people and nation. You have made them to be a kingdom and priests to serve our God, and they will reign on the earth" (REVELATION 5:9–10).

Imagine heaven: a parade of every people group in the world celebrating the wonder of being children of the living God— together! As believers in Jesus, may we celebrate that diversity today.   *BILL CROWDER*

What are the best things about the church being so diverse?
What can make that diversity occasionally challenging?

Father, I thank You that no people group is excluded from
Your great love. Teach us to truly love one another,
as You have so generously loved us.

Let's not have any quarreling between you and me . . .
for we are close relatives. [GENESIS 13:8]

UNITED IN SEPARATION

Thrown into a project with his colleague Tim, Alvin faced a major challenge: he and Tim had very different ideas of how to go about it. While they respected each other's opinions, their approaches were so different that conflict seemed imminent. Before conflict broke out, however, the two men agreed to discuss their differences with their boss, who put them on separate teams. It turned out to be a wise move. That day, Alvin learned this lesson: Being united doesn't always mean doing things together.

Abraham must have realized this truth when he suggested that he and Lot go their separate ways in Bethel (GENESIS 13:5–9). Seeing that there wasn't enough space for both their flocks, Abraham wisely suggested parting company. But first, he stressed that they were "close relatives" (V. 8), reminding Lot of their relationship. Then, with the greatest humility, he let his nephew have the first choice (V. 9) even though he, Abraham, was the senior man. It was, as one pastor described it, a "harmonious separation."

Being made uniquely by God, we may find that we sometimes work better separately to achieve the same goal. There's a unity in diversity. May we never forget, however, that we're still brothers and sisters in the family of God. We may do things differently, but we remain united in purpose. *LESLIE KOH*

How can humility help in a "harmonious separation"?
How can you remain united in purpose even when you disagree
with someone on a disputable matter? (ROMANS 14:1–10).

God, help me to work together with others in unity,
and help me to discern when it's best to serve separately.

Go, then, to all peoples everywhere
and make them my disciples. [MATTHEW 28:19 GNT]

LAUNDRY DAY

Driving through a low-income area near his church, Colorado pastor Chad Graham started praying for his "neighbors." When he noticed a small laundromat, he stopped to take a look inside and found it filled with customers. One asked Graham for a spare coin to operate the clothes dryer. That small request inspired a weekly "Laundry Day" sponsored by Graham's church. Members donate coins and soap to the laundromat, pray with customers, and support the owner of the laundry facility.

Their neighborhood outreach, which dares to include a laundromat, reflects Jesus' Great Commission to His disciples. As He said, "I have been given all authority in heaven and on earth. Go, then, to all peoples everywhere and make them my disciples: baptize them in the name of the Father, the Son, and the Holy Spirit" (MATTHEW 28:18–19 GNT).

His Holy Spirit's powerful presence enables "everywhere" outreach, including even a laundromat. Indeed, we don't go alone. As Jesus promised, "I will be with you always, to the end of the age" (V. 20 GNT).

Pastor Chad experienced that truth after praying at the laundromat for a customer named Jeff who is battling cancer. As Chad reported, "When we opened our eyes, every customer in the room was praying with us, hands stretched out toward Jeff. It was one of the most sacred moments I have experienced as a pastor."

The lesson? Let's go everywhere to proclaim Christ.

PATRICIA RAYBON

Where can you go in your neighborhood today to proclaim Christ? How could His powerful presence enable you?

Jesus, enable me to proclaim Your good news today—everywhere.

God opposes the proud but shows favor
to the humble. [JAMES 4:6]

PLAYING THE FOOL

My most humiliating experience ever was the day I addressed the faculty, students, and friends of a seminary on its fifty-year anniversary. I approached the lectern with my manuscript in hand and looked out on a vast crowd, but my eye fell on the distinguished professors seated in the front row, garbed in academic gowns and looking very serious. I immediately took leave of my senses. My mouth dried up and detached itself from my brain. I fumbled the first few sentences and then I began to improvise. Since I had no idea where I was in my lecture, I began frantically turning pages, while talking a line of nonsense that baffled everyone. Somehow I made it through, crept back to my chair, and stared at the floor. I wanted to die.

However, I learned that humiliation can be a good thing if it leads to humility, for this is the key that opens God's heart. The Scriptures say, "God opposes the proud but shows favor to the humble" (JAMES 4:6). He showers the humble with grace. God Himself said, "These are the ones I look on with favor: those who are humble and contrite in spirit, and who tremble at my word" (ISAIAH 66:2). As we humble ourselves before God, He lifts us up (JAMES 4:10).

Humiliation and shame can bring us to God for His shaping. When we fall, we have fallen into His hands.　　*DAVID H. ROPER*

What was your most humiliating and embarrassing moment?
What good thing did you see come from it?

*Loving God, help me to accept humiliation if it in some way
brings honor and glory to You.*

I have come that they may have life, and have it
to the full. I am the good shepherd. [JOHN 10:10–11]

★ *JULY TOPIC: CELEBRATION*

LIFE TO THE FULL

Seventeenth-century philosopher Thomas Hobbes famously wrote that human life in its natural state is "solitary, poor, nasty, brutish, and short." Hobbes argued that our instincts tend toward war in a bid to attain dominance over others; thus the establishment of government would be necessary to maintain law and order.

The bleak view of humanity sounds like the state of affairs that Jesus described when He said, "All who have come before me are thieves and robbers" (JOHN 10:8). But Jesus offers hope in the midst of despair. "The thief comes only to steal and kill and destroy," but then the good news: "I have come that they may have life, and have it to the full" (V. 10).

Psalm 23 paints a refreshing portrait of the life our Shepherd gives us. In Him, we "lack nothing" (V. 1) and are refreshed (V. 3). He leads us down the right paths of His perfect will, so that even when we face dark times, we need not be afraid; for He is present to comfort us (VV. 3–4). He causes us to triumph in the face of adversity and overwhelms us with blessings (V. 5). His goodness and love follow us every day, and we have the privilege of His presence forever (V. 6).

May we answer the Shepherd's call and experience the full, abundant life He came to give us.   *REMI OYEDELE*

**How would you describe the life that Jesus came to give?
How can you share this life with others?**

*Jesus, You're the source of true life, abundant and full.
Help me seek my fulfillment only in You.*

BIBLE IN A YEAR | PSALMS 13–15; ACTS 19:21–41

When a man found it, he . . . went and sold
all he had and bought that field. [MATTHEW 13:44]

COSTLY JOY

A t the sound of the digital melody, all six of us sprang into
action. Some slipped shoes on, others simply bolted for the
door bare-foot. Within seconds we were all sprinting down
the driveway chasing the ice cream truck. It was the first warm
day of summer, and there was no better way to celebrate than
with a cold, sweet treat! There are things we do simply because
of the joy it brings us, not out of discipline or obligation.

In the pair of parables found in Matthew 13:44–46, the
emphasis is *selling everything to gain something else.* We might
think the stories are about sacrifice. But that's not the point. In
fact, the first story declares it was "joy" that led the man to sell
everything and buy the field. Joy drives change—not guilt or duty.

Jesus isn't one segment of our lives; His claims on us are total.
Both men in the stories "sold all" (V. 44). But here's the best part:
the result of this selling of everything is actually gain. We may not
have guessed that. Isn't the Christian life about taking up your
cross? Yes. It is. But when we die, we live; when we lose our life,
we find it. When we "sell all," we gain the greatest treasure: Jesus!
Joy is the reason; surrender is the response. The treasure of
knowing Jesus is the reward.　　　　　　　　*GLENN PACKIAM*

**How have you experienced joy in your relationship with Jesus?
What is He inviting you to surrender to Him?**

*Dear Jesus, open my eyes to see the treasure that You are! Direct my
heart to You as the source of true and unfailing joy, and let me ever
be fixed on You. Grant me the grace to surrender all to You.*

You, LORD, keep my lamp burning; my God
turns my darkness into light. [PSALM 18:28]

LIGHT IN THE DARK

A severe thunderstorm passed through our new town, leaving high humidity and dark skies in its wake. I took our dog, Callie, for an evening stroll. The mounting challenges of my family's cross-country move grew heavier on my mind. Frustrated by the countless ways things had strayed so far from our high hopes and expectations, I slowed to let Callie sniff the grass. I listened to the creek that runs beside our house. Tiny lights flashed on and off while hovering over the patches of wildflowers climbing up the creek's bank. *Fireflies.*

The Lord wrapped me in peace as I watched the blinking lights cutting through the darkness. I thought of the psalmist David singing, "You, LORD, keep my lamp burning" (PSALM 18:28). Proclaiming that God turns his darkness into light, David demonstrated confident faith in the Lord's provision and protection (VV. 29–30). With God's strength, he could handle anything that came his way (VV. 32–35). Trusting the living Lord to be with him through all circumstances, David promised to praise Him among the nations and sing the praises of His name (VV. 36–49).

Whether we're enduring the unpredictable storms in life or enjoying the stillness after the rains have passed, the peace of God's constant presence lights our way through the darkness. Our living God will always be our strength, our refuge, our sustainer, and our deliverer.   XOCHITL DIXON

What verses help you trust God's constant presence? How can relying on God's sovereign goodness help us walk through storms with confident faith?

*Father, please help me trust Your goodness and love even when
I sometimes can't see You in the dark circumstances in life.*

Because of the LORD's great love we are not consumed,
for his compassions never fail. [LAMENTATIONS 3:22]

WHEN THE SPLENDOR IS GONE

I can never recapture the splendor that was our daughter Melissa. Fading from my memory are those wonderful times when we watched her joyfully playing high school volleyball. And it's sometimes hard to remember the shy smile of contentment that crossed her face when we were doing family activities. Her death at age seventeen dropped a curtain on the joy of her presence.

In the book of Lamentations, Jeremiah's words show he understood that the heart can be punctured. "My splendor is gone," he said, "and all that I had hoped from the LORD" (3:18). His situation was far different from yours and mine. He had preached God's judgment, and he saw Jerusalem defeated. The splendor was gone because he felt defeated (V. 12), isolated (V. 14), and abandoned by God (VV. 15–20).

But that's not the end of his story. Light shined through. Jeremiah, burdened and broken, stammered out "I have hope" (V. 21)—hope that comes from realizing that "because of the LORD's great love we are not consumed" (V. 22). And here is just what we need to remember when the splendor is gone: God's "compassions never fail. They are new every morning" (VV. 22–23).

Even in our darkest days, God's great faithfulness shines through.   *DAVE BRANON*

How has God encouraged you when you felt hopeless?
How might He want you to use that to encourage others?

Thank You, Father, that You're the God of compassion. Even while
I walk through the valley of darkness, morning will follow as
I remember Your compassion and Your faithfulness.

These commandments . . . are to be on your hearts.
Impress them on your children. [DEUTERONOMY 6:6–7]

ON OUR HEARTS

After a young boy faced some challenges in school, his dad began to teach him a pledge to recite each morning before school: "I thank God for waking me up today. I am going to school so I can learn . . . and be the leader that God has created me to be." The pledge is one way the father hopes to help his son apply himself and deal with life's inevitable challenges.

In a way, by helping his son to commit this pledge to memory, the father is doing something similar to what God commanded the Israelites in the desert: "These commandments . . . are to be on your hearts. Impress them on your children" (DEUTERONOMY 6:6–7).

After wandering in the wilderness for forty years, the next generation of Israelites was about to enter the Promised Land. God knew it wouldn't be easy for them to succeed—*unless* they kept their focus on Him. And so, through Moses, He urged them to remember and be obedient to Him—and to help their children to know and love God by talking about His Word "when you sit at home and when you walk along the road, when you lie down and when you get up" (V. 7).

Each new day, we too can commit to allowing Scripture to guide our hearts and minds as we live in gratitude to Him.

ALYSON KIEDA

What can you do to keep Scripture on your heart? Why is it important to read and talk about the Word with loved ones?

Dear God, thank You for giving me each new day. Help me to keep Your wisdom in my heart and on my mind.

Hear my voice when I call, LORD; be merciful to me
and answer me. [PSALM 27:7]

HOW TO WAIT

Frustrated and disappointed with church, seventeen-year-old Trevor began a years-long quest for answers. But nothing he explored seemed to satisfy his longings or answer his questions.

His journey did draw him closer to his parents. Still, he had problems with Christianity. During one discussion, he exclaimed bitterly, "The Bible is full of empty promises."

Another man faced disappointment and hardship that fueled his doubts. But as David fled from enemies who sought to kill him, his response was not to run from God but to praise Him. "Though war break out against me, even then I will be confident," he sang (PSALM 27:3).

Yet David's poem still hints at doubt. His cry, "Be merciful to me and answer me" (V. 7), sounds like a man with fears and questions. "Do not hide your face from me," David pleaded. "Do not reject me or forsake me" (V. 9).

David didn't let his doubts paralyze him, however. Even in those doubts, he declared, "I will see the goodness of the LORD in the land of the living" (V. 13). Then he addressed his readers: you, me, and the Trevors of this world. "Wait for the LORD; be strong and take heart and wait for the LORD" (V. 14).

We won't find fast, simple answers to our huge questions. But we will find—when we wait for Him—a God who can be trusted.

TIM GUSTAFSON

What do you do with your big questions? Where have you seen answers "in the land of the living" (PSALM 27:13), and where are you still waiting for answers?

Father, melt my heart along with my fears and my anger.

To all who did receive him, to those who
believed in his name, he gave the right to become
children of God. [JOHN 1:12]

A ROYAL ROLE

The closer someone in a royal family is to the throne, the more the public hears about him or her. Others are almost forgotten. The British royal family has a line of succession that includes nearly sixty people. One of them is Lord Frederick Windsor, who's forty-ninth in line for the throne. Instead of being in the limelight, he quietly goes about his life. Though he works as a financial analyst, he's not considered a "working royal"—one of the important family members who are paid for representing the family.

David's son Nathan (2 SAMUEL 5:14) is another royal who lived outside the limelight. Very little is known about him. But while the genealogy of Jesus in Matthew mentions his son Solomon (tracing Joseph's line, MATTHEW 1:6), Luke's genealogy, which many scholars believe is Mary's family line, mentions Nathan (LUKE 3:31). Though Nathan didn't hold a scepter, he still had a role in God's forever kingdom.

As believers in Christ, we're also royalty. The apostle John wrote that God gave us "the right to become children of God" (JOHN 1:12). Though we may not be in the spotlight, we're children of the King! God considers each of us important enough to represent Him here on earth and to one day reign with Him (2 TIMOTHY 2:11–13). Like Nathan, we may not wear an earthly crown, but we still have a part to play in God's kingdom.   *LINDA WASHINGTON*

**How does knowing you're royalty—God's child—make you feel?
As a child of the King, what do you see as your responsibilities
to the people around you?**

*Heavenly Father, I'm grateful that You adopted me into
Your forever family.*

BIBLE IN A YEAR | PSALMS 29–30; ACTS 23:1–15

Come, let us sing for joy to the LORD;
let us shout aloud to the Rock of our salvation. [PSALM 95:1]

★ *JULY TOPIC: CELEBRATION*

A SINGER'S HEART

The praise song drifted downstairs . . . at 6:33 on a Saturday morning. I didn't think anyone else was awake, but my youngest daughter's scratchy voice proved me wrong. She was barely conscious, but there was already a song on her lips.

My youngest is a singer. In fact, she can't *not* sing. She sings when she wakes up. When she goes to school. When she goes to bed. She was born with a song in her heart—and most of the time, her songs focus on Jesus. She'll praise God anytime, anywhere.

I love the simplicity, devotion, and earnestness of my daughter's voice. Her spontaneous and joyful songs echo invitations to praise God found throughout Scripture. In Psalm 95, we read, "Come let us sing for joy to the LORD; let us shout aloud to the Rock of our salvation" (V. 1). Reading further, we learn that this praise flows from an understanding of who He is ("For the LORD is the great God, the great King above all gods," v. 3)—and whose we are ("For he is our God and we are the people of his pasture," v. 7).

For my daughter, those truths are her first thought in the morning. By God's grace, this little worshiper offers us a profound reminder of the joy of singing to Him.   *ADAM R. HOLZ*

**What prompts you to praise God for His faithfulness to you?
What songs help you to remember and focus on His character
and goodness?**

*God, thank You for who You are and for what You've done for me—
and for all Your people—by inviting us to be sheep in Your pasture.
Let today be filled with my songs of praise for Your goodness.*

At that time you were separate from Christ....
without hope and without God in the world.
[EPHESIANS 2:12]

A GLIMMER ON THE SEA

"I lay on my bed full of stale liquor and despair," wrote journalist Malcolm Muggeridge of a particularly dismal evening during his work as a World War II spy. "Alone in the universe, in eternity, with no glimmer of light."

In such a condition, he did the only thing he thought sensible; he tried to drown himself. Driving to the nearby Madagascar coast, he began the long swim into the ocean until he grew exhausted. Looking back, he glimpsed the distant coastal lights. For no reason clear to him at the time, he started swimming back toward the lights. Despite his fatigue, he recalls "an overwhelming joy."

Muggeridge didn't know exactly how, but he knew God had reached him in that dark moment, infusing him with a hope that could only be supernatural. The apostle Paul wrote often about such hope. In Ephesians he noted that, before knowing Christ, each of us is "dead in [our] transgressions and sins . . . . without hope and without God in the world" (2:1, 12). But "God, who is rich in mercy, made us alive with Christ even when we were dead" (VV. 4–5).

This world tries to drag us into the depths, but there's no reason to succumb to despair. As Muggeridge said about his swim in the sea, "It became clear to me that there was no darkness, only the possibility of losing sight of a light which shone eternally."

TIM GUSTAFSON

**What has been your darkest moment? In what places have you
glimpsed the "light that shines eternally"?**

*Father, You're the source of all our genuine hope.
Fill us with Your light and joy.*

He was pierced for our transgressions, . . .
and by his wounds we are healed. [ISAIAH 53:5]

HIS SCARS

After my conversation with Grady, it occurred to me why his preferred greeting was a "fist bump" not a handshake. A hand-shake would've exposed the scars on his wrist—the result of his attempts to do himself harm. It's not uncommon for us to hide our wounds—external or internal—caused by others or self-inflicted.

In the wake of my interaction with Grady, I thought about Jesus' physical scars, the wounds caused by nails pounded into His hands and feet and a spear thrust into His side. Rather than hiding His scars, Christ called attention to them.

After Thomas initially doubted that Jesus had risen from the dead, He said to him, "Put your finger here; see my hands. Reach out your hand and put it into my side. Stop doubting and believe" (JOHN 20:27). When Thomas saw those scars for himself and heard Christ's amazing words, he was convinced that it was Jesus. He exclaimed in belief, "My Lord and my God!" (V. 28). Jesus then pronounced a special blessing for those who haven't seen Him or His physical wounds but still believe in Him: "Blessed are those who have not seen and yet have believed" (V. 29).

The best news ever is that His scars were for *our* sins—our sins against others or ourselves. The death of Jesus is for the forgiveness of the sins of all who believe in Him and confess with Thomas, "My Lord and my God!"   *ARTHUR JACKSON*

What circumstances led you to believe that Jesus' scars were for you? If you haven't believed in Him for the forgiveness of your sins, what keeps you from trusting Him today?

Father, I believe that Christ's scars were for my sin. I'm grateful!

"Am I not sending you?"
[JUDGES 6:14]

PLOD ON!

God loves to use people the world might overlook. William Carey was raised in a tiny village in the 1700s and had little formal education. He had limited success in his chosen trade and lived in poverty. But God gave him a passion for sharing the good news and called him to be a missionary. Carey learned Greek, Hebrew, and Latin and eventually translated the first New Testament into the Bengali language. Today he is regarded as a "father of modern missions," but in a letter to his nephew he offered this humble assessment of his abilities: "I can plod. I can persevere."

When God calls us to a task, He also gives us strength to accomplish it regardless of our limitations. In Judges 6:12 the angel of the Lord appeared to Gideon and said, "The LORD is with you, mighty warrior." The angel then told him to rescue Israel from the Midianites who were raiding their towns and crops. But Gideon, who hadn't earned the title of "mighty warrior," humbly responded, "How can I save Israel? . . . I am the least in my family" (V. 15). Still, God used Gideon to set His people free.

The key to Gideon's success was in the words, "the LORD is with you" (V. 12). As we humbly walk with our Savior and rely on His strength, He will empower us to accomplish what's only possible through Him.   *JAMES BANKS*

What's God calling you to do that you can't do in your own strength? How can you rely on His power today?

Thank You for empowering me, my Savior and my strength! Please help me to follow You closely.

Even my close friend, someone I trusted, one who
shared my bread, has turned against me. [PSALM 41:9]

BETRAYED

I n 2019, art exhibitions worldwide commemorated the five
hundredth anniversary of the death of Leonardo da Vinci.
While many of his drawings and scientific discoveries were
showcased, there are only five finished paintings universally credited to da Vinci, including *The Last Supper*.

This intricate mural depicts the final meal Jesus ate with His disciples, as described in the gospel of John. The painting captures the
disciples' confusion at Jesus' statement, "One of you is going to
betray me" (JOHN 13:21). Perplexed, the disciples discussed who the
betrayer might be—while Judas quietly slipped out into the night to
alert the authorities of the whereabouts of his teacher and friend.

Betrayed. The pain of Judas' treachery is evident in Jesus' words,
"He who shared my bread has turned against me (V. 18). A friend
close enough to share a meal used that connection to harm Jesus.

Each of us has likely experienced a friend's betrayal. How can
we respond to such pain? Psalm 41:9, which Jesus quoted to indi-
cate His betrayer was present during the shared meal (JOHN 13:18),
offers hope. After David poured out his anguish at a close friend's
duplicity, he took solace in God's love and presence that would
uphold and set him in God's presence forever (PSALM 41:11–12).

When friends disappoint, we can find comfort knowing God's
sustaining love and His empowering presence will be with us to
help us endure even the most devastating pain.   *LISA M. SAMRA*

**How have you experienced the betrayal of a friend?
How has the reassurance of God's love and presence
sustained you?**

*Heavenly Father, I'm thankful that Your love is stronger than
any betrayal. When I face rejection, help me find strength in the
knowledge that You are always with me.*

My eyes will flow unceasingly, without relief,
until the LORD looks down from heaven and sees.
[LAMENTATIONS 3:49–50]

TAKE YOUR TEARS TO GOD

Recently, an orca named Talequah gave birth. Talequah's pod of killer whales was endangered, and her newborn was their hope for the future. But the calf lived for less than an hour. In a show of grief that was watched by people around the world, Talequah pushed her dead calf through the cold waters of the Pacific Ocean for seventeen days before letting her go.

Sometimes believers in Jesus have a hard time knowing what to do with grief. Perhaps we fear that our sorrow might look like a lack of hope. But the Bible gives us many examples of humans crying out to God in grief. Lament and hope can both be part of a faithful response.

Lamentations is a book of five poems that express the sorrow of people who have lost their home. They've been hunted by enemies and were near death (3:52–54), and they weep and call on God to bring justice (V. 64). They cry out to God not because they have lost hope, but because they believe God is listening. And when they call, God does come near (V. 57).

It's not wrong to lament the broken things in our world or in your life. God is always listening, and you can be sure that God will look down from heaven and see you.   *AMY PETERSON*

**How can you practice bringing all your emotions to God?
When have you felt God draw near to you in your sadness?**

*Loving God, help us to remember that it's right to lament wrongness
before we can begin to change it.*

I know whom I have believed.
[2 TIMOTHY 1:12]

TRUSTING GOD IN TIMES OF SORROW

When a man known as "Papa John" learned he had terminal cancer, he and his wife, Carol, sensed God calling them to share their illness journey online. Believing that God would minister through their vulnerability, they posted their moments of joy *and* their sorrow and pain for two years.

When Carol wrote that her husband "went into the outstretched arms of Jesus," hundreds of people responded, with many thanking Carol for their openness. One person remarked that hearing about dying from a Christian point of view was healthy, for "we all have to die" someday. Another said that although she'd never met the couple personally, she couldn't express how much encouragement she'd received through their witness of trusting God.

Although Papa John sometimes felt excruciating pain, he and Carol shared their story so they could demonstrate how God upheld them. They knew their testimony would bear fruit for God, echoing what Paul wrote to Timothy when he suffered: "I know whom I have believed, and am convinced that he is able to guard what I have entrusted to him until that day" (2 TIMOTHY 1:12).

God can use even the death of a loved one to strengthen our faith in Him (and the faith of others) through the grace we receive in Christ Jesus (V. 9). If you're experiencing anguish and difficulty, know that He can bring comfort and peace. *AMY BOUCHER PYE*

How have you experienced God's joy even in times of deep sorrow? How do you explain this? How could you share what you learned with others?

Heavenly Father, fan into flame the gift of faith in me,
that I might share with love and power my testimony of
how You work in my life.

Mephibosheth ate at David's table
like one of the king's sons. [2 SAMUEL 9:11]

GRACE OUTSIDE THE BOX

Tom worked for a law firm that advised Bob's company. They became friends—until Tom embezzled thousands of dollars from the company. Bob was hurt and angry when he found out, but he received wise counsel from his vice president, a believer in Christ. The VP noticed Tom was deeply ashamed and repentant, and he advised Bob to drop the charges and hire Tom. "Pay him a modest salary so he can make restitution. You'll never have a more grateful, loyal employee." Bob did, and Tom was.

Mephibosheth, grandson of King Saul, hadn't done anything wrong, but he was in a tough spot when David became king. Most kings killed the royal bloodline. But David loved King Saul's son Jonathan, and treated his surviving son as his own (SEE 2 SAMUEL 9:1–13). His grace won a friend for life. Mephibosheth marveled that he "deserved nothing but death from my lord the king, but you gave your servant a place" (19:28). He remained loyal to David, even when David's son Absalom chased David from Jerusalem (2 SAMUEL 16:1–4; 19:24–30).

Do you want a loyal friend for life? Someone so extraordinary may require you to do something extraordinary. When common sense says punish, choose grace. Hold them accountable, but give the undeserving a chance to make things right. You may never find a more grateful, devoted friend. Think outside the box, with grace.   *MIKE WITTMER*

**Who has sinned against you? How might you hold them
accountable while also forgiving them?**

*Father, I've received extraordinary grace from You.
Help me show that grace to others—especially to those with
a repentant spirit.*

The one who is in [us] is greater
than the one who is in the world. [1 JOHN 4:4]

THE MOUSE THAT ROARED

S everal years ago my sons and I spent a few days camping in
the Selway-Bitterroot Wilderness in Northern Idaho. It's
grizzly bear habitat, but we carried bear spray, kept our
campsites clean, and anticipated no major grizzly encounters.

One evening, in the middle of the night, I heard Randy scramble
around trying to get out of his sleeping bag. I grabbed my flashlight
and turned it on, expecting to see him in the clutches of an
enraged grizzly.

There, sitting upright on its haunches and waving its paws in
the air was a field mouse about 4 inches tall. It had Randy's cap
firmly clenched in its teeth. The little creature had tugged and
tugged until he pulled Randy's cap from his head. As I laughed, the
mouse dropped the cap and scampered away. We crawled back
into our sleeping bags. I, however, fully adrenalized, couldn't get
back to sleep and thought about another predator—the devil.

Consider Satan's temptation of Jesus (MATTHEW 4:1–11). He
countered his enticements with the Scriptures. With each answer,
Jesus reminded Himself that God had spoken on this issue and
therefore He wouldn't disobey. This caused the devil to flee.

Although Satan wants to devour us, it's good to remember that
he's a created being like the little rodent. John said, "the one who
is in [us] is greater than the one who is in the world" (1 JOHN 4:4).

DAVID H. ROPER

**What are your greatest temptations? What does God say about
these issues and how might you use that when you're tempted?**

*Dear God, I'm grateful that You're greater than any temptation that
comes at me. Please provide the way out.*

They replied, "Let us start rebuilding."
So they began this good work. [NEHEMIAH 2:18]

HOW TO REBUILD

I t was nighttime when the leader set out by horseback to inspect the work that lay ahead. As he toured the destruction all around him, he saw city walls that had been destroyed and gates that had been burned. In some areas, the vast debris made it tough for his horse to get through. Saddened, the rider turned toward home.

When it came time to report the damage to the officials of the city, he began by saying, "You see the trouble we are in" (NEHEMIAH 2:17). He reported that the city was in ruins, and the protecting city wall had been rendered useless.

But then he made a statement that energized the troubled citizens: "I also told them about the gracious hand of my God on me." Immediately, the people replied, "Let us start rebuilding" (V. 18).

And they *did*.

With faith in God and all-out effort, despite enemy opposition and a seemingly impossible task, the people of Jerusalem—under Nehemiah's leadership—rebuilt the wall in just fifty-two days (6:15).

As you consider your circumstances, is there something that looks difficult but that you know God wants you to do? A sin you can't seem to get rid of? A relationship rift that's not God-honoring? A task for Him that looks too hard?

Ask God for guidance (2:4–5), analyze the problem (VV. 11–15), and recognize His involvement (V. 18). Then start rebuilding.

DAVE BRANON

What are a couple of "destroyed wall" situations that are troubling you? How will prayerfully asking for God's help and guidance help you start the rebuilding process?

God, I need Your help. I can't fix these problems alone. Help me to understand the situation, and then to seek Your help and guidance in resolving the challenges before me.

BIBLE IN A YEAR | PSALMS 54–56; ROMANS 3　　　221

FAMILY MATTERS

Every evening at 7:00, no matter where she is or how tired or busy she may be, Jo calls her elderly mother. If for some reason Jo isn't able to talk at that time, she makes sure to text her mom to let her know. Even though it can be a challenge to do this day after day, Jo does it gladly because she loves her mother and doesn't want her to worry.

When our children were young, my husband and I bought a home a distance away. But we needed to wait to move, and school was about to start. Knowing it would be stressful for our children to switch schools twice, for two weeks I made the long trek from home to their new schools and to my office and back because I wanted to minimize their stress.

No matter if we're married or single, have children or not, we have opportunities to show love to those God has placed in our lives—grandparents, parents, siblings, nephews, and nieces. Because God first loved us, He enables and empowers us through His Spirit to love our families and others (1 JOHN 4:7–21). And 1 Corinthians 13:4–7 offers some guidelines:

- Love is patient
- Love is kind
- Love does not dishonor others
- Love is not self-seeking
- Love is not easily angered
- Love keeps no record of wrongs

Loving our family through providing for their needs is also a God-given responsibility (1 TIMOTHY 5:8)—and that includes physically, mentally, emotionally, and spiritually.

Into what relationships can you give out of God's love for you this month? Think about the ways you can encourage others, and then take action.

ALYSON KIEDA, OUR DAILY BREAD *AUTHOR*

I am reminded of your sincere faith, which first lived
in your grandmother Lois and in your mother Eunice
and . . . now lives in you. [2 TIMOTHY 1:5]

★ *AUGUST TOPIC: FAMILY*

LOVE PASSED DOWN

My daughter has become fascinated with Nancy Drew. In the last three weeks, she's read at least a dozen of the novels featuring the girl sleuth. She comes by her love of detective stories honestly: I loved Nancy Drew too, and the blue-bound copies that my mom read in the 1960s still line a shelf in her house.

Seeing this affection passed down makes me wonder what else I'm passing down. In his second letter to Timothy, Paul wrote that when he thought of Timothy, he was reminded of the "sincere faith" that lived in Timothy's grandmother and mother. I hope that along with her love of mysteries, my daughter is also inheriting faith—that she will "serve" as her grandparents have, that she will pray, and that she will hold on "to the promise of life that is in Christ Jesus" (2 TIMOTHY 1:1).

I also see hope here for those who don't have parents or grandparents who know Jesus. Though Timothy's father isn't mentioned, Paul calls Timothy his "dear son" (V. 2). Those who don't have families to pass down faith can still find parents and grandparents in the church—people who will help us figure out how to live a "holy life" (V. 9), and to embrace the gifts God has given us of "power, love and self-discipline" (V. 7). Truly, we all have a beautiful inheritance.   *AMY PETERSON*

What are some things you've learned from fathers or mothers in the faith? How are you working to pass down a legacy of faith to your children or those in your church?

Heavenly Father, thank You for saving me by grace through faith in Jesus. Help me to pass down to the next generation the gifts I've received and the truth of the gospel.

BIBLE IN A YEAR | PSALMS 57–59; ROMANS 4   223

Whoever turns a sinner from the error of their way
will save them from death. [JAMES 5:20]

KIND CORRECTION

The early spring weather was refreshing and my traveling companion, my wife, couldn't have been better. But the beauty of those moments together could have quickly morphed into tragedy if it weren't for a red and white warning sign that informed me I was headed in the wrong direction. Because I hadn't turned wide enough, I momentarily saw a "Do Not Enter" sign staring me in the face. I quickly adjusted, but shudder to think of the harm I could have brought to my wife, myself, and others if I'd ignored the sign that reminded me I was going the wrong way.

The closing words of James emphasize the importance of correction. Who among us hasn't needed to be "brought back" by those who care for us from paths or actions, decisions or desires that could've been hurtful? Who knows what harm might have been done to ourselves or others had someone not courageously intervened at the right time.

James stresses the value of kind correction with these words, "Whoever turns a sinner from the error of their way will save them from death and cover over a multitude of sins" (5:20). Correction is an expression of God's mercy. May our love and concern for the well-being of others compel us to speak and act in ways that He can use to "bring that person back" (V. 19).   ARTHUR JACKSON

**What risks or rewards are associated with helping a wanderer
find his or her way back to where they belong? When did God use
someone to bring you back from a not-so-good place?**

*Father, keep me from straying from Your truth and grant me courage
to help bring back those who are wandering.*

We were . . . buried with him.
[ROMANS 6:4]

THE BATTLE'S OVER. REALLY.

For twenty-nine years after World War II ended, Hiroo Onoda hid in the jungle, refusing to believe his country had surrendered. Japanese military leaders had dispatched Onoda to a remote island in the Philippines (Lubang) with orders to spy on the Allied forces. Long after a peace treaty had been signed and hostilities ceased, Onoda remained in the wilderness. In 1974, Onoda's commanding officer traveled to the island to find him and convince him the war was over.

For three decades, Onoda lived a meager, isolated existence, because he refused to surrender—refused to believe the conflict was done. We can make a similar mistake. Paul proclaims the stunning truth that "all of us who were baptized into Christ Jesus were baptized into his death" (ROMANS 6:3). On the cross, in a powerful, mysterious way, Jesus put to death Satan's lies, death's terror, and sin's tenacious grip. Though we're "dead to sin" and "alive to God" (V. 11), we often live as though evil still holds the power. We yield to temptation, succumbing to sin's seduction. We listen to lies, failing to trust Jesus. But we don't have to yield. We don't have to live in a false narrative. By God's grace we can embrace the true story of Christ's victory.

While we'll still wrestle with sin, liberation comes as we recognize that Jesus has already won the battle. May we live out that truth in His power.   *WINN COLLIER*

How are you tempted to believe that death and sin still hold power over your life? Where can you see Christ's victory already present in the world?

Jesus, I know You've won the battle over evil and darkness. Would You help me to live this out?

BIBLE IN A YEAR | PSALMS 63–65; ROMANS 6   225

May the LORD judge between you and me.
[1 SAMUEL 24:12]

GOD'S MERCY AT WORK

My anger percolated when a woman mistreated me, blamed me, and gossiped about me. I wanted everyone to know what she'd done—wanted her to suffer as I'd suffered because of her behavior. I steamed with resentment until a headache pierced my temples. But as I began praying for my pain to go away, the Holy Spirit convicted me. How could I plot revenge while begging God for relief? If I believed He would care for me, why wouldn't I trust Him to handle this situation? Knowing that people who are hurting often hurt other people, I asked God to help me forgive the woman and work toward reconciliation.

The psalmist David understood the difficulty of trusting God while enduring unfair treatment. Though David did his best to be a loving servant, King Saul succumbed to jealousy and wanted to murder him (1 SAMUEL 24:1–2). David suffered while God worked things out and prepared him to take the throne, but still he chose to honor God instead of seeking revenge (VV. 3–7). He did his part to reconcile with Saul and left the results in God's hands (VV. 8–22).

When it seems others are getting away with wrongdoing, we struggle with the injustice. But with God's mercy at work in our hearts and the hearts of others, we can forgive as He's forgiven us and receive the blessings He's prepared for us. *XOCHITL DIXON*

How can trusting that God is perfect, loving, good, and in control help you when sin seems to be prevailing? Who do you need to forgive and place in God's mighty and merciful hands?

Merciful God, please help me trust You to determine how justice prevails.

The Spirit himself testifies with our spirit that
we are God's children. [ROMANS 8:16]

LOVED, BEAUTIFUL, GIFTED

Malcolm appeared confident as a teenager. But this confidence was a mask. In truth, a turbulent home left him fearful, desperate for approval, and feeling falsely responsible for his family's problems. "For as far back as I remember," he says, "every morning I would go into the bathroom, look in the mirror, and say out loud to myself, 'You are stupid, you are ugly, and it's your fault.'"

Malcolm's self-loathing continued until he was twenty-one, when he had a divine revelation of his identity in Jesus. "I realized that God loved me unconditionally and nothing would ever change that," he recalls. "I could never embarrass God, and He would never reject me." In time, Malcolm looked in the mirror and spoke to himself differently. "You are loved, you are beautiful, you are gifted," he said, "and it's not your fault."

Malcolm's experience illustrates what God's Spirit does for the believer in Jesus—He frees us from fear by revealing how profoundly loved we are (ROMANS 8:15, 38–39), and confirms that we are children of God with all the benefits that status brings (8:16–17; 12:6–8). As a result, we can begin seeing ourselves correctly by having our thinking renewed (12:2–3).

Years later, Malcolm still whispers those words each day, reinforcing who God says he is. In the Father's eyes he's loved, beautiful, and gifted. And so are we.   *SHERIDAN VOYSEY*

**What words come to mind when you see yourself in the mirror?
How different are they from Scripture's depiction of what God
sees in you?**

*Father, thank You for loving me, gifting me, and making me Your
child. May Your Spirit work in me today to truly, deeply believe it.*

But the Lord stood at my side and
gave me strength. [2 TIMOTHY 4:17]

FROM PITY TO PRAISE

At a coat drive for children, excited kids searched gratefully for
their favorite colors and proper sizes. They also gained self-
esteem, an organizer said, with new coats boosting their
acceptance by peers and school attendance on winter days.

The apostle Paul seemed to need a coat, as well, when he
wrote Timothy, "Bring the cloak that I left with Carpus at Troas"
(2 TIMOTHY 4:13). Held in a cold Roman prison, Paul needed warmth
but also companionship. "No one came to my support, but everyone deserted me," he lamented, when he faced a Roman judge
(V. 16). His words pierce our hearts with the honesty of this great
missionary's pain.

Yet in these final words of Paul's last recorded letter—his closing thoughts after an astounding ministry—he moves from pity to
praise. "But the Lord stood at my side," he adds (V. 17), and his
words rally our hearts. As Paul declared, "[God] gave me strength
so that I might preach the Good News in its entirety for all the
Gentiles to hear. And he rescued me from certain death" (V. 17 NLT).

If you're facing a crisis, lacking even the right clothing for
warmth or close friends to help, *remember God.* He's faithful to
revive, provide, and deliver. Why? For His glory *and* for our purpose in His kingdom.   *PATRICIA RAYBON*

**In what "cold" area of your life do you need God's great
and warming strength? As you praise Him, how does your
outlook change?**

*Our strong God, when life's circumstances overwhelm us, stand with
us, stir our praise, giving us Your strength to overcome.*

Precious in the sight of the LORD is the death of his
faithful servants. [PSALM 116:15]

LETTING GO

"**Y**our father is actively dying," said the hospice nurse.
"Actively dying" refers to the final phase of the dying
process and was a new term to me, one that felt strangely
like traveling down a lonely one-way street. On my dad's last day,
not knowing if he could still hear us, my sister and I sat by his bed.
We kissed the top of his beautiful bald head. We whispered God's
promises to him. We sang "Great Is Thy Faithfulness" and quoted
the 23rd Psalm. We told him we loved him and thanked him for
being our dad. We knew his heart longed to be with Jesus, and we
told him he could go. Speaking those words was the first painful
step in letting go. A few minutes later, our dad was joyously welcomed into his eternal home.

The final release of a loved one is painful. Even Jesus' tears
flowed when His good friend Lazarus died (JOHN 11:35). But because
of God's promises, we have hope beyond physical death. Psalm
116:15 says that God's "faithful servants"—those who belong to
Him—are "precious" to Him. Though they die, they'll be alive again.

Jesus promises, "I am the resurrection and the life. The one
who believes in me will live, even though they die; and whoever
lives by believing in me will never die" (JOHN 11:25–26). What comfort it brings to know we'll be in God's presence forever.

CINDY HESS KASPER

What did Jesus accomplish by His death on the cross?
How does His sacrifice affect every person who has ever lived?

Precious Father, thank You for the promise of eternal life
in Your presence.

Peacemakers who sow in peace reap
a harvest of righteousness. [JAMES 3:18]

★ *AUGUST TOPIC: FAMILY*

INSTRUMENTS OF PEACE

When World War I erupted in 1914, British statesman Sir Edward Grey declared, "The lamps are going out all over Europe; we shall not see them lit again in our lifetime." Grey was right. When the "war to end all wars" finally ended, some 20 million had been killed (10 million of them civilians) and another 21 million injured.

While not on the same scale or magnitude, devastation can also occur in our personal lives. Our home, workplace, church, or neighborhood can also be shrouded by the dark specter of conflict. This is one of the reasons God calls us to be difference-makers in the world. But to do so we must rely on His wisdom. The apostle James wrote, "The wisdom that comes from heaven is first of all pure; then peace-loving, considerate, submissive, full of mercy and good fruit, impartial and sincere. Peacemakers who sow in peace reap a harvest of righteousness" (JAMES 3:17–18).

The role of peacemaker is significant because of its harvest. The word *righteousness* means "right standing" or "right relationship." Peacemakers can help restore *relationships*. No wonder Jesus said, "Blessed are the peacemakers, for they will be called children of God" (MATTHEW 5:9). His children, relying on His wisdom, become instruments of His peace where it's needed most.   *BILL CROWDER*

In what personal conflicts do you need the light of God's wisdom? How can His peace enable you to be a peacemaker when people around you choose to fight?

Father, Your light penetrates the deepest darkness and Your peace calms the most troubled heart. Help me know Your wisdom and peace and carry it to others in their struggles as well.

The life appeared; we have seen it and testify to it,
and we proclaim to you the eternal life, which was
with the Father and has appeared to us. [1 JOHN 1:2]

TIME-TRAVELING LETTERS

More than a million young people take part in the International Letter-Writing Competition each year. In 2018, the theme of the competition was this: "Imagine you are a letter traveling through time. What message do you want to convey to your readers?"

In the Bible, we have a collection of letters that—thanks to the inspiration and guidance of the Holy Spirit—have made their way through time to us. As the Christian church grew, Jesus' disciples wrote to local churches across Europe and Asia Minor to help the people understand their new life in Christ; many of those letters were collected in the Bible we read today.

What did these letter-writers want to convey to readers? John explains, in his first letter, that he's writing about "that which was from the beginning, which we have heard, which we have seen with our eyes, which we have looked at and our hands have touched." He's writing about his encounter with the living Christ (1 JOHN 1:1). He writes so that his readers may "have fellowship" with one another, and with "the Father and with his Son, Jesus Christ" (V. 3). When we have fellowship together, he writes, our joy will be complete (V. 4). The letters in the Bible draw us into a fellowship that's beyond time—fellowship with the eternal God. *AMY PETERSON*

> **If God wrote a letter to you today, what would it say?**
> **If you wrote a letter to a friend telling about how you've**
> **encountered the living God, what would it say?**
>
> *Thank You, Father, for the fellowship I have with You.*

You are a chosen people, a royal priesthood, a holy nation,
God's special possession, that you may declare the praises of
him who called you . . . into his wonderful light. [1 PETER 2:9]

ON THE BUBBLE

A news article in May 1970 contained one of the first uses of
the idiom "on the bubble." Referring to a state of uncertainty, the expression was used in relation to rookie race
car driver Steve Krisiloff. He'd been "on the bubble," having
posted a slow qualifying lap for the Indianapolis 500. Later, it was
confirmed that his time—though the slowest of those who quali-
fied—allowed him to compete in the race.

We can feel at times that we're "on the bubble," uncertain we
have what it takes to compete in or finish the race of life. When
we're feeling that way, it's important to remember that in Jesus
we're never "on the bubble." As children of God, our place in His
kingdom is secure (JOHN 14:3). Our confidence flows from Him who
chose Jesus to be the "cornerstone" on which our lives are built,
and He chose us to be "living stones" filled with the Spirit of God,
capable of being the people God created us to be (1 PETER 2:5–6).

In Christ, our future is secure as we hope in and follow Him (V. 6).
For "[we] are a chosen people, a royal priesthood, a holy nation,
God's special possession, that [we] may declare the praises of him
who called [us] out of darkness into his wonderful light" (V. 9).

In Jesus' eyes we're not "on the bubble." We're precious and
loved (V. 4).   *RUTH O'REILLY-SMITH*

**In what areas of life have you found yourself "on the bubble"
and struggling with uncertainty? What can you do to regain your
confidence in Jesus?**

*Father God, when disappointments threaten to undermine
my identity as Your child, remind me to put my hope and confidence
in You alone.*

"Don't call me Naomi," she told them. "Call me Mara, because the Almighty has made my life very bitter." [RUTH 1:20]

NAMED BY GOD

Riptide. Batgirl. Jumpstart. These are a few names given to counselors at the summer camp our family attends every year. Created by their peers, the camp nicknames usually derive from an embarrassing incident, a funny habit, or a favorite hobby.

Nicknames aren't limited to camp—we even find them used in the Bible. For example, Jesus dubs the apostles James and John the "sons of thunder" (MARK 3:17). It's rare in Scripture for someone to give *themselves* a nickname, yet it happens when a woman named Naomi asks people to call her "Mara," which means "bitterness" (RUTH 1:20), because both her husband and two sons had died. She felt that God had made her life bitter (V. 21).

The new name Naomi gave herself didn't stick, however, because those devastating losses were not the end of her story. In the midst of her sorrow, God had blessed her with a loving daughter-in-law, Ruth, who eventually remarried and had a son, creating a family for Naomi again.

Although we might sometimes be tempted to give ourselves bitter nicknames, like "failure" or "unloved," based on difficulties we've experienced or mistakes we've made, those names are not the end of our stories. We can replace those labels with the name God has given each of us, "loved one" (ROMANS 9:25), and look for the ways He's providing for us in even the most challenging of times.   *LISA M. SAMRA*

Think of a nickname someone gave you. What did you like or not like about it? How does being called a beloved child of God change how you see yourself?

Heavenly Father, thank You that I'm not defined by the circumstances or experiences of my life. Thank You for calling me Your child.

From the ends of the earth I call to you.
[PSALM 61:2]

NEEDING HIS LEADING

Uncle Zaki was more than a friend to scholar Kenneth Bailey; he was his trusted guide on challenging excursions into the vast Sahara. By following Uncle Zaki, Bailey says that he and his team were demonstrating their complete trust in him. In essence, they were affirming, "We don't know the way to where we are going, and if you get us lost we will all die. We have placed our total trust in your leadership."

In a time of great weariness and heartache, David looked beyond any human guide, seeking direction from the God he served. In Psalm 61:2 we read, "From the ends of the earth I call to you, I call as my heart grows faint; lead me to the rock that is higher than I." He longed for the safety and relief of being ushered afresh into God's presence (VV. 3–4).

God's guidance in life is desperately needed for people the Scriptures describe as sheep that have "gone astray" (ISAIAH 53:6). Left to ourselves, we would be hopelessly lost in the desert of a broken world.

But we are not left to ourselves! We have a Shepherd who leads us "beside quiet waters," refreshes our souls, and guides us (PSALM 23:2–3).

Where do you need His leading today? Call on Him. He will never leave you.   *BILL CROWDER*

What was it like when you felt lost? How can you begin to trust God's desire to guide you like a shepherd in those times of seeking?

*Loving Father, thank You for being my Shepherd and Guide.
Help me to trust You and rest in Your wisdom, allowing Your Spirit
to guide me through the challenging moments of life.*

"I am carrying on a great project and cannot go down.
Why should the work stop while I leave it and go
down to you?" [NEHEMIAH 6:3]

A GREAT WORK

The security guard found and removed a piece of tape that
was keeping a door from clicking shut. Later, when he
checked the door, he found it had been taped again. He
called the police, who arrived and arrested five burglars.

Working at the Watergate building in Washington, D.C., the
headquarters of a major political party in the US, the young guard
had just uncovered the biggest political scandal of his lifetime
simply by taking his job seriously—and doing it well.

Nehemiah began rebuilding the wall around Jerusalem—a
task he took very seriously. Toward the end of the project, neigh-
boring rivals asked him to meet with them in a nearby village.
Under the guise of a friendly invitation was an insidious trap
(NEHEMIAH 6:1–2). Yet Nehemiah's response shows the depth of his
conviction: "I am carrying on a great project and cannot go
down. Why should the work stop while I leave it and go down to
you?" (V. 3).

Although he certainly possessed some authority, Nehemiah
may not have rated very high on the hero scale. He wasn't a great
warrior, not a poet or a prophet, not a king or a sage. He was a
cupbearer-turned-contractor. Yet he believed he was doing
something vital for God. May we take seriously what He's given
us to do and do it well in His power and provision.   *GLENN PACKIAM*

**What has God called you to do? Why is it important for you to
take it seriously—seeing it as a great work?**

*Dear God, help me to believe that I'm doing a great work.
I trust that You've called me to this in this season.
Give me the focus to stay the course.*

The desert and the parched land will be glad; the wilderness will rejoice and blossom. [ISAIAH 35:1]

HOPE BLOSSOMS

I n the city of Philadelphia, when weedy vacant lots were cleaned up and brightened with beautiful flowers and trees, nearby residents also brightened in overall mental health. This proved especially true for those who struggled economically.

"There's a growing body of evidence that green space can have an impact on mental health," said Dr. Eugenia South, "and that's particularly important for people living in poorer neighborhoods." South, a faculty member at the University of Pennsylvania's Perelman School of Medicine, is coauthor of a study on the subject.

The downtrodden people of Israel and Judah found fresh hope in the prophet Isaiah's vision of their beautiful restoration by God. Amid all the doom and judgment Isaiah foretold, this bright promise took root: "The desert and the parched land will be glad; the wilderness will rejoice and blossom. Like the crocus, it will burst into bloom; it will rejoice greatly and shout for joy" (ISAIAH 35:1–2).

No matter our situation today, we too can rejoice in the beautiful ways our heavenly Father restores us with fresh hope, including through His creation. When we feel down, reflecting on His glory and splendor will bolster us. "Strengthen the feeble hands, steady the knees that give way," Isaiah encouraged (V. 3).

Can a few flowers rekindle our hope? A prophet said yes. So does our hope-giving God.   *PATRICIA RAYBON*

When you feel hopeless, how do you usually respond? How could spending time outdoors in God's creation transform your despair to renewed hope in God?

Dear God, thank You for the splendor of Your creation, pointing me to Your glory, and reviving my hope in You.

As I have loved you, so you must love one another.
[JOHN 13:34]

★ *AUGUST TOPIC: FAMILY*

THE FAVORITE

My husband's brother lives about 1,200 miles away in the mountains of Colorado. Despite the distance, Gerrits has always been a beloved family member because of his great sense of humor and kind heart. As long as I can remember, however, his siblings have good-naturedly joked about his favored status in their mother's eyes. Several years ago, they even presented him with a T-shirt sporting the words, "I'm Mom's Favorite." While we all enjoyed the silliness of our siblings, true favoritism is no joking matter.

In Genesis 37, we read about Jacob who gave his son Joseph an ornate coat—an indication to his other children that Joseph was special (V. 3). Without a hint of subtlety, the coat's message shouted: "Joseph is my *favorite* son."

Displaying favoritism can be crippling in a family. Jacob's mother, Rebekah, had favored him over her son Esau, leading to conflict between the two brothers (25:28). The dysfunction was perpetuated when Jacob favored his wife Rachel (Joseph's mother) over his wife Leah, creating discord and heartache (29:30–31). No doubt this pattern was the unhealthy basis for Joseph's brothers to despise their younger brother, even plotting his murder (37:18).

When it comes to our relationships, we may sometimes find it tricky to be objective. But our goal must be to treat everyone without favoritism and to love every person in our life as our Father loves us (JOHN 13:34).

CINDY HESS KASPER

When have you struggled with showing favoritism? How is God helping you to treat everyone equally?

Loving God, as I interact with others help me to avoid showing unhealthy preferences. Help me to see others as You do and to treat everyone fairly and without favoritism.

BIBLE IN A YEAR | PSALMS 91–93; ROMANS 15:1-13

Let the little children come to me, and do not hinder them,
for the kingdom of God belongs to such as these. [LUKE 18:16]

BIG ENOUGH

My grandson ran to the roller coaster line and stood with his back against the height-requirement sign to see if he was big enough to ride. He squealed with joy when his head exceeded the mark.

So much of life is about being "big" enough, isn't it? To move from car seat to seatbelt and from the back seat to the front. To take a driver's test. To vote. To get married. Like my grandson, we can spend our lives longing to grow up.

In New Testament times, children were loved but not highly valued in society until they "became of age" and could contribute to the home and enter the synagogue with adult privileges. Jesus shattered the standards of His day by welcoming the impoverished, the diseased, and even children. Three gospels (Matthew, Mark, and Luke) tell of parents bringing little children to Jesus so that He might lay hands on them and pray for them (MATTHEW 19:13; MARK 10:16).

The disciples rebuked the adults for what they saw as an inconvenience. At this, Jesus was "indignant" (MARK 10:14) and opened His arms to the little ones. He elevated their value in His kingdom and challenged all to become like children themselves—to embrace their vulnerability and need for Him in order to know Him (LUKE 18:17). It's our childlike need that makes us "big" enough to receive His love. *ELISA MORGAN*

How might you need to remain small in order to know God?
What does His love, the love of a heavenly Father, mean to you?

Dear God, help me embrace my need for You today that You might
draw me closer, like a child, to Your heart.

These trials will show that your faith is genuine.
[1 PETER 1:7 NLT]

REFINED IN THE FIRE

Twenty-four-karat gold is nearly 100 percent gold with few impurities. But that percentage is difficult to achieve. Refiners most commonly use one of two methods for the purification process. The Miller process is the quickest and least expensive, but the resulting gold is only about 99.95 percent pure. The Wohlwill process takes a little more time and costs more, but the gold produced is 99.99 percent pure.

In Bible times, refiners used fire as a gold purifier. Fire caused impurities to rise to the surface for easier removal. In his first letter to believers in Jesus throughout Asia Minor (northern Turkey), the apostle Peter used the gold-refining process as a metaphor for the way trials work in the life of a believer. At that time, many believers were being persecuted by the Romans for their faith in Christ. Peter knew what that was like firsthand. But persecution, Peter explained, brings out the "genuineness of [our] faith" (1 PETER 1:7).

Perhaps you feel like you're in a refiner's fire—feeling the heat of setbacks, illness, or other challenges. But hardship is often the process by which God purifies the gold of our faith. In our pain we might beg God to quickly end the process, but He knows what's best for us, even when life hurts. Keep connected to the Savior, seeking His comfort and peace.   *LINDA WASHINGTON*

**What challenges have you faced that led to your growth?
How did you respond to them?**

*Father God, help me see how the trials of my life
bring out the gold in me.*

Be perfectly united in mind and thought.
[1 CORINTHIANS 1:10]

RIVALS OR ALLIES?

The city of Texarkana sits squarely on the state border between Texas and Arkansas. The city of 70,000 inhabitants has two mayors, two city councils, and two police and fire departments. The cross-town sporting rivalry between high schools draws an uncommonly high attendance, reflecting the deep allegiance each has to their own state's school. More significant challenges arise as well, such as disputes over the shared water system, governed by two sets of state laws. Yet the town is known for its unity despite the line that divides it. Residents gather annually for a dinner held on State Line Avenue to share a meal in celebration of their oneness as a community.

The believers in Corinth may not have drawn a line down their main thoroughfare, but they were divided. They'd been quarreling as a result of their allegiances to those who taught them about Jesus: Paul, Apollos, or Cephas (Peter). Paul called them all to oneness "in mind and thought" (1 CORINTHIANS 1:10), reminding them it was Christ who was crucified for them, not their spiritual leaders.

We behave similarly today, don't we? We sometimes oppose even those who share our singularly important belief—Jesus' sacrifice for our wrongdoings—making them rivals instead of allies. Just as Christ Himself is not divided, we, as His earthly representation—His body—mustn't allow differences over nonessentials to divide us. Instead, may we celebrate our oneness in Him.

KIRSTEN HOLMBERG

Over what nonessential spiritual issues are you likely to allow division? How can you foster unity instead?

God, help me to remain focused on You and Your sacrifice for Your people. May I not be distracted by the less important issues but call others to oneness as a community of faith.

So there was food every day for Elijah and for the
woman and her family. [1 KINGS 17:15]

ONLY TRUST

Three hundred children were dressed and seated for breakfast, and a prayer of thanks was offered for the food. But there was no food! Situations like this were not unusual for orphanage director and missionary George Mueller (1805–1898). Here was yet another opportunity to see how God would provide. Within minutes of Mueller's prayer, a baker who couldn't sleep the night before showed up at the door. Sensing that the orphanage could use the bread, he had made three batches. Not long afterward, the town milkman appeared. His cart had broken down in front of the orphanage. Not wanting the milk to spoil, he offered it to Mueller.

It's normal to experience bouts of worry, anxiety, and self-pity when we lack resources essential to our well-being—food, shelter, health, finances, friendships. First Kings 17:8–16 reminds us that God's help can come through unexpected sources like a needy widow. "I don't have any bread—only a handful of flour in a jar and a little olive oil in a jug" (V. 12). Earlier it was a raven that provided for Elijah (VV. 4–6). Concerns for our needs to be met can send us searching in many directions. A clear vision of God as the Provider who has promised to supply our needs can be liberating. Before we seek solutions, may we be careful to seek Him first. Doing so can save us time, energy, and frustration. ARTHUR JACKSON

**What's been your experience when you've focused on securing
provision *before* seeking the Provider in prayer? What current
needs will you bring before God?**

*Father, sharpen my vision of You as the Provider for all my needs.
Forgive me for times I have futilely sought to find my way without
seeking You first.*

Remember how the LORD your God led you
all the way. [DEUTERONOMY 8:2]

PEOPLE FORGET

A woman complained to her pastor that she'd noticed a lot of repetition in his sermons. "Why do you do that?" she queried. The preacher replied, *"People forget."*

There are lots of reasons we forget—the passage of time, growing older, or just being too busy. We forget passwords, names of people, or even where we parked our car. My husband says, "There's only so much I can fit in my brain. I have to delete something before I can remember something new."

The preacher was right. People forget. So we often need reminders to help us remember what God has done for us. The Israelites had a similar tendency. Even with the many miracles they'd seen, they still needed to be reminded of His care for them. In Deuteronomy 8, God reminded the Israelites that He'd allowed them to experience hunger in the wilderness, but then provided an amazing superfood for them every day—manna. He supplied clothing that never wore out. He led them through a wilderness of snakes and scorpions and provided water from a rock. They'd learned humility, as they realized how totally dependent they were on God's care and provision (VV. 2–4, 15–18).

God's faithfulness "continues through all generations" (PSALM 100:5). Whenever we find ourselves forgetting, we can think about the ways He's answered our prayers, and that reminds us of His goodness and faithful promises.   *CINDY HESS KASPER*

**In what areas do you struggle to trust God? What Bible verses
help you to remember how much He cares for you?**

*Dear Father, thank You for always being faithful.
Help me to trust You in whatever I face today.*

You, Lord, are forgiving and good, abounding in love
to all who call to you [PSALM 86:5]

BRIGHT SPOTS IN BLEAK PLACES

When my husband and I were exploring a small, rugged
corner of the state of Wyoming, I spied a sunflower in a
rocky, dry place where sagebrush, nettles, prickly cac-
tus, and other scraggly plants grew. It wasn't as tall as the domes-
tic sunflower, but it was just as bright—and I felt cheered.

This unexpected bright spot in rough terrain reminded me of
how life, even for the believer in Jesus, can seem barren and
cheerless. Troubles can seem insurmountable, and like the cries
of the psalmist David, our prayers sometimes seem to go
unheeded: "Hear me, LORD, and answer me, for I am poor and
needy" (PSALM 86:1). Like him, we too long for joy (V. 4).

But David goes on to declare that we serve a faithful (V. 11),
"compassionate and gracious God" (V. 15), who abounds in love for
all who call on Him (V. 5). He *does* answer (V. 7).

Sometimes in bleak places, God sends a sunflower—an
encouraging word or note from a friend; a comforting verse or
Bible passage; a beautiful sunrise—that helps us to move forward with a lighter step, with hope. Even as we await the day we
experience God's deliverance out of our difficulty, may we join
the psalmist in proclaiming, "You are great and do marvelous
deeds; you alone are God"! (V. 10).   *ALYSON KIEDA*

**Out of what difficult place has God delivered you? During that time,
did you experience any "sunflowers" that helped you persevere?**

*Loving God, thank You for being compassionate and gracious.
Help me to remember how You've been faithful and answered
my prayers in the past—and will again in the future.*

It is not good for the man to be alone.
I will make a helper suitable for him. [GENESIS 2:18]

★ *AUGUST TOPIC: FAMILY*

MADE FOR EACH OTHER

" I take care of him. When he's happy, I'm happy," says Stella. Merle replies, "I'm happy when she's around." Merle and Stella have been married for 79 years. When Merle was recently admitted to a nursing home, he was miserable—so Stella gladly brought him home. He's 101, and she's 95. Though she needs a walker to get around, she lovingly does what she can for her husband, such as preparing the food he likes. But she couldn't do it on her own. Grandchildren and neighbors help with the things Stella can't manage.

Stella and Merle's life together is an example of Genesis 2, where God said, "It is not good for the man to be alone. I will make a helper suitable for him" (V. 18). None of the creatures God brought before Adam fit that description. Only in Eve, made from the rib of Adam, did Adam find a suitable helper and companion (VV. 19–24).

Eve was the perfect companion for Adam, and through them God instituted marriage. This wasn't only for the mutual aid of individuals but also to begin a family and to care for creation, which includes other people (1:28). From that first family came a community so that, whether married or single, old or young, none of us would be alone. As a community, God has given us the privilege of sharing "each other's burdens" (GALATIANS 6:2). *ALYSON KIEDA*

How is it helpful to know that no matter our marital status, as believers in Jesus we're never alone? How have you seen the body of Christ in action?

Dear God, thank You for creating man and woman for each other and for instituting community so that none of us are truly alone.

[God will] hurl all our iniquities into
the depths of the sea. [MICAH 7:19]

NO FISHING ALLOWED

Holocaust survivor Corrie ten Boom knew the importance of forgiveness. In her book *Tramp for the Lord*, she says her favorite mental picture was of forgiven sins thrown into the sea. "When we confess our sins, God casts them into the deepest ocean, gone forever. . . . I believe God then places a sign out there that says No Fishing Allowed."

She points to an important truth that believers in Jesus can sometimes fail to grasp—when God forgives our wrongdoing, we're forgiven fully! We don't have to keep dredging up our shameful deeds, wallowing in any mucky feelings. Rather we can accept His grace and forgiveness, following Him in freedom.

We see this idea of "no fishing allowed" in Psalm 130. The psalmist proclaims that although God is just, He forgives the sin of those who repent: "But with you there is forgiveness" (V. 4). As the psalmist waits for God, putting his trust in Him (V. 5), he states in faith that He "himself will redeem Israel from all their sins" (V. 8). Those who believe will find "full redemption" (V. 7).

When we're caught in feelings of shame and unworthiness, we can't serve God with our whole hearts. Instead, we're restricted by our past. If you feel stymied by the wrong you've done, ask God to help you fully believe in His gift of forgiveness and new life. He's cast your sins into the ocean!   *AMY BOUCHER PYE*

Are you holding on to the false belief that God can't possibly
forgive you for some sin in your life? God wants you to
allow His forgiveness to set you free!

Forgiving God, You sent Your Son Jesus to save me from my sins and
shame. Help me to live in the freedom of being fully forgiven.

Shall we accept good from God,
and not trouble? [JOB 2:10]

HOW DID I GET HERE?

Tiffani awoke in the pitch-black darkness of an Air Canada jet. Still wearing her seat belt, she'd slept while the other passengers exited and the plane was parked. *Why didn't anyone wake her? How did she get here?* She shook the cobwebs from her brain and tried to remember.

Have you found yourself in a place you never expected? You're too young to have this disease, and there's no cure. Your last review was excellent; why is your position being eliminated? You were enjoying the best years of your marriage. Now you're starting over, as a single parent with a part-time job.

How did I get here? Job may have wondered as "he sat among the ashes" (JOB 2:8). He'd lost his children, his wealth, and his health, in no time flat. He couldn't have guessed how he got here; he just knew he had to remember.

Job remembered his Creator and how good He'd been. He told his wife, "Shall we accept good from God, and not trouble?" (V. 10). Job remembered he could count on this good God to be faithful. So he lamented. He screamed at the heavens. And he mourned in hope, "I know that my redeemer lives," and that "in my flesh I will see God" (19:25–26). Job clung to hope as he remembered how the story began and how it ends.　　　　　　　　　*MIKE WITTMER*

What situation fills you with agony and dread? How might you regain your bearings and live with hope and joy?

Father, You're not surprised by what surprises me.
You were good before, and You remain good now.

Open my eyes that I may see wonderful things
in your law. [PSALM 119:18]

WONDERFUL REWARD

Donelan, a teacher, had always been a reader, but one day it literally paid off. She was planning a trip and reviewing her lengthy travel insurance policy when on page seven she discovered a wonderful reward. As part of their "It Pays to Read" contest, the company was giving $10,000 to the first person to read that far into the contract. They also donated thousands of dollars to schools in Donelan's area for children's literacy. She says, "I've always been that nerd who reads contracts. I was the most surprised of anyone!"

The psalmist wanted his eyes opened to "see wonderful things" about God (PSALM 119:18). He must have had an understanding that God wants to be known, and so he longed for a deeper closeness to Him. His desire was to see more of who God is, what He'd already given, and how to follow Him more closely (VV. 24, 98). He wrote, "Oh, how I love your law! I meditate on it all day long" (V. 97).

We too have the privilege of taking time to ponder God, His character, and His provisions—to learn about and grow closer to Him. God longs to instruct us, guide us, and open our hearts to who He is. When we search for Him, He rewards us with greater wonder at who He is and the enjoyment of His presence!

ANNE CETAS

As you open your Bible and read, how is your heart and mind opened to God and His ways? What would you like to know or experience more of?

How I love Your Word, God. It's sweet to my taste,
sweeter than honey to my mouth.

Be very careful, then, how you live—not as unwise
but as wise, making the most of every opportunity,
because the days are evil. [EPHESIANS 5:15–16]

SPIRITUAL DRIVING

I don't remember many specifics about my driver's education class. But for some reason, an acronym we learned, S-I-P-D-E, remains firmly lodged in my memory.

The letters stood for **S**can, **I**dentify, **P**redict, **D**ecide, and **E**xecute, a process we were taught to practice continually. We were to *scan* the road, *identify* hazards, *predict* what the hazards might do, *decide* how we'd respond, and then, if necessary, *execute* that plan. It was a strategy for being intentional to avoid accidents.

I wonder how that idea might translate to our spiritual lives. In Ephesians 5, Paul told Ephesian believers, "Be very careful, then, how you live—not as unwise, but as wise" (V. 15). Paul knew certain hazards could derail the Ephesians—old ways of living at odds with their new life in Jesus (VV. 8, 10–11). So he instructed the growing church to pay attention.

The words translated "be very careful, then, how you live" literally mean "see how you walk." In other words, look around. Notice hazards, and avoid personal pitfalls like drunkenness and wild living (V. 18). Instead, the apostle said, we can seek to learn God's will for our lives (V. 17), while, with fellow believers, we sing to and give Him thanks (VV. 19–20).

No matter what hazards we face—and even when we stumble—we can experience our new life in Christ as we grow in dependence on His boundless power and grace.   *ADAM R. HOLZ*

What strategy do you use to recognize what might trip you up spiritually? What role do you think other believers play in identifying and resisting spiritual hazards? How might thanksgiving be an important part of avoiding spiritual pitfalls?

Heavenly Father, as I navigate the spiritual potholes on life's road, thank You for reminding me to look up to You for help.

Rescue the weak and the needy; deliver them
from the hand of the wicked. [PSALM 82:4]

RESCUE THE WEAK

Which would you choose—a skiing holiday in Switzerland
or rescuing children from danger in Prague? Nicholas
Winton, just an ordinary man, chose the latter. In 1938,
war between Czechoslovakia and Germany seemed on the horizon. After Nicholas visited refugee camps in Prague, where many
Jewish citizens lived in horrible conditions, he felt compelled to
come up with a plan to help. He raised money to transport hundreds of children safely out of Prague to Great Britain to be cared
for by British families before the onset of World War II.

His actions exemplified those called for in Psalm 82: "Uphold
the cause of the poor and the oppressed" (V. 3). Asaph, the writer
of this psalm, wanted to stir his people to champion the cause of
those in need: "Rescue the weak and the needy; deliver them from
the hand of the wicked" (V. 4). Like the children Nicholas worked
tirelessly to rescue, the psalmist spoke for those who couldn't
speak for themselves—the poor and the widowed who needed
justice and protection.

Everywhere we look today we see people in need due to war,
storms, and other hardships. Although we can't solve every problem, we can prayerfully consider what we can do to help in the
situations God brings into our lives.   *LINDA WASHINGTON*

**What are some immediate needs of others you can help meet?
How has God uniquely prepared you to rescue and care for others?**

Loving God, open my eyes to the needs of those around me.

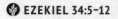

I will rescue them from all the places where they were scattered. [EZEKIEL 34:12]

GOD OUR RESCUER

In the open sea, a rescuer positioned her kayak to assist panicked swimmers competing in a triathlon. "Don't grab the middle of the boat!" she called to swimmers, knowing such a move would capsize her craft. Instead, she directed weary swimmers to the bow, or front, of the kayak. There they could grab a loop, allowing the safety kayaker to help rescue them.

Whenever life or people threaten to pull us under, as believers in Jesus, we know we have a Rescuer. "For this is what the Sovereign LORD says: I myself will search for my sheep.... I will rescue them from all the places where they were scattered" (EZEKIEL 34:11–12).

This was the prophet Ezekiel's assurance to God's people when they were in exile. Their leaders had neglected and exploited them, plundering their lives and caring "for themselves rather than for [God's] flock" (V. 8). As a result, the people "were scattered over the whole earth, and no one searched or looked for them" (V. 6).

But "I will rescue my flock," declared the Lord (V. 10), and His promise still holds.

What do we need to do? Hold fast to almighty God and His promises. "I myself will search for my sheep and look after them," He says (V. 11). That's a saving promise worth holding tightly.

PATRICIA RAYBON

When you feel panicked, what's your typical reaction?
What problem can you release today as you reach instead for God?

Our rescuing God, when life makes me panic, encourage me to turn from the rolling waves and always reach for You.

The gospel is bearing fruit and growing.
[COLOSSIANS 1:6]

THE ULTIMATE WAVE

People love doing "the wave." At sporting events and concerts around the world, it begins when a few people stand and raise their hands. A moment later, those seated beside them do the same. The goal is to have one sequential flowing movement work its way around an entire stadium. Once it reaches the end, those who started it smile and cheer—and keep the movement going.

The first recorded incident of the wave occurred at a professional baseball game between the Oakland Athletics and the New York Yankees in 1981. I love joining in the wave because it's fun. But it's also occurred to me that the happiness and togetherness we experience while doing it is reminiscent of the gospel—the good news of salvation in Jesus that unites believers everywhere in praise and hope. This "ultimate wave" started over twenty centuries ago in Jerusalem. Writing to the members of the church in Colossae, Paul described it this way: "The gospel is bearing fruit and growing throughout the whole world—just as it has been doing among you since the day you heard it" (COLOSSIANS 1:6). The natural result of this good news is "faith and love that spring from the hope stored up for [us] in heaven" (V. 5).

As believers in Jesus, we're part of the greatest wave in history. Keep it going! Once it's done, we'll see the smile of the One who started it all. *JAMES BANKS*

From whom did you first hear the good news of Jesus? How can you share it with another person close to you this week?

I praise You for the wonderful gift of my salvation, Father. Please send me to someone who needs to hear of Your kindness today!

Let us examine our ways and test them, and let us return to the LORD. [LAMENTATIONS 3:40]

SELF-CHECKING

Recently I read through a stack of World War II-era letters my dad sent to my mother. He was in North Africa and she was in West Virginia. Dad, a second lieutenant in the US Army, was tasked with censoring soldiers' letters—keeping sensitive information from enemy eyes. So it was rather humorous to see—on the outside of his letters to his wife—a stamp that said, "Censored by 2nd Lt. John Branon." Indeed, he had cut out lines from his own letters!

Self-censoring is really a good idea for all of us. Several times in Scripture, the writers mention the importance of taking a good long look at ourselves to find what's not right—not God-honoring. The psalmist, for example, prayed, "Search me, God, and know my heart ....See if there is any offensive way in me" (PSALM 139:23–24). Jeremiah put it like this: "Let us examine our ways and test them, and let us return to the LORD" (LAMENTATIONS 3:40). And Paul, speaking of our heart condition at the time of communion, said, "Everyone ought to examine themselves" (1 CORINTHIANS 11:28).

The Holy Spirit can help us turn from any attitudes or actions that don't please God. So before we head out into the world today, let's stop and seek the Spirit's help in doing some self-checking so we can "return to the LORD" in fellowship with Him. *DAVE BRANON*

How will you pursue healthy spiritual self-examination today? What are two things that come to mind that you could remove to improve your fellowship with God?

Search me, O God, and know my heart. See if there are any changes I need to make today as I seek to know You more and serve You better.

The LORD came and stood there, calling as at the other times, "Samuel! Samuel!" Then Samuel said, "Speak, for your servant is listening." [1 SAMUEL 3:10]

THE SERVANT HEARS

Had the wireless radio been on, they would have known the *Titanic* was sinking. Cyril Evans, the radio operator of another ship, had tried to relay a message to Jack Phillips, the radio operator on the *Titanic*—letting him know they had encountered an ice field. But Phillips was busy relaying passengers' messages and rudely told Evans to be quiet. So Evans reluctantly turned off his radio and went to bed. Ten minutes later, the *Titanic* struck an iceberg. Their distress signals went unanswered because no one was listening.

In 1 Samuel we read that the priests of Israel were corrupt and had lost their spiritual sight and hearing as the nation drifted into danger. "The word of the LORD was rare; there were not many visions" (1 SAMUEL 3:1). Yet God wouldn't give up on His people. He began to speak to a young boy named Samuel who was being raised in the priest's household. Samuel's name means "the Lord hears"—a memorial to God's answering his mother's prayer. But Samuel would need to learn how to hear God.

"Speak, for your servant is listening" (V. 10). It's the servant who hears. May we also choose to listen to and obey what God has revealed in the Scriptures. Let's submit our lives to Him and take the posture of humble servants—those who have their "radios" turned on.   *GLENN PACKIAM*

Why is it vital for you to obey what God has revealed in Scripture? How can you stay "tuned in" to His voice?

Dear Jesus, thank You for being a speaking God. Thank You for the Scriptures that help me follow You in obedience. Speak, Your servant is listening.

THE CHURCH:
GOD'S PEOPLE AND POSSESSION

When we hear the word *church*, it's common to have an image of a physical structure. From what we read in Scripture, however, we're compelled to think "people" over "place," "believers" instead of "buildings." Indeed, the Greek word *ekklesia* (translated "church") means "assembly," and in most cases in the New Testament it refers to a gathering of believers in Jesus in a specific location.

God's special relationship with and plans for the church are reflected in the words and word pictures used to describe it. "You are a chosen people, a royal priesthood, a holy nation, God's special possession, that you may declare the praises of him who

> *"You are a chosen people, a royal priesthood, a holy nation..."*

called you out of darkness into his wonderful light" (1 PETER 2:9). Peter's language is reminiscent of the way God had spoken of His covenant people in the Old Testament (SEE EXODUS 19:5–6). Furthermore, believers in Christ are welcomed into a family of people who are crowned with mercy (1 PETER 2:10) and dubbed as "beloved" (V. 11 ESV).

What does this mean for how believers interact with each other? Those who are precious to God are to value and care for each other. Like other New Testament writers, Peter uses "one another" phrases to emphasize how we should relate to each other. First Peter 4:8–11 states that those who belong to the family of God should "love each other deeply" (V. 8), "offer hospitality to one another without grumbling" (V. 9), and use their gifts to serve each other so that God is honored in everything (VV. 10–11).

ARTHUR JACKSON, OUR DAILY BREAD *AUTHOR*

Rejoice before the LORD your God
for seven days. [LEVITICUS 23:40]

★ *SEPTEMBER TOPIC: THE CHURCH*

SACRED GATHERING

O ur group of friends reunited for a long weekend together on the shores of a beautiful lake. The days were spent playing in the water and sharing meals, but it was the evening conversations I treasured the most. As darkness fell, our hearts opened to one another with uncommon depth and vulnerability, sharing the pains of faltering marriages and the aftermath of trauma some of our children were enduring. Without glossing over the brokenness of our realities, we pointed one another to God and His faithfulness throughout such extreme difficulties. Those evenings are among the most sacred in my life.

I imagine those nights are similar to what God intended when He instructed His people to gather each year for the Festival of Tabernacles. This feast, like many others, required the Israelites to travel to Jerusalem. Once they arrived, God instructed His people to gather together in worship and to "do no regular work" for the duration of the feast—about a week! (LEVITICUS 23:35). The Festival of Tabernacles celebrated God's provision and commemorated their time in the wilderness after leaving Egypt (VV. 42–43).

This gathering cemented the Israelites' sense of identity as God's people and proclaimed His goodness despite their collective and individual hardships. When we gather with those we love to recall God's provision and presence in our lives, we too are strengthened in faith. *KIRSTEN HOLMBERG*

**Who can you gather with for worship and encouragement?
How has your faith been strengthened in community with others?**

*Father God, thank You for the people You've put in my life.
Please help us to encourage one another.*

In my distress I called to the LORD;
I cried to my God for help. [PSALM 18:6]

THE WHISPERING GALLERY

In the towering dome of London's St. Paul's Cathedral, visitors can climb 259 steps to access The Whispering Gallery. There you can whisper and be heard by another person anywhere along the circular walkway, even across the enormous abyss nearly one hundred feet away. Engineers explain this anomaly as a result of the spherical shape of the dome and the low intensity sound waves of a whisper.

How we long to be confident that God hears our agonized whispers! The Psalms are filled with testimonies that He hears us—our cries, prayers, and whispers. David writes, "In my distress I called to the LORD; I cried to my God for help" (PSALM 18:6). Over and over again, he and other psalmists plead, "Hear my prayer" (4:1), my voice (5:3), my groans (102:20). Sometimes the expression is more of a whispered, "Hear me" (77:1), where the "heart meditated and [the] spirit asked" (77:6).

In answer to these pleas, the psalmists—like David in Psalm 18:6—reveal that God is listening: "From his temple he heard my voice; my cry came before him, into his ears." Since the actual temple wasn't yet built, might David have been referring to God listening in His heavenly dwelling?

From His very own "whispering gallery" in the dome of the heavens above the earth, God bends to our deepest murmurs, even our *whispers* . . . and listens. ELISA MORGAN

What do you long to whisper to God today? How can you know that He hears?

*Dear God, give me courage to whisper to You today,
trusting You to hear and respond.*

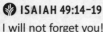
I will not forget you!
[ISAIAH 49:15]

IRRATIONAL FEARS

It makes no logical sense, but when my parents died within a three-month period, I feared they would forget me. Of course they were no longer on earth, but that left me with a large uncertainty. I was a young, unmarried adult and wondered how to navigate life without them. Feeling *really* single and alone, I sought God.

One morning I told Him about my irrational fear and the sadness it brought (even though He knew it already). The Scripture passage that came from the devotional I read that day was Isaiah 49: "Can a mother forget the baby at her breast ... ? Though she may forget, I will not forget you!" (V. 15). God reassured His people through Isaiah that He had not forgotten them and later promised to restore them to Himself through sending His Son Jesus. But the words ministered to my heart too. It's rare for a mother or a father to forget their child, yet it's possible. But God? No way. "I have engraved you on the palms of my hands," He said.

God's answer to me could have brought more fear. But the peace He gave because of His own remembrance of me was exactly what I needed. It was the start of discovering that God is even closer than a parent or anyone else, and He knows the way to help us with everything—even our irrational fears.

ANNE CETAS

**What fears do you face? How might you seek God's help
to address them?**

*Father, my emotions and fears can be overwhelming and controlling.
Thank You for being kind by helping me with them.*

Pray…that God may open a door
for our message, so that we may proclaim
the mystery of Christ. [COLOSSIANS 4:3]

SPEAK UP!

Brittany exclaimed to her coworker at the restaurant, "There's that man! There's that man!" She was referring to Melvin, who first encountered her under different circumstances. While he was tending to the lawn of his church, the Spirit prompted him to start a conversation with a woman who appeared to be a prostitute. Her reply when he invited her to church was: "Do you know what I do? They wouldn't want me in there." As Melvin told her about the love of Jesus and assured her of His power to change her life, tears streamed down her face. Now, some weeks later, Brittany was working in a new environment, living proof of the power of Jesus to change lives.

In the context of encouraging believers to be devoted to prayer, the apostle Paul made a twofold request: "Pray for us, too, that God may open a door for our message, so that we may proclaim the mystery of Christ, for which I am in chains. Pray that I may proclaim it clearly, as I should" (COLOSSIANS 4:3–4).

Have you prayed for opportunities to speak boldly and clearly for Jesus? What a fitting prayer! Such prayers can lead believers, like Melvin, to speak about Him in unexpected places and to unexpected people. Speaking up for Jesus can seem uncomfortable, but the rewards—changed lives—have a way of compensating for our discomforts. *ARTHUR JACKSON*

When did you share the love of Jesus with someone even though it was unexpected and uncomfortable? What role does prayer play in our preparation to boldly speak up for Him?

Jesus, help me to see opportunities and step through the doors You open to speak boldly and clearly about You!

Great is our Lord and mighty in power;
his understanding has no limit. [PSALM 147:5]

GOD UNDERSTANDS

After a recent move, Mabel's seven-year-old son, Ryan, fussed as he prepared to attend a summer camp at his new school. Mabel encouraged him, assuring him that she understood change was hard. But one morning, Ryan's out-of-character grumpiness seemed excessive. With compassion, Mabel asked, "What's bothering you, Son?"

Staring out of the window, Ryan shrugged. "I don't know, Mom. I just have too many feelings."

Mabel's heart ached as she comforted him. Desperate for a way to help him, she shared that the move was hard for her too. She assured Ryan that God would stay close, that He knows everything, even when they couldn't understand or voice their frustrations. "Let's set up a visit with your friends before school starts," she said. They made plans, grateful that God understands even when His children have "too many feelings."

The writer of Psalm 147 experienced overwhelming emotions throughout his faith journey and recognized the benefits of praising the all-knowing Maker and Sustainer of all, the Healer of physical and emotional wounds (VV. 1–6). He praised God for the ways He provides and "delights in those who fear him, who put their hope in his unfailing love" (V. 11).

When we're struggling to make sense of our emotions, we don't have to feel alone or discouraged. We can rest in the unlimited understanding of our unchanging, loving God.   *XOCHITL DIXON*

How does knowing God understands your most intimate needs help you trust Him while you process your emotions? What emotions seem most difficult for you to place into God's mighty and merciful hands?

Sovereign God, thank You for assuring me that You understand and care about my emotional and physical needs.

After beginning by means of the Spirit,
are you now trying to finish by means of the flesh?
[GALATIANS 3:3]

FAILED AGAIN

Back in my sermon-making days I approached some Sunday mornings feeling like a lowly worm. During the week before, I had not been the best husband, father, or friend. I felt that before God could use me again I had to establish a track record of right living. So I vowed to get through the sermon as best I could and try to live better the coming week.

That was not the right approach. In Galatians 3 it's said that God continually supplies us with His Spirit and works powerfully through us as a free gift—not because we've done anything or deserve it.

Abraham's life demonstrates this. At times he failed as a husband. For example, he twice put Sarah's life in jeopardy by lying to save his own skin (GENESIS 12:10–20; 20:1–18). Yet his faith "was credited to him as righteousness" (GALATIANS 3:6). Abraham put himself in God's hands despite his failures, and God used him to bring salvation to the world through his lineage.

There's no justification for behaving badly. Jesus has asked us to follow Him in obedience, and He supplies the means to do so. A hard, unrepentant heart will always hinder His purposes for us, but His ability to use us doesn't depend on a lengthy pattern of good behavior. It's based solely on God's willingness to work through us as we are: saved and growing by grace. You don't have to work for His grace—it's free. *DAVID H. ROPER*

Think of those situations in which you've felt disqualified. How does God look at those occasions? How do you?

I'm thankful, God, that You bless me and use me in spite of my failures. Your grace is amazing!

There is the sea, vast and spacious, teeming with creatures beyond number. [PSALM 104:25]

A WORLD OF PROVISION

I t's 2 a.m. when Nadia, a farmer of sea cucumbers, walks into a roped-off pen in the ocean shallows near her Madagascar village to harvest her "crop." The early hour doesn't bother her. "Life was very hard before I started farming," she says. "I didn't have any source of income." Now, as a member of a marine-protection program called Velondriake, meaning "to live with the sea," Nadia sees her income growing and stabilizing. "We thank God that this project appeared," she adds.

It appeared in large part because God's creation provided what their project needs—a natural supply of sea life. In praise of our providing God, the psalmist wrote, "He makes grass grow for the cattle, and plants for people to cultivate" (PSALM 104:14). As well, "there is the sea…teeming with creatures beyond number—living things both large and small" (V. 25).

It's a wonder, indeed, how God's wondrous creation also provides for us. The humble sea cucumber, for example, helps form a healthy marine food chain. Careful harvesting of sea cucumbers, in turn, grants Nadia and her neighbors a living wage.

Nothing is random in God's creation. He uses it all for His glory and our good. Thus, "I will sing to the LORD all my life," says the psalmist (V. 33). We too can praise Him today as we ponder all that He provides.   *PATRICIA RAYBON*

In what ways does God provide for you through His creation? How can you thank Him for that today?

O Creator God, we're humbled by Your vast creation and all the ways You provide for our needs.

Let the peace of Christ rule in your hearts, since as members of one body you were called to peace. [COLOSSIANS 3:15]

★ *SEPTEMBER TOPIC: THE CHURCH*

THRIVING TOGETHER

My husband, Alan, stood below the towering lights illuminating the athletic field, as a member of the opposing team hit a ball into the air. With his eyes fixed on the ball, Alan ran full speed toward the darkest corner of the field—and slammed into the chain link fence.

Later that night, I handed him an ice pack. "Are you feeling okay?" I asked. He rubbed his shoulder. "I'd feel better if my buddies had warned me that I was getting near the fence," he said.

Teams function best when they work together. Alan's injury could have been avoided, if only one of his teammates had yelled out a warning as he approached the fence.

Scripture reminds us that members of the church are designed to work together and watch out for each other like a team. The apostle Paul tells us that God cares about how we interact with each other, because the actions of one person can impact the whole community of believers (COLOSSIANS 3:13–14). When we all embrace opportunities to serve each other, fully devoted to unity and peace, the church flourishes (V. 15).

Paul instructed his readers to "let the message of Christ dwell among you richly as you teach and admonish one another with all wisdom through psalms, hymns, and songs from the Spirit" (V. 16). In this way we can inspire and protect one another through loving and honest relationships, obeying and praising God with grateful hearts—thriving together.   XOCHITL DIXON

How can you share Scripture this week with others to encourage unity and love in the body of Christ? What does it mean for you to have "the message of Christ [dwelling] among you richly"?

Father God, thank You for using Scripture to instruct me, Your Spirit to guide me, and Your people to keep me focused and accountable.

Bind them on your fingers; write them
on the tablet of your heart. [PROVERBS 7:3]

PRINTED ON OUR HEARTS

When Johannes Gutenberg combined the printing press with moveable type in 1450, he ushered in the era of mass communications in the West, spreading learning into new social realms. Literacy increased across the globe and new ideas produced rapid transformations in social and religious contexts. Gutenberg produced the first-ever printed version of the Bible. Prior to this, Bibles were painstakingly hand-copied, taking scribes up to a year to produce.

For centuries since, the printing press has provided people like you and me the privilege of direct access to Scripture. While we also have electronic versions available to us, many of us often hold a physical Bible in our hands because of his invention. What was once inaccessible given the sheer cost and time to have a Bible copied is readily at our fingertips today.

Having access to God's truth is an amazing privilege. The writer of Proverbs indicates we should treat His instructions to us in the Scriptures as something to be cherished, as "the apple of [our] eye" (PROVERBS 7:2) and to write His words of wisdom on "the tablet of [our] heart" (V. 3). As we seek to understand the Bible and live according to its wisdom, we, like scribes, are drawing God's truth from our "fingers" down into our hearts, to be taken with us wherever we go.   *KIRSTEN HOLMBERG*

**How has having Scripture stored in your heart benefitted you?
How can you begin to internalize more of God's wisdom?**

*Loving God, help me to know Your Word intimately that I might live
in the way You desire.*

We all . . . are being transformed into his image.
[2 CORINTHIANS 3:18]

MAKING HIS MUSIC

C hoir director Arianne Abela spent her childhood sitting on her hands—to *hide* them. Born with fingers missing or fused together on both hands, she also had no left leg and was missing toes on her right foot. A music lover and lyric soprano, she'd planned to major in government at Smith College. But one day her choir teacher asked her to conduct the choir, which made her hands quite visible. From that moment, she found her career, going on to conduct church choirs and serving now as director of choirs at another university. "My teachers saw something in me," Abela explains.

Her inspiring story invites believers to ask, *What does God, our holy Teacher, see in us, regardless of our "limits"?* More than anything, He sees Himself. "So God created human beings in his own image. In the image of God he created them; male and female he created them" (GENESIS 1:27 NLT).

As His glorious "image bearers," when others see us, we should reflect Him. For Abela, that means Jesus, not her hands—or her lack of fingers—matters most. The same is true for all believers. "And we all, who with unveiled faces contemplate the Lord's glory, are being transformed into his image," says 2 Corinthians 3:18.

Similar to Abela, we can conduct our lives by Christ's transforming power (V. 18), offering a life song that rings out to the honor of God.   *PATRICIA RAYBON*

How does knowing you are God's "image-bearer" help you to see yourself differently? How does it help you in your interactions with others?

Thank You, God, for making me in Your image. Help me to apply this fact to all of my life.

I am sending you to Pharaoh to bring my people
the Israelites out of Egypt. [EXODUS 3:10]

FIRE IN THE DESERT

While riding in the Chihuahuan Desert in the late 1800s, Jim
White spotted a strange cloud of smoke spiraling skyward.
Suspecting a wildfire, the young cowboy rode toward the
source, only to learn that the "smoke" was a vast swarm of bats spill-
ing from a hole in the ground. White had come across New Mexico's
Carlsbad Caverns, an immense and spectacular system of caves.

As Moses was tending sheep in a Middle Eastern desert, he
too saw an odd sight that grabbed his attention—a flaming bush
that didn't burn up (EXODUS 3:2). When God Himself spoke from
the bush, Moses realized he had come to something far grander
than it had first appeared. He told Moses, "I am the God of your
father, the God of Abraham" (V. 6). God was about to lead an
enslaved people to freedom and show them their true identity as
His children (V. 10).

More than six hundred years earlier, God had made this promise to Abraham: "All peoples on earth will be blessed through you"
(GENESIS 12:3). The flight of the Israelites from Egypt was but one
step in that blessing—God's plan to rescue His creation through
the Messiah, Abraham's descendant.

Today we can enjoy the benefits of that blessing, for God
offers this rescue to everyone. Christ came to die for the sins of
the whole world. By faith in Him, we too become children of the
living God.   *TIM GUSTAFSON*

**What surprising things have helped you learn about God? How are
you living in the knowledge that you are one of His children?**

*Thank You, Father, for making Yourself accessible to me despite Your
great power, holiness, and overwhelming presence.*

We urge you, brothers and sisters, . . .
encourage the disheartened. [1 THESSALONIANS 5:14]

DAY OF ENCOURAGEMENT

First responders show dedication and courage daily by being on the front lines when disasters occur. In the attack on the World Trade Center in New York City in 2001 when thousands of people were killed or injured, more than four hundred emergency workers also lost their lives. In honor of first responders, the US Senate designated September 12 as the National Day of Encouragement.

While it may seem unique that a government would declare a national day of encouragement, the apostle Paul certainly thought this was needed for the growth of a church. He commended the young church in Thessalonica, a city in Macedonia, to "encourage the disheartened, help the weak, be patient with everyone" (1 THESSALONIANS 5:14). Although they were going through persecution, Paul encouraged the believers to "always strive to do what is good for each other and for everyone else" (V. 15). He knew that as humans, they would be prone to despair, selfishness, and conflict. But he also knew they would not be able to uplift one another without God's help and strength.

Things are no different today. We all need to be uplifted, and we need to do the same for those around us. Yet we can't do it in our own strength. That's why Paul's encouragement that "the one who calls you [Jesus] is faithful, and he will do it" is so reassuring (V. 24). With His help, we can encourage one another every day.

ESTERA PIROSCA ESCOBAR

**How can a word of encouragement keep despair away?
Who can you encourage today?**

*Jesus, thank You for the encouragement You give me each day.
Show me who I need to encourage as well.*

Am I my brother's keeper?
[GENESIS 4:9]

FRIENDLY FIN

A marine biologist was swimming near the Cook Islands in the South Pacific when a 50,000-pound humpback whale suddenly appeared and tucked her under its fin. The woman thought her life was over. But after swimming slowly in circles, the whale let her go. It's then that the biologist saw a tiger shark leaving the area. The woman believes the whale had been protecting her—keeping her from danger.

In a world of danger, we're called to watch out for others. But you might ask yourself, *Should I really be expected to be responsible for someone else?* Or in Cain's words: "Am I my brother's keeper?" (GENESIS 4:9). The rest of the Old Testament resounds with the thunderous response: *Yes!* Just as Adam was to care for the garden, so Cain was to care for Abel. Israel was to keep watch over the vulnerable and care for the needy. Yet they did the opposite— exploiting the people, oppressing the poor, and abdicating the calling to love their neighbors as themselves (ISAIAH 3:14–15).

Yet, in the Cain and Abel story, God continued to watch over Cain, even after he was sent away (GENESIS 4:15–16). God did for Cain what Cain should have done for Abel. It's a beautiful foreshadowing of what God in Jesus would come to do for us. Jesus keeps us in His care, and He empowers us to go and do likewise for others.

GLENN PACKIAM

Who has God entrusted to your care? How have you embraced that responsibility? How have you tried to evade or avoid it?

Compassionate God, thank You for Your care for me. You keep me and watch over me. Help me to do the same for others.

God himself will be with them and be their God.
"He will wipe every tear from their eyes." [REVELATION 21:3–4]

GOODBYES AND HELLOS

When my brother David suddenly died of cardiac failure, my perspectives on life changed dramatically. Dave was the fourth of seven children, but he was the first of us to pass—and the unexpected nature of that passing gave me much to ponder. It became apparent that as age began to catch up with us our family's future was going to be marked more by loss than by gain. It was going to be characterized as much by goodbyes as hellos.

None of this was a surprise intellectually—that is just how life works. But this realization was an emotional lightning bolt to the brain. It gave a fresh, new significance to every moment life gives us and every opportunity time allows. And it placed a huge new value on the reality of a future reunion, where no goodbyes will ever be needed.

This ultimate reality is at the heart of what we find in Revelation 21:3–4: "God himself will be with them and be their God. 'He will wipe every tear from their eyes. There will be no more death' or mourning or crying or pain, for the old order of things has passed away."

Though today we may find ourselves experiencing seasons of long goodbyes, our trust in Christ's death and resurrection promises an eternity of hellos.   *BILL CROWDER*

How do you cope with grief and the loss of loved ones? What comfort does it bring to know that you will one day see them again?

Father, I thank You that You're the living God who gives everlasting life. I pray that You would use our eternal hope to comfort us in our seasons of loss and grief.

Rejoice with those who rejoice;
mourn with those who mourn. [ROMANS 12:15]

★ *SEPTEMBER TOPIC: THE CHURCH*
IN IT TOGETHER

During a two-month period in 1994, as many as one million Tutsis were slain in Rwanda by Hutu tribe members bent on killing their fellow countrymen. In the wake of this horrific genocide, Bishop Geoffrey Rwubusisi approached his wife about reaching out to women whose loved ones had been slain. Mary's reply was, "All I want to do is cry." She too had lost members of her family. The bishop's response was that of a wise leader and caring husband: "Mary, gather the women together and cry with them." He knew his wife's pain had prepared her to uniquely share in the pain of others.

The church, the family of God, is where all of life can be shared—the good and not-so-good. The New Testament words "one another" are used to capture our interdependence. "Be devoted to one another in love. Honor one another above yourselves. . . . Live in harmony with one another" (ROMANS 12:10, 16). The extent of our connectedness is expressed in verse 15: "Rejoice with those who rejoice; mourn with those who mourn."

While the depth and scope of our pain may pale in comparison with those affected by genocide, it's nonetheless personal and real. And, as with the pain of Mary, because of what God has done for us it can be embraced and shared for the comfort and good of others.   *ARTHUR JACKSON*

**When have you allowed someone else to share your sorrow?
How does the body of Christ—the church—help you deal with the
hard times in life?**

*Gracious God, forgive me for my reluctance to enter the pain of others.
Help me to live more fully as a connected member of Your church.*

[Christ Jesus] made himself nothing.
[PHILIPPIANS 2:7]

TRULY HUMBLE, TRULY GREAT

As the American Revolution concluded with England's improbable surrender, many politicians and military leaders maneuvered to make General George Washington a new monarch. The world watched, wondering if Washington would stick to his ideals of freedom and liberty when absolute power was within his grasp. England's King George III saw another reality, however. He was convinced that if Washington resisted the power pull and returned to his Virginia farm, he would be "the greatest man in the world." The king knew that the greatness evidenced in resisting the allure to power is a sign of true nobility and significance.

Paul knew this same truth and encouraged us to follow Christ's humble way. Even though Jesus was "in very nature God," he "did not consider equality with God something to be used to his own advantage" (PHILIPPIANS 2:6). Instead, He surrendered His power, became "a servant" and "humbled himself by becoming obedient to death" (VV. 7–8) The One who held all power surrendered every bit of it for the sake of love.

And yet, in the ultimate reversal, God exalted Christ from a criminal's cross "to the highest place" (V. 9). Jesus, who could demand our praise or force us to be obedient, laid down His power in a breathtaking act that won our worship and devotion. Through absolute humility, Jesus demonstrated true greatness, turning the world upside down.　　　　　　　　　　　　　*WINN COLLIER*

How does the depth of Jesus' humility surprise you?
How does His humility force you to reconsider your
definition of greatness?

Thank You, Jesus, that in Your most destitute and (seemingly)
disgraceful moment, You demonstrated Your true power
and greatness.

[The devil] is a liar and the father of lies.
[JOHN 8:44]

DON'T BE DECEIVED

The spotted lanternfly is a pretty insect with speckled outer wings and a splotch of bright red on its inner wings that flashes when it flies. But its beauty is a bit deceptive. This insect, first seen in the US in 2014, is considered invasive to North America, which means it has the potential to harm the environment and economy. The lanternfly will "eat the innards of practically any woody plant," which includes cherry and other fruit trees, and leaves a sticky goo that leads to mold—killing trees outright or leaving them with little energy to grow fruit.

In the story of Adam and Eve, we learn of a different kind of menace. The serpent, Satan, deceived the couple into disobeying God and eating the forbidden fruit so they would "be like God" (GENESIS 3:1–7). But why listen to a serpent? Did his words alone entice Eve, or was there also something attractive about him? Scripture hints at Satan being created beautiful (EZEKIEL 28:12). Yet Satan fell by the same temptation he used to entice Eve: "I will make myself like [God]" (ISAIAH 14:14; EZEKIEL 28:9).

Any beauty Satan now has is used to deceive (GENESIS 3:1; JOHN 8:44; 2 CORINTHIANS 11:14). Just as he fell, he seeks to pull others down—or keep them from growing. But we have someone far more powerful on our side! We can run to Jesus, our beautiful Savior.   *ALYSON KIEDA*

When have you been deceived by a person or group's seemingly attractive idea? What helps you to recognize deception?

Dear God, help me to weigh what I see and hear by the truths of the gospel. Thank You for triumphing over evil through the cross.

Love your neighbor as yourself. I am the LORD.
[LEVITICUS 19:18]

FIXING ELEVATORS

Sarah has a rare condition that causes her joints to dislocate, making her reliant on an electric wheelchair to get around. On her way to a meeting recently, Sarah rode her wheelchair to the train station but found the elevator broken. Again. With no way of getting to the platform, she was told to take a taxi to another station forty minutes away. The taxi was called but never arrived. Sarah gave up and went home.

Unfortunately, this is a regular occurrence for Sarah. Broken elevators stop her from boarding trains, forgotten ramps leave her unable to get off them. Sometimes Sarah is treated as a nuisance by railway staff for needing assistance. She's often close to tears.

Out of the many biblical laws governing human relationships, "love your neighbor as yourself" is key (LEVITICUS 19:18; ROMANS 13:8–10). And while this love stops us from lying, stealing, and abusing others (LEVITICUS 19:11, 14), it also changes how we work. Employees must be treated fairly (V. 13), and we should all be generous to the poor (VV. 9–10). In Sarah's case, those who fix elevators and drag out ramps aren't doing inconsequential tasks but offering important service to others.

If we treat work as just a means to a wage or other personal benefit, we will soon treat others as annoyances. But if we treat our jobs as opportunities to love, then the most everyday task becomes a holy enterprise. *SHERIDAN VOYSEY*

Why do you think we can become annoyed at someone needing extra assistance? How can you turn your job into a channel of love today?

Father, a job is never just a job to You but an opportunity to love You and serve others. Help me to see my work as an opportunity to benefit others today.

By faith in the name of Jesus, this man whom you
see and know was made strong. [ACTS 3:16]

IN FOCUS

Author Mark Twain suggested that whatever we look at in life—
and how we see it—can influence our next steps, even our
destiny. As Twain said, "You can't depend on your eyes when
your imagination is out of focus."

Peter too spoke of vision when he replied to a lame beggar, a
man whom he and John encountered at the busy temple gate
called Beautiful (ACTS 3:2). As the man asked them for money,
Peter and John looked directly at the man. "Then Peter said, 'Look
at us!' " (V. 4).

Why did he say that? As Christ's ambassador, Peter likely
wanted the beggar to stop looking at his own limitations—yes,
even to stop looking at his need for money. As he looked at the
apostles, he would see the reality of having faith in God.

As Peter told him, "Silver or gold I do not have, but what I do
have I give you. In the name of Jesus Christ of Nazareth, walk"
(V. 6). Then Peter "helped him up, and instantly the man's feet and
ankles became strong. He jumped to his feet and began to walk"
and give praise (VV. 7–8).

What happened? The man had faith in God (V. 16). As evangelist
Charles Spurgeon urged, "Keep your eye simply on Him." When
we do, we don't see obstacles. We see God, the One who makes
our way clear.　　　　　　　　　　　　　　　　　*PATRICIA RAYBON*

**What are you focused on instead of God? With refocused faith,
what could you see in Him for your life?**

*Heavenly Father, when my eyes wander from You, focus my gaze on
Your unlimited power.*

Do not spread false reports.
[EXODUS 23:1]

STOPPING RUMORS

After Charles Simeon (1759–1836) was named the minister of Holy Trinity Church in Cambridge, England, he faced years of opposition. As most in the congregation had wanted the associate minister to be appointed rather than Simeon, they spread rumors about him and rejected his ministry—even at times locking him out of the church. But Simeon, who desired to be filled by God's Spirit, sought to cope with the gossip by creating some principles to live by. One was never to believe rumors unless they were absolutely true and another was "always to believe, that if the other side were heard, a very different account would be given of the matter."

In this practice, Simeon followed God's instructions to His people to cease the gossip and malicious talk He knew would erode their love for each other. One of God's Ten Commandments reflects His desire for them to live truthfully: "You shall not give false testimony against your neighbor" (EXODUS 20:16). Another instruction in Exodus reinforces this commandment: "Do not spread false reports" (23:1).

Think of how different the world would be if each of us never spread rumors and false reports and if we stopped them the moment we heard them. May we rely on the Holy Spirit to help us speak the truth in love as we use our words to bring glory to God.

AMY BOUCHER PYE

**What has helped you when you've faced opposition?
How do you react when you hear gossip?**

*Jesus, help me to speak Your truth in love. Give me words that bring
peace, grace, and encouragement.*

In this world you will have trouble. But take heart!
I have overcome the world. [JOHN 16:33]

MAKING PEACE WITH TROUBLE

We were almost home when I noticed it: the needle of our car's temperature gauge was rocketing up. As we pulled in, I killed the engine and hopped out. Smoke wafted from the hood. The engine sizzled like bacon. I backed the car up a few feet and found a puddle beneath: oil. Instantly, I knew what had happened: The head gasket had blown.

I groaned. We'd just sunk money into other expensive repairs. *Why can't things just work?* I grumbled bitterly. *Why can't things just stop breaking?*

Can you relate? Sometimes we avert one crisis, solve one problem, pay off one big bill, only to face another. Sometimes those troubles are much bigger than an engine self-destructing: an unexpected diagnosis, an untimely death, a terrible loss.

In those moments, we yearn for a world less broken, less full of trouble. That world, Jesus promised, is coming. But not *yet:* "In this world you will have trouble," He reminded His disciples in John 16. "But take heart! I have overcome the world" (V. 33). Jesus spoke in that chapter about grave troubles, such as persecution for your faith. But such trouble, He taught, would never have the last word for those who hope in Him.

Troubles small and large may dog our days. But Jesus' promise of a better tomorrow with Him encourages us not to let our troubles define our lives today.   *ADAM R. HOLZ*

What does it look like for you to surrender your troubles to God? What might you use as a prompt to remind yourself to offer up your anxieties to Him throughout the day?

Father, troubles never seem far away. But when they're close, You're even closer. Please help me to cling to You in trust today.

If one part suffers, every part suffers with it.
[1 CORINTHIANS 12:26]

★ *SEPTEMBER TOPIC: THE CHURCH*

SUFFERING TOGETHER

I n 2013, seventy-year-old James McConnell, a British Royal Marine veteran, died. McConnell had no family, and staff from his nursing home feared no one would attend his funeral. A man tapped to officiate McConnell's memorial service posted a Facebook message: "In this day and age it is tragic enough that anyone has to leave this world with no one to mourn their passing, but this man was family. . . . If you can make it to the graveside . . . to pay your respects to a former brother in arms, then please try to be there." Two hundred Royal Marines packed the pews!

These British compatriots exhibited a biblical truth: we're tied to one another. "The body is not made up of one part, but of many," Paul says (1 CORINTHIANS 12:14). We're not isolated. Just the opposite: we're bound in Jesus. Scripture reveals organic inter-connection: "If one member suffers, all the members suffer" (V. 26 NASB). As believers in Jesus, members of God's new family, we move toward one another into the pain, into the sorrow, into those murky places where we would fear to go alone. But thank-fully we do *not* go alone.

Perhaps the worst part of suffering is when we feel we're drowning in the dark all by ourselves. God, however, creates a new community that suffers together. A new community where no one should be left in the dark.　　　*WINN COLLIER*

When have you felt most alone? How does God's grace, kindness, and friendship help you deal with loneliness?

Is it true, God? Have You really placed me in a new community that knows and loves me in my suffering? Help me to believe this.

Assemble the people before me to hear my words
so that they may learn to revere me. [DEUTERONOMY 4:10]

GOD-PAVED MEMORIES

When my grown son faced a difficult situation, I reminded him about God's constant care and provision during his dad's year of unemployment. I recounted the times God strengthened our family and gave us peace while my mom fought and lost her battle with leukemia. Highlighting the stories of God's faithfulness stitched into Scripture, I affirmed He was good at keeping His word. I led my son down our family's God-paved memory lane, reminding him about the ways He remained reliable through our valley and mountaintop moments. Whether we were struggling or celebrating, God's presence, love, and grace proved sufficient.

Although I'd like to claim this faith-strengthening strategy as my own, God designed the habit of sharing stories to inspire the future generations' belief in Him. As the Israelites remembered all they'd seen God do in the past, He placed cobblestones of confidence down their divinely paved memory lanes.

The Israelites had witnessed God holding true to His promises as they followed Him (DEUTERONOMY 4:3–6). He'd always heard and answered their prayers (V. 7). Rejoicing and reminiscing with the younger generations (V. 9), the Israelites shared the holy words breathed and preserved by the one true God (V. 10).

As we tell of our great God's majesty, mercy, and intimate love, our convictions and the faith of others can be strengthened by the confirmation of His enduring trustworthiness.   XOCHITL DIXON

Who's invested in your spiritual growth by sharing what God has done in their lives? What creative ways can you share His faithfulness and love across generational lines?

Sovereign God, thank You for empowering me to walk with sure-footed faith that crosses generational lines.

You are a forgiving God . . . abounding in love.
[NEHEMIAH 9:17]

NEVER TOO SINFUL

"If I touched a Bible, it would catch fire in my hands," said my community college English professor. My heart sank. The novel we'd been reading that morning referenced a Bible verse, and when I pulled out my Bible to look it up, she noticed and commented. My professor seemed to think she was too sinful to be forgiven. Yet I wasn't bold enough to tell her about God's love—and that the Bible tells us we can *always* seek God's forgiveness.

There's an example of repentance and forgiveness in Nehemiah. The Israelites had been exiled because of their sin, but now they were allowed to return to Jerusalem. When they'd "settled in," Ezra the scribe read the law to them (NEHEMIAH 7:73–8:3). They confessed their sins, remembering that despite their sin God "did not desert" or "abandon them" (9:17, 19). He "heard them" when they cried out; and in compassion and mercy, He was patient with them (VV. 27–31).

In a similar way, God is patient with us. He won't abandon us if we choose to confess our sin and turn to Him. I wish I could go back and tell my professor that, no matter her past, Jesus loves her and wants her to be part of His family. He feels the same way about you and me. We can approach Him seeking forgiveness—and He will give it!   *JULIE SCHWAB*

Do you know someone who feels they're too sinful for Jesus to forgive them? How does the truth that Jesus has come not for "the righteous, but sinners" (MARK 2:17) **speak to this way of thinking?**

Dear Father, thank You for forgiving my sins and for Your assurance that no one is too sinful to be forgiven.

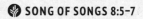

Place me like a seal over your heart,
like a seal on your arm. [SONG OF SONGS 8:6]

LOVE LOCKS

I stood amazed at the hundreds of thousands of padlocks, many engraved with the initials of sweethearts, attached to every imaginable part of the Pont des Arts bridge in Paris. The pedestrian bridge across the Seine River was inundated with these symbols of love, a couple's declaration of "forever" commitment. In 2014, the love locks were estimated to weigh a staggering fifty tons and had even caused a portion of the bridge to collapse, necessitating the locks' removal.

The presence of so many love locks points to the deep longing we have as human beings for assurance that love is secure. In Song of Songs, an Old Testament book that depicts a dialogue between two lovers, the woman expresses her desire for secure love by asking her beloved to "place me like a seal over your heart, like a seal on your arm" (SONG OF SONGS 8:6). Her longing was to be as safe and secure in his love as a seal impressed on his heart or a ring on his finger.

The longing for enduring romantic love expressed in Song of Songs points us to the New Testament truth in Ephesians that we are marked with the "seal" of God's Spirit (1:13). While human love can be fickle, and locks can be removed from a bridge, Christ's Spirit living in us is a permanent seal demonstrating God's never-ending, committed love for each of His children. *LISA M. SAMRA*

How have you experienced the secure love of your heavenly Father? How might you allow His love to guide and encourage you today?

Heavenly Father, thank You that even though the security of human love often remains elusive, Your love for me is strong, steadfast, and eternal.

After waiting patiently, Abraham received
what was promised. [HEBREWS 6:15]

PROMISE-KEEPER

ripped by the gravity of the promises he was making to
LaShonne, Jonathan found himself stumbling as he repeated
his wedding vows. He thought, *How can I make these promises and not believe they're possible to keep?* He made it through
the ceremony, but the weight of his commitments remained.
After the reception, Jonathan led his wife to the chapel where he
prayed—for more than two hours—that God would help him keep
his promise to love and care for LaShonne.

Jonathan's wedding-day fears were based on the recognition
of his human frailties. But God, who promised to bless the
nations through Abraham's offspring (GALATIANS 3:16), has no such
limitations. To challenge his Jewish Christian audience to perseverance and patience to continue in their faith in Jesus, the writer
of Hebrews recalled God's promises to Abraham, the patriarch's
patient waiting, and the fulfillment of what had been promised
(HEBREWS 6:13–15). Abraham and Sarah's status as senior citizens
was no barrier to the fulfillment of God's promise to give Abraham
"many descendants" (V. 14).

Are you challenged to trust God despite being weak, frail, and
human? Are you struggling to keep your commitments, to fulfill
your pledges and vows? In 2 Corinthians 12:9, God promises to
help us: "My grace is sufficient for you, for my power is made perfect in weakness." For more than thirty-six years God has helped
Jonathan and LaShonne to remain committed to their vows. Why
not trust Him to help you?   *ARTHUR JACKSON*

**Why do we find God's promises to help us difficult to embrace? What
promises are you challenged to keep in this season of your life?**

*God, thank You for being faithful in Your commitments to me. Help
me to be faithful in my commitments to You and others.*

Rejoice with me; I have found
my lost sheep. [LUKE 15:6]

WANDERING OFF

iving near cattle ranches as he did, humorist Michael Yaconelli noticed how cows were prone to wander while grazing. A cow would keep moving, always looking for the fabled "greener pastures." Near the edge of the property, the cow might discover some cool fresh grass under a shade tree. Just beyond a broken-down part of the fence was a tasty clump of foliage. Then the cow might push far beyond the fence and out to the road. It slowly "nibbled" its way into being lost.

Cows aren't alone in their roaming problem. Sheep also wander, and it's likely that people have the biggest tendency of all to stray.

Perhaps that's one of the reasons God compares us to sheep in the Bible. It can be easy to meander and "nibble our way" through reckless compromises and foolish decisions, never noticing how far away from the truth we've strayed.

Jesus told the Pharisees the story of a lost sheep. The sheep was of such value to the shepherd that he left his other sheep behind while he searched for the wandering one. And when he found the one that had strayed, He celebrated! (LUKE 15:1–7).

Such is the happiness of God over those who turn back to Him. Jesus said, "Rejoice with me; I have found my lost sheep" (V. 6). God has sent us a Savior to rescue us and bring us home.

CINDY HESS KASPER

**In what way might you be wandering in the wrong direction?
What's the first step you need to take to get back where you belong?**

*Father in heaven, I feel lost. Have I wandered too far?
Redirect my heart and show me the way home.*

The eye never has enough of seeing.
[ECCLESIASTES 1:8]

NEVER ENOUGH

Frank Borman commanded the first space mission that circled the moon. He wasn't impressed. The trip took two days both ways. Frank got motion sickness and threw up. He said being weightless was cool—for thirty seconds. Then he got used to it. Up close he found the moon drab and pockmarked with craters. His crew took pictures of the gray wasteland, then became bored.

Frank went where no one had gone before. It wasn't enough. If he quickly tired of an experience that was out of this world, perhaps we should lower our expectations for what lies in this one. The teacher of Ecclesiastes observed that no earthly experience delivers ultimate joy. "The eye never has enough of seeing, nor the ear its fill of hearing" (1:8). We may feel moments of ecstasy, but our elation soon wears off and we seek the next thrill.

Frank had one exhilarating moment, when he saw the earth rise from the darkness behind the moon. Like a blue and white swirled marble, our world sparkled in the sun's light. Similarly, our truest joy comes from the Son shining on us. Jesus is our life, the only ultimate source of meaning, love, and beauty. Our deepest satisfaction comes from out of this world. Our problem? We can go all the way to the moon, yet still not go far enough.   *MIKE WITTMER*

**When have you felt the most joy? Why didn't it last?
What can you learn from its fleeting nature?**

Jesus, shine the light of Your love on me.

Open my eyes that I may see
wonderful things in your law. [PSALM 119:18]

EYES TO SEE

I recently discovered the wonder of anamorphic art. Appearing at first as an assortment of random parts, an anamorphic sculpture only makes sense when viewed from the correct angle. In one piece, a series of vertical poles align to reveal a famous leader's face. In another, a mass of cable becomes the outline of an elephant. Another artwork, made of hundreds of black dots suspended by wire, becomes a woman's eye when seen correctly. The key to anamorphic art is viewing it from different angles until its meaning is revealed.

With thousands of verses of history, poetry, and more, the Bible can sometimes be hard to understand. But Scripture itself tells us how to unlock its meaning. Treat it like an anamorphic sculpture: view it from different angles and meditate on it deeply.

Christ's parables work this way. Those who care enough to ponder them gain "eyes to see" their meaning (MATTHEW 13:10–16). Paul told Timothy to "reflect" on his words so God would give him insight (2 TIMOTHY 2:7). And the repeated refrain of Psalm 119 is how meditating on Scripture brings wisdom and insight, opening our eyes to see its meaning (119:18, 97–99).

How about pondering a single parable for a week or reading a gospel in one sitting? Spend some time viewing a verse from all angles. Go deep. Biblical insight comes from meditating on Scripture, not just reading it.

Oh, God, give us eyes to see.   SHERIDAN VOYSEY

What do you think the difference is between reading Scripture and meditating on it? How will you spend time meditating on today's verse?

God, open my eyes to see each wonderful thing within the Scriptures. Guide me down the paths connecting each one.

I pray that you, being rooted and
established in love, may have power...to grasp...
the love of Christ. [EPHESIANS 3:17–18]

ROOTED IN LOVE

"**T**hat's all it takes!" Megan said. She had clipped a stem from her geranium plant, dipped the cut end into honey, and stuck it into a pot filled with compost. Megan was teaching me how to propagate geraniums: how to turn one healthy plant into many plants, so I would have flowers to share with others. The honey, she said, was to help the young plant establish roots.

Watching her work, I wondered what kinds of things help us establish spiritual roots. What helps us mature into strong, flourishing people of faith? What keeps us from withering up or failing to grow? Paul, writing to the Ephesians, says that we are "rooted and established in love" (EPHESIANS 3:17). This love comes from God, who strengthens us by giving us the Holy Spirit. Christ dwells in our hearts. And as we begin to "grasp how wide and long and high and deep is the love of Christ" (V. 18), we can have a rich experience of God's presence as we're "completely filled and flooded with God Himself" (V. 19 AMP).

Growing spiritually requires rooting into the love of God—meditating on the truth that we are beloved by the God who is able to do "immeasurably more than all we ask or imagine" (V. 20). What an incredible basis for our faith!　　　　　*AMY PETERSON*

**How can you cultivate a habit of meditating on God's love?
Who could you share the truth of God's love with today?**

God, thank You for Your love for me. Help me to meditate on the truth of that love. May Your love grow in my heart, bringing beauty to my life and to a world in need.

LIVING FREE

A believer in Jesus experiences ongoing tension between living by the Spirit and giving in to selfish desires. There are only two ways to resolve this issue. The first is to die and be with God. The second is to give up the struggle and give in to the flesh. This is the option we must avoid!

Our battle against the flesh is not hopeless, for we're no longer under the authority of sin. In Romans 6, Paul explains why sin no longer has authority over us. If we've died with Christ, we have been set free from sin (V. 7). While sin is no longer our master (V. 14), the pull to sin is real and powerful. But we don't have to give in.

Sin once ruled over us, but in Christ we're no longer slaves to sin. We live this life of tension between the Spirit and our former rulers, sin and the flesh. We're to go on choosing the Spirit because we belong to Christ now.

> *The presence of the Holy Spirit in our lives points to a glorious future.*

The second reason our battle against the flesh is not hopeless is that it will one day come to an end. As Paul says in Ephesians 1:13–14, the Spirit is a seal marking the fact that we belong to Christ. The Spirit is proof of our future. We know that Spirit-filled people will one day be fully transformed, with new resurrection bodies, and we'll be, once and for all, totally free from sinning.

The presence of the Holy Spirit in our lives points to a glorious future without sin, suffering, or shame as the glorified children of God.

ADAPTED FROM LIVE FREE: A FRESH LOOK AT THE FRUIT OF THE SPIRIT, *BY **CONSTANTINE R. CAMPBELL**, © 2014 OUR DAILY BREAD MINISTRIES.*

God has chosen to make known . . .
the glorious riches of this mystery, which is
Christ in you, the hope of glory. [COLOSSIANS 1:27]

★ *OCTOBER TOPIC: FRUIT OF THE SPIRIT*

HOW TO REFLECT CHRIST

Thérèse of Lisieux was a joyful and carefree child—until her mother died when she was just four years old. She became timid and easily agitated. But many years later on Christmas Eve, all of that changed. After celebrating the birth of Jesus with her church community, she experienced God releasing her from her fear and giving her joy. She attributed the change to the power of God leaving heaven and becoming a man, Jesus, and through His dwelling in her.

What does it mean for Christ to dwell within us? It's a mystery, said Paul to the Colossian church. It's one that God "kept hidden for ages and generations" (COLOSSIANS 1:26), but which He disclosed to God's people. To them God revealed "the glorious riches of this mystery, which is Christ in you, the hope of glory" (V. 27). Because Christ now dwelled in the Colossians, they experienced the joy of new life. No longer were they enslaved to the old self of sin.

If we've asked Jesus to be our Savior, we too live out this mystery of His dwelling in us. Through His Spirit, He can release us from fear, as He did Thérèse, and grow within us the fruit of His Spirit, such as joy, peace, and self-control (GALATIANS 5:22–23).

Let's give thanks for the wonderful mystery of Christ within us.

AMY BOUCHER PYE

How do you see Jesus reflected in your life? In the lives of those you love who follow Him?

Jesus, thank You for lowering Yourself and becoming a man, and for living within me. Help me to understand more of Your work in my life.

I give them eternal life, and they shall never perish;
no one will snatch them out of my hand. [JOHN 10:28]

HE WON'T LET US GO

J ulio was biking across the George Washington Bridge—a busy,
double-decked thoroughfare connecting New York City and
New Jersey—when he encountered a life-or-death situation. A
man was standing on a ledge over the Hudson River preparing to
jump. Knowing that the police wouldn't arrive in time, Julio acted
quickly. He recalls getting off his bike and spreading out his arms,
saying something like: "Don't do it. We love you." Then, like a shepherd with a crook, he grabbed the distraught man, and with the
help of another passerby, brought him to safety. According to
reports, Julio wouldn't let go of the man, even after he was safe.

Two millennia earlier, in a life-or-death situation, Jesus, the
Good Shepherd, said He would lay down His life to save and never
let go of those who believed in Him. He summarized how He
would bless His sheep: they would know Him personally, have the
gift of eternal life, would never perish, and would be secure in His
care. This security didn't depend on the ability of the frail and
feeble sheep, but on the sufficiency of the Shepherd who'll never
let one be snatched "out of [His] hand" (JOHN 10:28–29).

When we were distraught and feeling hopeless, Jesus rescued
us; now we can feel safe and secure in our relationship with Him.
He loves us, pursues us, finds us, saves us, and promises to never
let us go.   *MARVIN WILLIAMS*

**What makes you feel insecure in your relationship with Jesus?
How do you feel knowing that your security in Him depends on His
sufficiency and not your weakness?**

*Jesus, when I let go of You because of my sin, You never let go of me
because of Your grace.*

BIBLE IN A YEAR | ISAIAH 14–16; EPHESIANS 5:1–16

Husbands, love your wives, just as Christ loved the
church and gave himself up for her. [EPHESIANS 5:25]

REMOVING THE INTRUDER

I t wasn't quite dawn when my husband rose from bed and went
into the kitchen. I saw the light flip on and off and wondered at
his action. Then I recalled that the previous morning I'd yelped
at the sight of an "intruder" on our kitchen counter. Translated: an
undesirable creature of the six-legged variety. My husband knew
my paranoia and immediately arrived to remove it. This morning
he'd risen early to ensure our kitchen was bug-free so I could
enter without concern. What a guy!

My husband awoke with me on his mind, putting my need
before his own. To me, his action illustrates the love Paul describes
in Ephesians 5:25, "Husbands, love your wives, just as Christ loved
the church and gave himself up for her." Paul goes on, "Husbands
ought to love their wives as their own bodies. He who loves his
wife loves himself" (V. 28). Paul's comparison of a husband's love
to the love of Christ pivots on how Jesus put our needs before His
own. My husband knows I'm afraid of certain intruders, and so he
made my concern his priority.

That principle doesn't apply to husbands only. After the example of Jesus, each of us can lovingly sacrifice to help remove an
intruder of stress, fear, shame, or anxiety so that someone can
move more freely in the world. 　　　　　　　　　　*ELISA MORGAN*

**What "intruder" might God be asking you to address to help
another? How might you allow someone to help rid your life of
certain "intruders"?**

*Dear God, thank You for the gift of Your Son who's removed the
intruder of sin from my life and reconciled me to You!*

Open his eyes, LORD, so that he may see.
[2 KINGS 6:17]

STRANGE COMFORT

The verse on the card Lisa received didn't seem to match her situation: "Then the LORD opened the servant's eyes, and he looked and saw the hills full of horses and chariots of fire all around Elisha" (2 KINGS 6:17). *I have cancer!* she thought in confusion. *I've just lost a baby! A verse about angel soldiers doesn't apply.*

Then the "angels" began to show up. Cancer survivors gave her their time and a listening ear. Her husband got released early from an overseas military assignment. Friends prayed with her. But the moment she most felt God's love was when her friend Patty walked in with two boxes of tissues. Placing them on the table, she started crying. Patty *knew*. She'd endured miscarriages too.

"That meant more than anything," Lisa says. "The card made sense now. My 'angel soldiers' had been there all along."

When an army besieged Israel, a host of literal angels protected Elisha. But Elisha's servant couldn't see them. "What shall we do?" he cried to the prophet (V. 15). Elisha simply prayed, "Open his eyes, LORD, so that he may see" (V. 17).

When we look to God, our crisis will show us what truly matters and that we're not alone. We learn that God's comforting presence never leaves us. He shows us His love in infinitely surprising ways.

TIM GUSTAFSON

**What's your first reaction when you receive bad news?
When you endured a crisis, how did you view God in new ways?**

*Loving God, thank You for the complete reliability of Your presence.
Open my eyes so that I may see You in a new way today.*

He who began a good work in you
will carry it on to completion until
the day of Christ Jesus. [PHILIPPIANS 1:6]

BEGIN WITH THE END

"**W**hat do you want to be when you grow up?" I was often asked that question as a child. And the answers changed like the wind. A doctor. A firefighter. A missionary. A worship leader. A physicist—or actually, MacGyver! (a favorite TV character). Now, as a dad of four kids, I think of how difficult it must be for them to be asked that question. There are times when I want to say, "I know what you'll be great at!" Parents can sometimes see more in their children than the children can see in themselves.

This resonates with what Paul saw in the Philippian believers—those he loved and prayed for (PHILIPPIANS 1:3). He could see the end; he knew what they'd be when all was said and done. The Bible gives us a grand vision of the end of the story—resurrection and the renewal of all things (SEE 1 CORINTHIANS 15 AND REVELATION 21). But it also tells us who's writing the story.

Paul, in the opening lines of a letter he wrote from prison, reminded the Philippian church that "he who began a good work in you will carry it on to completion until the day of Christ Jesus" (PHILIPPIANS 1:6). Jesus started the work and He'll complete it. The word *completion* is particularly important—the story doesn't just end, for God leaves nothing unfinished. 　　　　*GLENN PACKIAM*

Where are you in your story? How can you trust Jesus to take the "pen" from your hand and to bring your story to completion?

Dear Jesus, You're in charge of my story. It's not up to me to make it happen. I surrender my life to You. Help me to trust You.

For as in Adam all die, so in Christ all will be
made alive. [1 CORINTHIANS 15:22]

YOU'LL SEE HER AGAIN

The room was dim and silent as I pulled a chair close to Jacquie's bed. Before a three-year battle with cancer, my friend had been a vibrant person. I could still picture her laughing—eyes full of life, her face lit with a smile. Now she was quiet and still, and I was visiting her in a special care facility.

Not knowing what to say, I decided to read some Scripture. I pulled my Bible out of my purse and turned to a reference in 1 Corinthians and began to read.

After the visit and an emotional time in the seclusion of my parked car, a thought came to mind that slowed my tears: *You'll see her again.* Caught up in sadness, I had forgotten that death is only temporary for believers (1 CORINTHIANS 15:21–22). I knew I'd see Jacquie again because both of us had trusted in Jesus' death and resurrection for the forgiveness of our sin (VV. 3–4). When Jesus came back to life after His crucifixion, death lost its ultimate power to separate believers from each other and from God. After we die, we'll live again in heaven with God and all of our spiritual brothers and sisters—forever.

Because Jesus is alive today, believers in Him have hope in times of loss and sorrow. Death has been swallowed up in the victory of the cross (V. 54).   *JENNIFER BENSON SCHULDT*

**How has God comforted you in times of sorrow? How might He
want to use you to comfort someone who's grieving today?**

*Dear Jesus, thank You for dying for my sin. I believe that You're alive
today because God raised You from the dead.*

Satisfy us in the morning with your unfailing love,
that we may sing for joy and be glad all our days.
[PSALM 90:14]

DO WE MATTER?

For some months now I've been corresponding with a young man who's thinking deeply about faith. On one occasion he wrote, "We're no more than teeny, tiny, infinitesimal blips on the timeline of history. Do we matter?"

Moses, Israel's prophet, would agree: "Our days . . . quickly pass, and we fly away" (PSALM 90:10). The brevity of life can worry us and cause us to wonder if we matter.

We *do*. We matter because we're deeply, eternally loved by the God who made us. In this poem, Moses prays, "Satisfy us . . . with your unfailing love" (V. 14). We matter because we matter to God.

We also matter because we can show God's love to others. Though our lives are short, they're not meaningless if we leave a legacy of God's love. We're not here on earth to make money and retire in style, but to "show God" to others by showing them His love.

And finally, though life here on earth is transient, we're creatures of eternity. Because Jesus rose from the dead, we'll live forever. That's what Moses meant when he assured us that God will "satisfy us in the morning with [His] unfailing love." On that "morning" we'll rise to live and love and be loved forever. And if that doesn't create meaning, I don't know what does.　　*DAVID H. ROPER*

**When have you struggled with wondering if your life counts?
How does Psalm 90 help?**

*I'm grateful, loving God, that I matter to You.
Help me to share You with others.*

That person is like a tree planted by streams of water,
which yields its fruit in season. [PSALM 1:3]

★ *OCTOBER TOPIC: FRUIT OF THE SPIRIT*
THE TREE WHISPERER

Some call him the "tree whisperer." Tony Rinaudo is, in fact, World Vision Australia's tree maker. He's a missionary and agronomist engaged in a thirty-year effort to share Jesus by combating deforestation across Africa's Sahel, south of the Sahara.

Realizing stunted "shrubs" were actually dormant trees, Rinaudo started pruning, tending, and watering them. His work inspired hundreds of thousands of farmers to save their failing farms by restoring nearby forests, reversing soil erosion. Farmers in Niger, for example, have doubled their crops and their income, providing food for an additional 2.5 million people per year.

In John 15, Jesus, the creator of agriculture, referred to similar farming tactics when He said, "I am the true vine, and my Father is the gardener. He cuts off every branch in me that bears no fruit, while every branch that does bear fruit he prunes so that it will be even more fruitful" (VV. 1–2).

Without the daily tending of God, our souls grow barren and dry. When we delight in His law, however, meditating on it day and night, we are "like a tree planted by streams of water" (PSALM 1:3). Our leaves will "not wither" and "whatever [we] do prospers" (V. 3). Pruned and planted in Him, we're evergreen—revived and thriving.   *PATRICIA RAYBON*

**Where and how do you sense your soul being tended by God?
What do you do to "delight" in God's Word?**

O Gardener God, I yield my stunted places to Your pruning and watering, surrendering my dry places to grow green and revived in You.

The one who is patient calms a quarrel.
[PROVERBS 15:18]

A CRITICAL REACTION

Tough words hurt. So my friend—an award-winning author—struggled with how to respond to the criticism he received. His new book had earned five-star reviews plus a major award. Then a respected magazine reviewer gave him a back-handed compliment, describing his book as well-written yet still criticizing it harshly. Turning to friends, he asked, "How should I reply?"

One friend advised, "Let it go." I shared advice from writing magazines, including tips to ignore such criticism or learn from it even while continuing to work and write.

Finally, however, I decided to see what Scripture—which has the best advice of all—has to say about how to react to strong criticism. The book of James advises, "Everyone should be quick to listen, slow to speak and slow to become angry" (1:19). The apostle Paul counsels us to "live in harmony with one another" (ROMANS 12:16).

An entire chapter of Proverbs, however, offers extended wisdom on reacting to disputes. "A gentle answer turns away wrath," says Proverbs 15:1. "The one who is patient calms a quarrel" (V. 18). Also, "The one who heeds correction gains understanding" (V. 32). Considering such wisdom, may God help us hold our tongues, as my friend did. More than all, however, wisdom instructs us to "fear the LORD" because "humility comes before honor" (V. 33).

PATRICIA RAYBON

**What's your typical reaction when you're criticized?
In a dispute, what's a humble way you can guard your tongue?**

*Dear God, when criticism strikes or a dispute hurts,
guard my tongue in humble honor of You.*

Having disarmed the powers and authorities,
he made a public spectacle of them, triumphing over
them by the cross. [COLOSSIANS 2:15]

FIGHTING LIFE'S DRAGONS

Have you ever fought a dragon? If you answered no, author Eugene Peterson disagrees with you. In *A Long Obedience in the Same Direction,* he wrote, "Dragons are projections of our fears, horrible constructions of all that might hurt us....A peasant confronted by a magnificent dragon is completely outclassed." Peterson's point? Life is *filled* with dragons: the life-threatening health crisis, the sudden job loss, the failed marriage, the estranged prodigal child. These "dragons" are the supersized dangers and frailties of life that we're inadequate to fight alone.

But in those battles, we have a Champion. Not a fairy tale champion—the ultimate Champion who has fought on our behalf and conquered the dragons that seek to destroy us. Whether they're dragons of our own failures or the spiritual enemy who desires our destruction, our Champion is greater, allowing Paul to write of Jesus, "Having disarmed the powers and authorities, he made a public spectacle of them, triumphing over them by the cross" (COLOSSIANS 2:15). The destructive forces of this broken world are no match for Him!

The moment we realize that the dragons of life are too big for us is the moment we can begin to rest in Christ's rescue. We can confidently say, "But thanks be to God! He gives us the victory through our Lord Jesus Christ" (1 CORINTHIANS 15:57).   *BILL CROWDER*

What "dragons" are you facing in life? How can Christ's victory on the cross provide encouragement as you deal with them?

Father, thank You for being more than enough for the threats I will face today. Give me the wisdom and strength to walk with You, trusting You for the grace I need.

Give your servant a discerning heart...
to distinguish between right and wrong. [1 KINGS 3:9]

MISSING: WISDOM

Two-year-old Kenneth went missing. Yet within three minutes of his mom's 9-1-1 call, an emergency worker found him just two blocks from home at the county fair. His mom had promised he could go later that day with his grandpa. But he'd driven his toy tractor there, and parked it at his favorite ride. When the boy was safely home, his dad wisely removed the toy's battery.

Kenneth was actually rather smart to get where he wanted to go, but two-year-olds are missing another key quality: wisdom. And as adults we sometimes lack it too. Solomon, who'd been appointed king by his father David (1 KINGS 2), admitted he felt like a child. God appeared to him in a dream and said, "Ask for whatever you want me to give you" (3:5). He replied, "I am only a little child and do not know how to carry out my duties. . . . So give your servant a discerning heart to govern your people and to distinguish between right and wrong" (VV. 7–9). God gave Solomon "a breadth of understanding as measureless as the sand on the seashore" (4:29).

Where can we get the wisdom we need? Solomon said the beginning of wisdom is a "fear" or awe of God (PROVERBS 9:10). So we can start by asking Him to teach us about Himself and to give us wisdom beyond our own.   *ANNE CETAS*

In what areas do you need God's wisdom?
What might give you a teachable heart?

I'm always in need of wisdom, God. I want to follow Your ways.
Please show me which way to go.

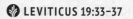

Love them as yourself, for you were
foreigners in Egypt. [LEVITICUS 19:34]

LOVING THE STRANGER

When I moved to a new country, one of my first experiences
left me feeling unwelcome. After finding a seat in the little
church where my husband was preaching that day, a gruff
older gentleman startled me when he said, "Move along down."
His wife apologized as she explained that I was sitting in the pew
they always occupied. Years later I learned that congregations
used to rent out pews, which raised money for the church and also
ensured no one could take another person's seat. Apparently
some of that mentality carried on through the decades.

Later, I reflected on how God instructed the Israelites to welcome foreigners, in contrast to cultural practices such as I encountered. In setting out the laws that would allow His people to
flourish, He reminded them to welcome foreigners because they
themselves were once foreigners (LEVITICUS 19:34). Not only were
they to treat strangers with kindness (V. 33), but they were also to
"love them as [themselves]" (V. 34). God had rescued them from
oppression in Egypt, giving them a home in a land "flowing with
milk and honey" (EXODUS 3:17). He expected His people to love others who also made their home there.

As you encounter strangers in your midst, ask God to reveal
any cultural practices that might keep you from sharing His love
with them.   *AMY BOUCHER PYE*

**Why is it so important that we welcome people into our homes
and churches? What do you find most challenging and most
rewarding in this?**

*Father God, You welcome me with open arms, for You love me day
after day. Give me Your love to share with others.*

I will uphold you with my
righteous right hand. [ISAIAH 41:10]

GOD HOLDS US

South African Fredie Blom turned 114 in 2018, widely recognized as the oldest living man. Born in 1904, the year the Wright Brothers built their Flyer II, he's lived through both World Wars, apartheid, and the Great Depression. When asked for the secret for his longevity, Blom only shrugs. Like many of us, he hasn't always chosen the foods and practices that promote wellness. However, Blom does offer one reason for his remarkable health: "There's only one thing, it's [God]. He's got all the power....He holds me."

Blom echoes words similar to what God spoke to Israel, as the nation wilted under the oppression of fierce enemies. "I will strengthen you and help you," God promised. "I will uphold you with my righteous right hand" (ISAIAH 41:10). No matter how desperate their situation, how impossible the odds that they would ever find relief, God assured His people that they were held in His tender care. "Do not fear, for I am with you," He insisted. "Do not be dismayed, for I am your God" (V. 10).

No matter how many years we're given, life's hardships will come knocking at our door. A troubled marriage. A child abandoning the family. Terrifying news from the doctor. Even persecution. However, our God reaches out to us and holds us firmly. He gathers us and holds us in His strong, tender hand.   *WINN COLLIER*

When have you felt isolated or exposed? How does it encourage you to know that your life is being held in God's strong hand?

God, assure me that You're holding me because I feel like I'm only hanging on by a thread. I trust that You'll help and uphold me.

Then they cried out to the LORD in their trouble,
and he delivered them from their distress.
[PSALM 107:6]

THE PICTURE OF DESPAIR

During the Great Depression in the United States, famed photographer Dorothea Lange snapped a photo of Florence Owens Thompson and her children. This well-known photograph, *Migrant Mother,* is the picture of a mother's despair in the aftermath of the failed pea harvest. Lange took it in Nipomo, California, while working for the Farm Security Administration, hoping to make them aware of the needs of the desperate seasonal farm laborers.

The book of Lamentations presents another snapshot of despair—that of Judah in the wake of the destruction of Jerusalem. Before the army of Nebuchadnezzar swept in to destroy the city, the people had suffered from starvation thanks to a siege (2 KINGS 24:10–11). Though their turmoil was the result of years of disobedience to God, the writer of Lamentations cried out to God on behalf of his people (LAMENTATIONS 2:11–12).

While the author of Psalm 107 also describes a desperate time in Israel's history (during Israel's wanderings in the wilderness, vv. 4–5), the focus shifts to an action step to be taken in hard times: "Then they cried out to the LORD in their trouble" (V. 6). And what a wonderful result: "he delivered them from their distress."

In despair? Don't stay silent. Cry out to God. He hears and waits to restore your hope. Though He doesn't always take us out of hard situations, He promises to be with us always.

LINDA WASHINGTON

When have you experienced God's help in a stressful time? How will you encourage someone this week who's facing a crisis?

Heavenly Father, I'm grateful for Your comforting presence.

I am the vine; you are the branches. If you remain in me and I in you, you will bear much fruit. [JOHN 15:5]

★ *OCTOBER TOPIC: FRUIT OF THE SPIRIT*

FRUIT JUICE

A thrift-store bargain, the lamp seemed perfect for my home office—the right color, size, and price. Back at home, however, when I plugged in the cord, nothing happened. No light. No power. No juice.

No problem, my husband assured me. "I can fix that. Easy." As he took the lamp apart, he saw the trouble immediately. The plug wasn't connected to anything. Without wiring to a source of power, the "perfect" pretty lamp was useless.

The same is true for us. Jesus told His disciples. "I am the vine; you are the branches. If you remain in me and I in you, you will bear much fruit." But then he added this reminder. "Apart from me you can do nothing" (JOHN 15:5).

This teaching was given in a grape-growing region, so His disciples readily understood it. Grapevines are hardy plants, and their branches tolerate vigorous pruning. Cut off from their life source, however, the branches are worthless deadwood. So it is with us.

As we remain in Jesus and let His words dwell in us, we're wired to our life source—Christ Himself. "This is to my Father's glory," said Jesus, "that you bear much fruit, showing yourselves to be my disciples" (V. 8). Such a fruitful outcome needs daily nourishment, however. Freely, God provides it through the Scriptures and His love. So plug in and let the juice flow!   *PATRICIA RAYBON*

**What does it mean for you to remain in Jesus?
How has He equipped you to bear fruit for Him?**

*All-powerful God, empower me to remain in You
and allow Your loving Word to yield good fruit in me.*

Though it is the smallest of all seeds,
yet when it grows, it is the largest of garden plants
and becomes a tree. [MATTHEW 13:32]

SLOW, BUT SURE

I ran into an old friend who told me what he'd been up to, but I confess it seemed too good to be true. Within a few months of that conversation, however, his band was everywhere—from charting top singles on the radio to having a hit song pulsing under TV ads. His rise to fame was meteoric.

We can be obsessed with significance and success—the big and the dramatic, the quick and the meteoric. But the parables of the mustard seed and yeast compare the way of the kingdom (God's reign on earth) to small, hidden, and seemingly insignificant things whose work is slow and gradual.

The kingdom is like its King. Christ's mission culminated in His life, like a seed, being buried in the ground; like yeast, being hidden in the dough. Yet He rose. Like a tree breaking through the dirt, like bread when the heat is turned up. Jesus *rose*.

We're invited to live according to His way, the way that's persisting and permeating. To resist the temptation to take matters into our own hands, to grasp for power and to justify our dealings in the world by the outcomes they may produce. The outcome—"a tree . . . that the birds come and perch in its branches" (V. 32) and the bread that provides a feast—will be Christ's doing, not ours.   *GLENN PACKIAM*

What small and seemingly insignificant things could you do to encourage or bless the people in your life? Where do you need to turn away from comparison with others or from a false picture of significance and success?

Dear Jesus, thank You for often working in small, hidden, and seemingly insignificant ways. Help me to trust You're at work even when I can't see You. Grant me the grace to remain faithful.

I have swept away your offenses.
[ISAIAH 44:22]

A WIDE, SWEEPING GRACE

Alexa, Amazon's voice-controlled device, has an interesting feature: it can erase everything you say. Whatever you've asked Alexa to do, whatever information you've asked Alexa to retrieve, one simple sentence ("Delete everything I said today") sweeps it all clean, as if it never happened. It's too bad that the rest of our life doesn't have this capability. Every misspoken word, every disgraceful act, every moment we wish we could erase—we'd just speak the command, and the entire mess would disappear.

There's good news, though. God does offer each of us a clean start. Only, He goes far deeper than merely deleting our mistakes or bad behavior. God provides redemption, a deep healing that transforms us and makes us new. "Return to me," He says, "I have redeemed you" (ISAIAH 44:22). Even though Israel rebelled and disobeyed, God reached out to them with lavish mercy. He "swept away [their] offenses like a cloud, [their] sins like the morning mist" (V. 22). He gathered all their shame and failures and washed them away with His wide, sweeping grace.

God will do the same with our sin and blunders. There's no mistake He can't mend, no wound He can't heal. God's mercy heals and redeems the most painful places in our soul—even the ones we've hidden for so very long. His mercy sweeps away all our guilt, washes away every regret. *WINN COLLIER*

Where are you most aware of your failures? How does the image of God sweeping away all your mistakes give you hope?

So many regrets, so many things I'd do differently.
God, You tell me that You can forgive and heal me.
Thank You for Your mercy and grace.

Seek the LORD while he may be found.
[ISAIAH 55:6]

LISTENING BEYOND THE STARS

Imagine life without mobile phones, Wi-Fi, GPS, Bluetooth devices, or microwave ovens. That's the way it is in the little town of Green Bank, West Virginia, known as "the quietest town in America." It's also the location of the Green Bank Observatory, the world's largest steerable radio telescope. The telescope needs "quiet" to "listen" to naturally occurring radio waves emitted by the movement of pulsars and galaxies in deep space. It has a surface area larger than a football field and stands in the center of the National Radio Quiet Zone, a 13,000-square-mile area established to prevent electronic interference to the telescope's extreme sensitivity.

This intentional quiet enables scientists to hear "the music of the spheres." It also reminds me of our need to quiet ourselves enough to listen to the One who created the universe. God communicated to a wayward and distracted people through the prophet Isaiah, "Give ear and come to me; listen, that you may live. I will make an everlasting covenant with you" (ISAIAH 55:3). God promises His faithful love to all who will seek Him and turn to Him for forgiveness.

We listen intentionally to God by turning from our distractions to meet Him in Scripture and in prayer. God isn't distant. He longs for us to make time for Him so He can be the priority of our daily lives and then for eternity.   *JAMES BANKS*

Why is listening to God so vital in your life? In what ways do you plan to take time for Him?

Help me to be quiet before You today, loving God, even if it's only for a moment! Nothing matters more than being with You!

The Lord bless you and keep you.
[NUMBERS 6:24]

ANCIENT PROMISES

I n 1979, Dr. Gabriel Barkay and his team discovered two silver scrolls in a burial ground outside the Old City of Jerusalem. In 2004, after twenty-five years of careful research, scholars confirmed that the scrolls were the oldest biblical text in existence, having been buried in 600 bc. What I find particularly moving is what the scrolls contain—the priestly blessing that God wanted spoken over His people: "The Lord bless you and keep you; the Lord make his face shine on you" (NUMBERS 6:24–25).

In giving this benediction, God showed Aaron and his sons (through Moses) how to bless the people on His behalf. The leaders were to memorize the words in the form God gave so they would speak to them just as God desired. Note how these words emphasize that God is the one who blesses, for three times they say, "the Lord." And six times He says, "you," reflecting just how much God wants His people to receive His love and favor.

Ponder for a moment that the oldest existing fragments of the Bible tell of God's desire to bless. What a reminder of God's boundless love and how He wants to be in a relationship with us. If you feel far from God today, hold tightly to the promise in these ancient words. May the Lord bless *you*; may the Lord keep *you*.   AMY BOUCHER PYE

**What does it mean to you that God desires to bless you?
How can you share His love with others?**

*Father God, I give thanks for the many blessings You give to me.
Help me to notice the ways You bring me joy and peace, that I might
praise You.*

If I must boast, I will boast of the things
that show my weakness. [2 CORINTHIANS 11:30]

GOLDEN SCARS

I n the Netherlands, a group of fashion designers offer a "Golden Joinery" workshop. Inspired by the Japanese technique Kintsugi, where broken porcelain is visibly repaired with gold, participants collaborate in mending clothes in ways that highlight the mending work rather than trying to mask it. Those who are invited bring "a dear but broken garment and mend it with gold." As they remake their clothes, the repair becomes ornamental, a "golden scar."

Articles of clothing are transformed in ways that highlight the places where they were torn or frayed. Perhaps this is something like what Paul meant when he said that he would "boast" in the things that showed his weakness. Although he'd experienced "surpassingly great revelations," he doesn't brag about them (2 CORINTHIANS 12:6). He is kept from getting proud and overconfident, he says, by a "thorn" in his flesh (V. 7). No one knows exactly what he was referring to—perhaps depression, a form of malaria, persecution from enemies, or something else. Whatever it was, he begged God to take it away. But God said, "My grace is sufficient for you, for my power is made perfect in weakness" (V. 9).

Just as the rips and tears in old clothes can become sights of beauty as they're remade by designers, the broken and weak places in our lives can become places where God's power and glory may shine. He holds us together, transforms us, and makes our weaknesses beautiful.   AMY PETERSON

What are some weaknesses you try to keep hidden from the world? How has God revealed His power through your weakness?

God, may all my scars become golden as You heal and repair me in ways that bring glory to Your name.

Christ Jesus came into the world to save sinners—
of whom I am the worst. [1 TIMOTHY 1:15]

WHAT'S WRONG WITH THE WORLD?

There is an oft-heard story that *The London Times* posed a question to readers at the turn of the twentieth century. *What's wrong with the world?*

That's quite the question, isn't it? Someone might quickly respond, "Well, how much time do you have for me to tell you?" And that would be fair, as there seems to be so much that's wrong with our world. As the story goes, *The Times* received a number of responses, but one in particular has endured in its brief brilliance. The English writer, poet, and philosopher G. K. Chesterton penned this four-word response, a refreshing surprise to the usual passing-of-the-buck: "Dear Sirs, I am."

Whether the story is factual or not is up for debate. But that response? It's nothing but true. Long before Chesterton came along, there was an apostle named Paul. Far from a lifelong model citizen, Paul confessed his past shortcomings: "I was once a blasphemer and a persecutor and a violent man" (V. 13). After naming who Jesus came to save ("sinners"), he goes on to make a very Chesterton-like qualification: "of whom *I am* the worst" (V. 15). Paul knew exactly what was and is wrong with the world. And he further knew the only hope of making things right—"the grace of our Lord" (V. 14). What an amazing reality! This enduring truth lifts our eyes to the light of Christ's saving love.   *JOHN BLASE*

What *is* wrong with the world? Can you own the answer Paul and Chesterton gave? What is one way you can accept that without sliding into self-hatred?

God, thank You for Your immense patience with me, a sinner.
To You be honor and glory forever and ever.

Since we live by the Spirit, let us keep in step
with the Spirit. [GALATIANS 5:25]

★ *OCTOBER TOPIC: FRUIT OF THE SPIRIT*

IN TUNE WITH THE SPIRIT

As I listened to the piano tuner work on the elegant grand
piano, I thought about the times when I'd heard that very
same piano pour out the incredible sound of the "Warsaw
Concerto" and the rich melody of "How Great Thou Art." But now
the instrument desperately needed to be tuned. While some
notes were right on pitch, others were sharp or flat, creating an
unpleasant sound. The piano tuner's responsibility wasn't to
make each of the keys play the same sound but to assure that
each note's unique sound combined with others to create a pleasing harmonious whole.

Even within the church, we can observe notes of discord. People
with unique ambitions or talents can create a jarring dissonance
when they're joined together. In Galatians 5, Paul pleaded with
believers to do away with "discord, jealousy, fits of rage, [and] selfish ambition," which would destroy fellowship with God or relationships with others. Paul went on to encourage us to embrace the
fruit of the Spirit: "love, joy, peace, forbearance, kindness, goodness, faithfulness, gentleness and self-control" (VV. 20, 22–23).

When we live by the Spirit, we'll find it easier to avoid unneces-
sary conflict on nonessential matters. Our shared sense of purpose can be greater than our differences. And with God's help,
each of us can grow in grace and unity as we keep our hearts in
tune with Him.   *CINDY HESS KASPER*

**In what ways might I be causing discord among the body of
believers? How can I spread harmony?**

*Gracious God, teach me how to "get in tune" with the Spirit's leading
and live in harmony with others.*

To him who struck down the firstborn
of Egypt *His love endures forever.* [PSALM 136:10]

NICE SHOT?

When Walt Disney's *Bambi* was re-released, moms and dads relived childhood memories with their sons and daughters. A young mother, whose husband was an avid outdoorsman with an impressive trophy room, was one of those parents. With her little ones at her side, she experienced with them the gasp and groan of the moment when Bambi lost his mother to a hunter. To this day she's reminded at family gatherings of her embarrassment when, in all innocence, her little boy shouted out in the theater, "Nice shot!"

In time, we laugh at the embarrassing things our children say. But what are we to say when the people of Psalm 136 do something similar? Israel, God's chosen and rescued people, celebrate a love that endures for all creation and for themselves—but not for their enemies. The psalm sings the praises of "him who struck down the firstborn of Egypt" (V. 10; SEE ALSO EXODUS 12:29–30).

Doesn't that sound a bit like a shout of "nice shot" at the expense of someone else's mother, sister, father, brother?

That's why we need the rest of the story. Only when the lights come up in the resurrection of Jesus can the whole world be invited into the joy of one family's stories, tears, and laughter. Only when we receive Jesus as our Savior and are made alive in Him can we share the wonder of a God who loves everyone—at His own expense.   *MART DEHAAN*

What reason is given twenty-six times for this song?
What lyrics show that the heart of God reaches beyond those who sing the words?

Unseen Father, thank You for giving me reasons to believe that Your vision and love for all are better and wider than my love for myself and my own.

The one who trusts in the LORD ... will be like a tree
planted by the water. [JEREMIAH 17:7–8]

SURVIVING DROUGHT

In April 2019, a suburban neighborhood in Victorville, California, became buried in tumbleweeds. High winds pushed the rolling thistles into the development from the adjacent Mojave Desert where the plant grows. At maturity, the pesky weed can grow to up to six feet in height—a formidable size when it releases itself from its roots to "tumble" with the wind to scatter its seeds.

Tumbleweeds are what I picture when I read Jeremiah's description of a person "whose heart turns away from the Lord" (JEREMIAH 17:5). He says that those who draw their strength from "mere flesh" will be like "a bush in the wastelands" and be unable to "see prosperity when it comes" (VV. 5–6). In sharp contrast are those who put their trust in God instead of people. Like trees, their strong, deep roots draw strength from Him, enabling them to remain full of life, even in the midst of drought-like circumstances.

Tumbleweeds and trees both have roots. Tumbleweeds, however, don't stay connected to their life-source, causing them to dry out and die. Trees, on the other hand, remain connected to their roots, enabling them to flourish and thrive, anchored to that which will sustain them in times of difficulty. When we hold fast to God, drawing strength and encouragement from the wisdom found in the Bible and talking to Him in prayer, we too can experience the life-giving, life-sustaining nourishment He provides.

KIRSTEN HOLMBERG

How has God sustained you in times of drought? What can you do today to drive your roots more deeply into relationship with Him?

Life-giving God, You're my sustainer. Thank You for giving me what I need to navigate my struggles and hardships.

As I was with Moses, so I will be with you;
I will never leave you nor forsake you. [JOSHUA 1:5]

STRONG AND COURAGEOUS

Each night, as young Caleb closed his eyes, he felt the darkness envelop him. The silence of his room was regularly suspended by the creaking of the wooden house in Costa Rica. Then the bats in the attic became more active. His mother had put a night-light in his room, but the young boy still feared the dark. One night Caleb's dad posted a Bible verse on the footboard of his bed. It read: "Be strong and courageous. Do not be afraid; . . . for the LORD your God will be with you" (JOSHUA 1:9). Caleb began to read those words each night—and he left that promise from God on his foot-board until he went away to college.

In Joshua 1, we read of the transition of leadership to Joshua after Moses died. The command to "be strong and courageous" was repeated several times to Joshua and the Israelites to empha-size its importance (VV. 6–7, 9). Surely, they felt trepidation as they faced an uncertain future, but God reassuringly said, "As I was with Moses, so I will be with you; I will never leave you nor forsake you" (V. 5).

It's natural to have fears, but it's detrimental to our physical and spiritual health to live in a state of constant fear. Just as God encouraged His servants of old, we too can be strong and coura-geous because of the One who promises to always be with us.

CINDY HESS KASPER

What are your deepest and most persistent fears? How can meditating on God's promises help you overcome your fear and anxiety?

Faithful Father, thank You that You're always with me. Help me to remember Your promises and to trust in You when I'm afraid.

Let them praise the name of the LORD,
for his name alone is exalted. [PSALM 148:13]

PRAYERS ON LA PLAYA

During a trip to celebrate our twenty-fifth anniversary, my husband and I read our Bibles on the beach. As vendors passed and called out the prices of their wares, we thanked each one but didn't buy anything. One vendor, Fernando, smiled wide at my rejection and insisted we consider buying gifts for friends. After I declined his invitation, Fernando packed up and began walking away . . . still grinning. "I pray God will bless your day," I said.

Fernando turned toward me and said, "He has! Jesus changed my life." Fernando knelt between our chairs. "I feel His presence here." He then shared how God had delivered him from drug and alcohol abuse more than fourteen years earlier.

My tears flowed as he recited entire poems from the book of Psalms and prayed for us. Together, we praised God and rejoiced in His presence . . . on *la playa*.

Psalm 148 is a prayer of praise. The psalmist encourages all of creation to "praise the name of the LORD, for at his command [everything was] created" (V. 5), "for his name alone is exalted; his splendor is above the earth and the heavens" (V. 13).

Though God invites us to bring our needs before Him and trust He hears and cares for us, He also delights in prayers of grateful praise wherever we are. Even on the beach.   *XOCHITL DIXON*

What will you praise God for today? How has He inspired you to praise Him after hearing someone else's story?

Help me praise You with every breath You've given me, God.

But as for me, I watch in hope for the LORD.
[MICAH 7:7]

CHOOSING HOPE

I am one of millions of people worldwide who suffer from SAD (seasonal affective disorder), a type of depression common in places with limited sunlight due to short winter days. When I begin to fear winter's frozen curse will never end, I'm eager for any evidence that longer days and warmer temperatures are coming.

The first signs of spring—flowers successfully braving their way through the lingering snow—also powerfully remind me of the way God's hope can break through even our darkest seasons. The prophet Micah confessed this even while enduring a heart-rending "winter" as the Israelites turned away from God. As Micah assessed the bleak situation, he lamented that "not one upright person" seemed to remain (MICAH 7:2).

Yet, even though the situation appeared dire, the prophet refused to give up hope. He trusted that God was at work (V. 7)— even if, amid the devastation, he couldn't yet see the evidence.

In our dark and sometimes seemingly endless "winters," when spring doesn't appear to be breaking through, we face the same struggle as Micah. Will we give into despair? Or will we "watch in hope for the LORD"? (V. 7).

Our hope in God is never wasted (ROMANS 5:5). He's bringing a time with no more "winter": a time with no more mourning or pain (REVELATION 21:4). Until then, may we rest in Him, confessing, "My hope is in you" (PSALM 39:7).　　　　　　　　　　*LISA M. SAMRA*

Where do you find hope in dark times? In what "winter" season has God given you the hope you needed?

Heavenly Father, during difficult seasons of life, it's easy for me to be discouraged; in those hard times, help me place my hope in You. And in every season of my life, help me share with others the peace found in life with You.

He poured it out before the LORD.
[2 SAMUEL 23:16]

WHO'S IT FOR?

The picture made me laugh out loud. Crowds had lined a Mexican avenue, waving flags and throwing confetti as they waited for the pope. Down the middle of the street strolled a stray puppy, appearing to grin as if the cheering was entirely for him. Yes! Every dog should have its day, and it should look like this.

It's cute when a puppy "steals the show," but hijacking another's praise can destroy us. David knew this, and he refused to drink the water his mighty warriors had risked their lives to get. He had wistfully said it would be great if someone would fetch a drink from the well in Bethlehem. Three of his soldiers took him literally. They broke through enemy lines, drew the water, and carried it back. David was overwhelmed by their devotion, and he had to pass it on. He refused to drink the water, but "poured it out before the LORD" as a drink offering (2 SAMUEL 23:16).

How we respond to praise and honor says a lot about us. When praise is directed toward others, especially God, stay out of the way. The parade isn't for us. When the honor is directed toward us, thank the person and then amplify that praise by giving all the glory to Jesus. The "water" isn't for us either. Give thanks, then pour it out before God.   *MIKE WITTMER*

What praise for yourself or others did you hear today?
How did your heart respond?

God, may words of praise to You be continually on my lips.
You alone deserve the praise!

We have different gifts, . . . if it is to show mercy, do it cheerfully. [ROMANS 12:6, 8]

A TRUCK DRIVER'S HANDS

The news came as a shock. Having already survived prostate cancer, my father had now been diagnosed with pancreatic cancer. To complicate matters, my father is my mother's full-time caregiver, attending to her own chronic illnesses. With both parents needing care, there would be some difficult days ahead.

After flying home to be with them, I visited my parents' church one Sunday. There, a man named Helmut approached me, saying he'd like to help. Two days later, Helmut visited our home with a checklist. "You'll need some meals when the chemotherapy starts," he said. "I'll arrange a cooking roster. What about the mowing? I can do that. And what day is your rubbish collected?" Helmut was a retired truck driver, but to us he became an angel. We discovered he often helped others—single mothers, the homeless, the elderly.

While believers in Jesus are called to help others (LUKE 10:25–37), some have a special capacity to do so. The apostle Paul calls it the gift of mercy (ROMANS 12:8). People with this gift spot needs, rally practical assistance, and can serve over time without getting overwhelmed. Moved by the Holy Spirit, they're the hands of the body of Christ, reaching out to touch our wounds (VV. 4–5).

Dad recently had his first day of chemotherapy. Helmut drove him to the hospital. That night my parents' fridge was full of meals. God's mercy through a truck driver's hands.   *SHERIDAN VOYSEY*

What spiritual gifts do you have? (If unsure, check out Romans 12:3–8; 1 Corinthians 12; and Ephesians 4:7–13.) How are you using them to serve others?

Heavenly Father, help me to be filled with Your mercy, so that I might serve those in need powerfully and cheerfully, revealing who You are.

To Titus, my true son in our common faith.
[TITUS 1:4]

EVERYONE NEEDS A MENTOR

As I walked into my new supervisor's office, I was feeling wary and emotionally raw. My old supervisor had run our department with harshness and condescension, often leaving me (and others) in tears. Now I wondered, *What would my new boss be like?* Soon after I stepped into my new boss' office, I felt my fears dissipate as he welcomed me warmly and asked me to share about myself and my frustrations. He listened intently, and I *knew* by his kind expression and gentle words that he truly cared. A believer in Jesus, he became my work mentor, encourager, and friend.

The apostle Paul was a spiritual mentor to Titus, his "true son in our common faith" (TITUS 1:4). In his letter to Titus, Paul offered him helpful instructions and guidelines for his role in the church. He not only taught but modeled how to "teach what is appropriate to sound doctrine" (2:1), set "an example by doing what is good," and "show integrity, seriousness and soundness of speech" (VV. 7–8). As a result, Titus became his partner, brother, and coworker (2 CORINTHIANS 2:13; 8:23)—and a mentor of others.

Many of us have benefited from a mentor—a teacher, coach, grandparent, youth leader, or pastor—who guided us with their knowledge, wisdom, encouragement, and faith in God. Who could benefit from the spiritual lessons you've learned in your journey with Jesus?   *ALYSON KIEDA*

Who's been a spiritual mentor to you? For whom have you been a mentor? And whom might you mentor?

Father, I'm thankful for all those who mentored me when I needed them most. Guide me to someone who might need my encouragement today.

The LORD gave and the LORD has taken away;
may the name of the LORD be praised. [JOB 1:21]

STICKS, BRICKS, AND GOD

After praying about what God was calling them to do in the next phase of their lives, Mark and Nina determined that moving to the urban core of the city was what they needed to do. They purchased a vacant house and renovation was well underway—then came the storm. Mark wrote in a text message to me: "We had a surprise this morning. The tornado that came through Jefferson City, took out our renovation—down to sticks and bricks. God is up to something."

Uncontrollable storms are not the only things that surprise us and create confusion in our lives. Not losing sight of God in the midst of misfortune, however, is one of the keys of survival.

The weather catastrophe in Job's life that resulted in his loss of property and the death of his children (JOB 1:19) was but one of the shocking surprises he faced. Prior to that, three messengers had come bearing bad news (VV. 13–17).

On any given day, we can go from feasting to mourning, from celebrating life to processing death, or some other life challenge. Our lives can swiftly be reduced to "sticks and bricks"—financially, relationally, physically, emotionally, spiritually. But God is mightier than any storm. Surviving life's trials requires faith that's focused on Him—faith that enables us to say with Job and others, "May the name of the LORD be praised" (V. 21).   *ARTHUR JACKSON*

What has helped to clear your vision when you've lost sight of God? What can you learn from Job that will help you when the storms of life come?

Father, forgive me for the times I lose sight of You in the midst of life's difficulties. Help me to see You with fresh eyes.

SELFLESS SERVICE

Anita glanced at the bags of unopened food in the cafeteria, and then at the only other volunteer available to help me host a breakfast event for eighty people. Time was short. Sensing our need, she smiled as she offered her assistance.

As we mixed batter and flipped pancakes, I learned Anita was providing in-home care for her mother who had dementia. She also said she'd hired a caretaker that morning so she could have some free time, but had gladly given it up to help with the event.

Anita's selflessness reflected Jesus' attitude as He served others during His earthly ministry. In one memorable example, He set aside His own concerns to wash the disciples' feet during the Last Supper. Jesus knew He would soon face intense physical, mental, and emotional distress. Despite this burden, He considered what His followers needed most and taught them an important lesson.

> *May we listen even better to others...*

As Jesus prepared to wash their feet, He shed His right to be served as easily as He took off His outer garment (JOHN 13:4). He was the most important person present—the wise rabbi, *divinity in human flesh.* Yet Jesus gave up His rights, as He knelt down to rub dirt from callouses, to rinse dust from aching arches. Afterward He said, "Now that I, your Lord and Teacher, have washed your feet, you also should wash one another's feet" (JOHN 13:14).

Jesus wasn't simply advocating for good deeds. He was showing us that servanthood—in big or small things—is most meaningful when we leave our "selves" behind to lift others up. This month, by God's power, may we listen even better to others, accept them, and provide for them—pointing them to Jesus. He's the One who "did not come to be served, but to serve, and to give His life as a ransom for many" (MARK 10:45).

JENNIFER BENSON SCHULDT, OUR DAILY BREAD *AUTHOR*

If anyone gives even a cup of cold water...
that person will certainly not
lose their reward. [MATTHEW 10:42]

★ *NOVEMBER TOPIC: SERVICE*

EVEN A TACO

Ashton and Austin Samuelson graduated from a Christian college with a strong desire to serve Jesus. However, neither felt called to a traditional ministry in the church. But what about ministry in the world? Absolutely. They blended their burden to end childhood hunger with their God-given entrepreneurial skills, and in 2014 launched a restaurant that serves tacos. But this isn't just any restaurant. The Samuelsons operate from a buy-one-give-one philosophy. For every meal bought, they donate money to provide a meal specifically designed to meet the nutritional needs of malnourished children. So far, they've made contributions in more than sixty countries. Their goal is to be a part of ending childhood hunger—one taco at a time.

Jesus' words in Matthew 10 are not cryptic. They are astoundingly clear: devotion is evidenced by actions, not words (VV. 37–42). One of those actions is giving to the "little ones." For the Samuelsons, that focus is giving to children. But take note, the "little ones" isn't a phrase limited to chronological age. Christ is calling us to give to any who are of "little account" in the eyes of this world: the poor, the sick, the prisoner, the refugee, those disadvantaged in any way. And give what? Well, Jesus says "even a cup of cold water" (V. 42). If something as small and simple as a cup of cold water classifies, then a taco surely fits right in line too.

JOHN BLASE

**Who in your life are little in the eyes of the world? What's
something small you can do today to serve these "little ones"?**

*Jesus, give me eyes to see and ears to hear today, so that I can serve,
even in a small way, the least of these who cross my path.*

Let it be known today that you are God.
[1 KINGS 18:36]

GOD HEARS EVERYTHING

One of the longest-recorded postal delays in history lasted eighty-nine years. In 2008 a homeowner in the UK received an invitation to a party originally mailed in 1919 to a former resident of her address. The note was placed in her mailbox via the Royal Mail, but the reason behind its long delay remains a mystery.

Even the best human efforts at communication sometimes let us down, but Scripture makes clear that God never fails to hear His faithful people. In 1 Kings 18, Elijah demonstrated the striking contrast between the pagan god Baal and Jehovah God. In a showdown to demonstrate who the true God was, after Baal's prophets had prayed for hours, Elijah taunted them: "Shout louder! . . . Surely he is a god! Perhaps he is deep in thought, or busy, or traveling. Maybe he is sleeping and must be awakened" (V. 27). Then Elijah prayed for Jehovah to answer so that His people might return to faith, and God's power was clearly displayed.

While our prayers may not always be answered as immediately as Elijah's was, we can be assured that God hears them (PSALM 34:17). The Bible reminds us that He treasures our prayers so much that He keeps them before Him in "golden bowls," like precious incense (REVELATION 5:8). God will answer every prayer in His own perfect wisdom and way. There are no lost letters in heaven.   *JAMES BANKS*

What does it mean to you that God cares enough to listen to your prayers? How will you thank Him for His faithfulness to hear you today?

Father, how amazing You are to always hear my prayers! I praise You because my prayers are precious to You.

Let your gentleness be evident to all.
[PHILIPPIANS 4:5]

ZAX NATURE

I n one of Dr. Seuss' whimsical stories, he tells of a "North-Going Zax and a South-Going Zax" crossing the Prairie of Prax. Upon meeting nose to nose, neither Zax will step aside. The first Zax angrily vows to stay put—even if it makes "the whole world stand still." (Unfazed, the world moves on and builds a highway around them.)

The tale offers an uncomfortably accurate picture of human nature. We possess a reflexive "need" to be right, and we're prone to stubbornly cling to that instinct in rather destructive ways!

Happily for us, God lovingly chooses to soften stubborn human hearts. The apostle Paul knew this, so when two members of the Philippian church were squabbling, he loved them enough to call them out (PHILIPPIANS 4:2). Then, having earlier instructed the believers to have "the same mindset" of self-giving love as Christ (2:5–8), Paul asked them to "help these women," valued coworkers with him in sharing the gospel (4:3). It seems peacemaking and wise compromise call for team effort.

Of course there are times to take a firm stand, but a Christlike approach will look a lot different than an unyielding Zax! So many things in life aren't worth fighting over. We can bicker with each other over every trivial concern until we destroy ourselves (GALATIANS 5:15). Or we can swallow our pride, graciously receive wise counsel, and seek unity with our brothers and sisters.

TIM GUSTAFSON

**What are the things you're fighting over right now?
How could wise friends help you resolve your situation?**

*Soften my hardened, stubborn heart, loving God, so I can truly live in
unity. And help me to be open to wise counsel.*

Four things on earth are small,
yet they are extremely wise. [PROVERBS 30:24]

RELAXING WITH PURPOSE

Ramesh loves to tell others about Jesus. He boldly speaks with coworkers, and one weekend each month returns to his village to evangelize from house to house. His enthusiasm is contagious—especially since he's learned the value of taking time to rest and relax.

Ramesh used to spend every weekend and most evenings proclaiming the gospel. His wife and children missed him when he was out, and they found him exhausting when he was around. He needed to make every minute and conversation count. He couldn't enjoy games or small talk. Ramesh was wound too tight.

He was awakened to his imbalance by the honest words of his wife, the counsel of friends, and somewhat obscure passages of Scripture. Proverbs 30 mentions trivial things, such as ants, roosters, and locusts. It marvels how "a lizard can be caught with the hand, yet it is found in kings' palaces" (V. 28).

Ramesh wondered how something so mundane made it into the Bible. Observing lizards required significant downtime. Someone saw a lizard darting around the palace and thought *that's interesting*, and paused to watch some more. Perhaps God included it in His Word to remind us to balance work with rest. We need hours to daydream about lizards, catch one with our kids, and simply relax with family and friends. May God give us wisdom to know when to work, serve, and relax!   *MIKE WITTMER*

How are you balancing work and rest? Would those closest to you say that you love them? Why or why not?

Jesus, Your love frees me for productive work and meaningful rest.

Destroy this temple, and I will raise it again
in three days. [JOHN 2:19]

DESTROY THIS HOUSE

I n Pontiac, Michigan, a demolition company bulldozed the wrong
building. Investigators believe that the owner of a house sched-
uled to be demolished nailed the numbers of his own address
to a neighbor's house to avoid demolition.

Jesus did the opposite. He was on a mission to let his own
"house" be torn down for the sake of others. Imagine the scene
and how confused everyone must have been, including Jesus' own
disciples. Picture them eyeing one another as He challenged the
religious leaders: "Destroy this temple," Christ said, "and I will raise
it again in three days" (JOHN 2:19). The leaders retorted indignantly,
"It has taken forty-six years to build this temple, and you are going
to raise it in three days?" (V. 20). But Jesus knew He was referring to
the temple of His own body (V. 21). They didn't.

They didn't understand He had come to show that the harm we
do to ourselves and to one another would ultimately fall on Him.
He would atone for it.

God has always known our hearts far better than we do. So He
didn't entrust the fullness of His plans even to those who saw His
miracles and believed in Him (VV. 23–25). Then as now He was slowly
revealing the love and goodness in Jesus' words that we couldn't
understand even if He told us.   *MART DEHAAN*

**What emotions do you usually associate with Jesus' "cleansing
of the temple"? How can you see something more merciful and
compassionate now that you understand what Jesus meant?**

*Father in heaven, please help me to believe that You are always
working in the background doing far more—and much better—
than I know or understand.*

"I am the vine; you are the branches.
If you remain in me and I in you, you will bear
much fruit." [JOHN 15:5]

THE SWEETEST HARVEST

When we purchased our home, we inherited an established grapevine. As gardening novices, my family invested considerable time learning how to prune, water, and care for it. When our first harvest came, I popped a grape from the vine into my mouth—only to be disappointed with an unpleasant, sour taste.

The frustration I felt about painstakingly tending a grapevine, only to have a bitter harvest, echoes the tone of Isaiah 5. There we read an allegory of God's relationship to the nation of Israel. God, pictured as a farmer, had cleared the hillside of debris, planted good vines, built a watchtower for protection, and crafted a press to enjoy the results of His harvest (ISAIAH 5:1–2). To the farmer's dismay, the vineyard, representing Israel, produced sour-tasting grapes of selfishness, injustice, and oppression (V. 7). Eventually, God reluctantly destroyed the vineyard while saving a remnant of vines that someday would produce a good harvest.

In the gospel of John, Jesus revisits the vineyard illustration, saying, "I am the vine; you are the branches. If you remain in me and I in you, you will bear much fruit" (JOHN 15:5). In this parallel imagery, Jesus pictures believers in Him as grapevine branches connected to Him, the main vine. Now, as we remain connected to Jesus through prayerful reliance on His Spirit, we have direct access to the spiritual nourishment that will produce the sweetest fruit of all, love.

LISA M. SAMRA

How does remaining connected to Jesus produce love in your life? What are the other blessings of being connected to Him?

Jesus, thank You for creating good fruit in my life as I remain connected to You. May Your life flow through me to produce an even greater harvest of love in my life.

Do not rejoice that the spirits submit to you,
but rejoice that your names are written in heaven.
[LUKE 10:20]

LEAVE THE RESULTS TO GOD

Years ago, I was invited to speak to the residents of a university's fraternity house. They had a reputation for rowdiness so I brought along a friend for support. They were in a celebratory mood, having just won a football championship. At dinner, chaos reigned! Eventually, the president of the house announced: "There are two guys here that want to talk about God."

I rose on rubbery legs and began to tell them of God's love, and the room grew still. There was rapt attention. A vigorous and honest Q & A followed. Later, we started a Bible study there and in subsequent years many received salvation in Jesus.

I recall many days like that when I "saw Satan fall like lightning from heaven" (LUKE 10:18), but there were other days when it was I who fell—flat on my face.

Luke 10 tells of Jesus' disciples returning from a mission to report great success. Many had been brought into the kingdom, demons were put to flight, and people were healed. The disciples were pumped! Jesus replied, "I saw Satan fall like lightning from heaven." But then He issued a caveat: "Do not rejoice that the spirits submit to you, but rejoice that your names are written in heaven" (V. 20).

We delight in success. But we may despair when we seem to fail. Keep doing what God has called you to do—and leave the results to Him. He has your name in His book! *DAVID H. ROPER*

Picture your name written on God's heart.
How does that encourage you to carry on when things go well?
And when things go wrong?

Thank You, God, when You grant me victory over my enemies, but also help me to be strong when I fail. I'm grateful to be in Your family.

We are co-workers in God's service; you are God's field, God's building. [1 CORINTHIANS 3:9]

★ *NOVEMBER TOPIC: SERVICE*

WORKING WITH GOD

During his 1962 visit to Mexico, Bill Ashe helped fix windmill hand pumps at an orphanage. Fifteen years later, inspired by a deep desire to serve God by helping provide clean water to villages in need, Bill founded a nonprofit organization. He said, "God awoke me to 'make the most of the time' by finding others with a desire to bring safe drinking water to the rural poor." Later, having learned about the global need for safe water through the requests of thousands of pastors and evangelists from more than 100 countries, Bill invited others to join the ministry's efforts.

God welcomes us to team up to serve with Him and others in various ways. When the people of Corinth argued over which teachers they preferred, the apostle Paul affirmed his role as a servant of Jesus and a teammate of Apollos, fully dependent on God for spiritual growth (1 CORINTHIANS 3:1–7). He reminds us that all work has God-given value (V. 8). Acknowledging the privilege of working with others while serving Him, Paul encourages us to build each other up as He transforms us in love (V. 9).

Though our mighty Father doesn't *need* our help to accomplish His great works, He equips us and invites us to partner with Him.

XOCHITL DIXON

How does leaving the results to God give you the courage to risk doing what seems impossible? What hard thing has He invited you to do with His help?

Father, thank You for providing all I need as You continue to accomplish great things in me.

Each of you should use whatever gift you have received to serve others, as faithful stewards of God's grace. [1 PETER 4:10]

DOING OUR ROLE

When two of my grandchildren tried out for the musical *Alice in Wonderland Jr.*, their hearts were set on getting leading roles. Maggie wanted to be young Alice, and Katie thought Mathilda would be a good role. But they were chosen to be *flowers*. Not exactly a ticket to Broadway.

Yet my daughter said the girls were "excited for their friends who got the [leading roles]. Their joy seemed greater cheering for their friends and sharing in their excitement."

What a picture of how our interactions with each other in the body of Christ should look! Every local church has what might be considered key roles. But it also needs the flowers—the ones who do vital but not-so-high-profile work. If others get roles we desire, may we choose to encourage them even as we passionately fulfill the roles God has given us.

In fact, helping and encouraging others is a way to show love for Him. Hebrews 6:10 says, "[God] will not forget your work and the love you have shown him as you have helped his people." And no gift from His hand is unimportant: "Each of you should use whatever gift you have received to serve others, as faithful stewards of God's grace" (1 PETER 4:10).

Imagine a church of encouragers diligently using their God-given gifts to His honor (HEBREWS 6:10). That makes for joy!　　*DAVE BRANON*

Do you know someone who received a position, task, or role you wanted, yet could use your encouragement? Why is it good to thank God for the tasks He's given you in serving others?

Sovereign God, help me not to focus on other roles, but to serve You in the sacred calling You've given me. Enable me to help others by a word of encouragement for what they do for You.

Blessed is the one whose transgressions
are forgiven, whose sins are covered. [PSALM 32:1]

THE TRIUMPH OF FORGIVENESS

Mack, having struggled with drug abuse and sexual sin, was desperate. Relationships he valued were in disarray, and his conscience was beating him up. In his misery, he found himself unannounced at a church asking to speak with a pastor. There he found relief in sharing his complicated story and in hearing about God's mercy and forgiveness.

Psalm 32 is believed to have been composed by David after his sexual sin. He compounded his wrongdoing by devising a sinister strategy that resulted in the death of the woman's husband (SEE 2 SAMUEL 11–12). While these ugly incidents were behind him, the effects of his actions remained. Psalm 32:3–4 describes the deep struggles he experienced before he acknowledged the ugliness of his deeds; the gnawing effects of unconfessed sin were undeniable. What brought relief? Relief began with confession to God and accepting the forgiveness He offers (V. 5).

What a great place for us to start—at the place of God's mercy— when we say or do things that cause hurt and harm to ourselves and others. The guilt of our sin need not be permanent. There's One whose arms are open wide to receive us when we acknowledge our wrongs and seek His forgiveness. We can join the chorus of those who sing, "Blessed is the one whose transgressions are forgiven, whose sins are covered" (V. 1).   *ARTHUR JACKSON*

Where do you run when you find yourself burdened by something you've done or said? When someone comes to you who's struggling with guilt, how do you advise them?

Father, forgive me for the times when temptation has won in my life. Help me always to run to You for forgiveness and to seek the forgiveness of others when needed.

In distant lands they will remember me...
and they will return. [ZECHARIAH 10:9]

RETURNING HOME

Walter Dixon had five days to honeymoon before he shipped off to the Korean War. Less than a year later, troops found Dixon's jacket on the battlefield, with letters from his wife stuffed in the pockets. Military officials informed his young wife that her husband had been killed in action. Actually, Dixon was alive and spent the next 2.5 years as a POW. Every waking hour, he plotted to get home. Dixon escaped five times but was always recaptured. Finally, he was set free. You can imagine the shock when he returned home!

God's people knew what it was to be captured, moved far away, and to long for home. Due to their rebellion against God, they were exiles. They woke each morning yearning to return, but they had no way to rescue themselves. Thankfully, God promised He'd not forgotten them. "I will restore them because I have compassion on them" (ZECHARIAH 10:6). He would meet the people's relentless ache for home, not because of their perseverance, but because of His mercy: "I will signal for them...and they will return" (VV. 8–9).

Our sense of exile may come because of our bad decisions or because of hardships beyond our control. Either way, God hasn't forgotten us. He knows our desire and will call to us. And if we'll answer, we'll find ourselves returning to Him—returning home.

WINN COLLIER

Where do you sense exile in your life? How are you hearing God calling you, showing you how to return home?

God, I feel far away from You. I know You're near, but I feel so distant. Would You help me to hear Your call? Would You bring me home?

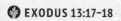

God did not lead them on the road through the
Philistine country, though that was shorter. [EXODUS 13:17]

THE LONG WAY

A s his peers were promoted one by one, Benjamin couldn't help but feel a little envious. "How come you're not a manager yet? You deserve it," friends told him. But Ben decided to leave his career to God. "If this is God's plan for me, I'll just do my job well," he replied.

Several years later, Ben was finally promoted. By then, his added experience enabled him to do his job confidently and won him the respect of subordinates. Some of his peers, meanwhile, were still struggling with their supervisory responsibilities, as they had been promoted before they were ready. Ben realized God had taken him the "long way around" so that he would be better prepared for his role.

When God led the Israelites out of Egypt (EXODUS 13:17–18), He chose a longer way because the "shortcut" to Canaan was fraught with risk. The longer journey, note Bible commentators, also gave them more time to strengthen themselves physically, mentally, and spiritually for subsequent battles.

The shortest way isn't always the best. Sometimes God lets us take the longer route in life, whether it's in our career or other endeavors, so that we'll be better prepared for the journey ahead. When things don't seem to happen quickly enough, we can trust in God—the One who leads and guides us.   *LESLIE KOH*

How might God be strengthening you by letting you take the "longer way" in life? How can you remind yourself to keep trusting Him?

Loving God, You know how I feel when things don't seem to happen quickly enough. Grant me the patience to trust in You and in Your sovereign plan and purpose.

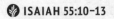

So is my word that goes out from my mouth:
It will not return to me empty. [ISAIAH 55:11]

WHEN GOD SPEAKS

Lily, a Bible translator, was flying home to her country when she was detained at the airport. Her mobile phone was searched, and when the officials found an audio copy of the New Testament on it, they confiscated the phone and questioned her for two hours. At one point they asked her to play the Scripture app, which happened to be set at Matthew 7:1–2: "Do not judge, or you too will be judged. For in the same way you judge others, you will be judged, and with the measure you use, it will be measured to you." Hearing these words in his own language, one of the officers turned pale. Later, she was released and no further action was taken.

We don't know what happened in that official's heart at the airport, but we know that the "word that goes out from [God's] mouth" accomplishes what He desires (ISAIAH 55:11). Isaiah prophesied these words of hope to God's people in exile, assuring them that even as the rain and snow make the earth bud and grow, so too what goes "out from [His] mouth" achieves His purposes (VV. 10–11).

We can read this passage to bolster our confidence in God. When we're facing unyielding circumstances, such as Lily with the airport officials, may we trust that God is working—even when we don't see the final outcome. *AMY BOUCHER PYE*

When was the last time you saw God at work? How have you received God's love through the words He has declared?

Heavenly Father, thank You for what You've revealed, which brings me hope, peace, and love. Help me to grow in my love for You.

I see four men walking around in the fire,
unbound and unharmed. [DANIEL 3:25]

INSIDE THE FIRE

A wildfire in Andilla, Spain, scorched nearly 50,000 acres of woodland. However, in the middle of the devastation, a group of nearly 1,000 bright green cypress trees remained standing. The trees' ability to retain water had allowed them to safely endure the fire.

During King Nebuchadnezzar's reign in Babylon, a small cluster of friends survived the flames of the king's wrath. Shadrach, Meshach, and Abednego refused to worship a statue Nebuchadnezzar had created, and they told him, "If we are thrown into the blazing furnace, the God we serve is able to deliver us from it" (DANIEL 3:17). Infuriated, the monarch cranked up the heat seven times hotter than normal (V. 19).

The soldiers who carried out the king's orders and tossed the friends into the blaze were burned up, yet onlookers watched Shadrach, Meshach, and Abednego walk around *inside* the flames "unbound and unharmed." Someone else was in the furnace as well—a fourth man who looked "like a son of the gods" (V. 25). Many scholars believe this was a preincarnate appearance of Jesus.

Jesus is with us when we face intimidation and trials. In the moments when we're urged to give in to pressure, we don't have to be afraid. We may not always know how or when God will help us, but we know He's with us. He'll give us the strength to stay faithful to Him through every "fire" we endure.   *JENNIFER BENSON SCHULDT*

Why is the supernatural comfort of God's presence encouraging to you? How can you support others who may be facing opposition?

Dear God, fill me with Your Spirit so that I can persevere when I feel pressured to give in. I want to honor You by standing strong.

Serve one another humbly in love.
[GALATIANS 5:13]

★ *NOVEMBER TOPIC: SERVICE*

BORROWED SHOES

I n the chaos of fleeing his home during the California wildfires of 2018, Gabe, a high school senior, missed the state-qualifying cross-country race for which he'd been training. Missing this meet meant he wouldn't have the chance to compete at the state meet—the culminating event of his four-year running career. In light of the circumstances, the state athletics board gave Gabe another chance: he'd have to run a qualifying time by himself, on a rival high school's track, in "street shoes" because his running shoes were in the charred rubble of his home. When he showed up to "race," Gabe was surprised by his competitors who had come to supply him with proper shoes and to run alongside him to ensure he kept the pace necessary to be entered in the state meet.

Gabe's opponents had no obligation to help him. They could have given into their natural desires to look out for themselves (GALATIANS 5:13); doing so might have improved their own odds of winning. But Paul urges us to display the fruit of the Spirit in our lives—to "serve one another humbly in love" and to demonstrate "kindness" and "goodness" (VV. 13, 22). When we lean on the Spirit to help us not act on our natural instincts, we're better able to love those around us.   *KIRSTEN HOLMBERG*

How are you showing the "fruit of the Spirit" in the way you treat others? How can you better love your "neighbor"?

Dear God, my natural desire is to look out for myself. Help me to serve others out of love for You.

Now faith is confidence in what we hope for and
assurance about what we do not see. [HEBREWS 11:1]

NO IMPOSSIBLE OBSTACLES

As an adult leader, I arranged a student field trip to an obstacle
course. We instructed students to slip into safety gear and
scale an eight-foot wall. Those who went first encouraged
each climber to trust the harness and keep moving forward without
looking down. One of our students stared at the barrier as we
secured belts and buckles around her waist. "There's no way I can
do this," she said. Affirming the strength of her harness, we encouraged her and cheered when she climbed up the wall and stepped
onto the high platform.

When we face problems that seem impossible to conquer,
fears and insecurities can cause doubts. The assurance of God's
unchanging might, goodness, and faithfulness creates a strong
harness of trust. This confident assurance fueled the courage of
the Old Testament saints, who demonstrated that faith trumps
our need to know every detail of God's plan (HEBREWS 11:1–13, 39).
With conviction, we seek God earnestly, often standing alone
when we trust Him. We can adjust the way we approach our challenges by viewing our circumstances with an eternal perspective—knowing our trials are only temporary (VV. 13–16).

Focusing on the steep climbs in life can prevent us from believing that God will bring us through. But knowing He's with us, we
can harness our uncertainties by faith as we trust God to help us
overcome obstacles that once seemed impossible.   XOCHITL DIXON

**How can you become more courageous in the face of an
impossible task? How do you feel when you've accomplished
something you didn't think you could do?**

*Father, thank You for being the Author and Perfecter of my faith,
so that the measure of my faith—when I face obstacles—is reliant on
Your strength not my own.*

The LORD is the strength of his people.
[PSALM 28:8]

IF ONLY WE COULD . . .

The weeping Alaskan cedar tree whipped from side to side in the storm's strong winds. Regie loved the tree that had not only provided shelter from the summer sun but also given her family privacy. Now the fierce storm was tearing the roots from the ground. Quickly, Regie, with her fifteen-year-old son in tow, ran to try to rescue the tree. With her hands and ninety-pound frame firmly planted against it, she and her son tried to keep it from falling over. But they weren't strong enough.

God was King David's strength when he called out to Him in another kind of storm (PSALM 28:8). Some commentators say he wrote this during a time when his world was falling apart. His own son rose in rebellion against him and tried to take the throne (2 SAMUEL 15). He felt so vulnerable and weak that he feared God might remain silent, and he would die (PSALM 28:1). "Hear my cry for mercy as I call to you for help," he said to God (V. 2). God gave David strength to go on, even though his relationship with his son never mended.

How we long to prevent bad things from happening! If only we could. But in our weakness, God promises we can always call to Him to be our Rock (VV. 1–2). When we don't have the strength, He's our shepherd and will carry us forever (VV. 8–9).   ANNE CETAS

**When have you felt vulnerable and unable to fix a situation?
How did you see God come through for you?**

*It seems there's always something for which I need extra strength
from You, O God. Help me to remember that without You I can
do nothing.*

I consider everything a loss because of the surpassing
worth of knowing Christ Jesus my Lord, for whose
sake I have lost all things. [PHILIPPIANS 3:8]

FALSE CONFIDENCE

A few years ago, my doctor gave me a stern talk about my
health. I took his words to heart and began going to the gym
and adjusting my diet. Over time, both my cholesterol and
my weight went down, and my self-esteem went up. But then
something not so good happened: I began noticing other people's
dietary choices and judging them. Isn't it funny that often when we
find a scoring system that grades us well, we use it to lift ourselves
up and put others down. It seems to be an innate human tendency
to cling to self-made standards in an attempt to justify ourselves—
systems of self-justification and guilt-management.

Paul warned the Philippians about doing such things. Some were
putting their confidence in religious performance or cultural confor-
mity, and Paul told them he had more reason to boast of such things:
"If someone else thinks they have reasons to put confidence in the
flesh, I have more" (3:4). Yet Paul knew his pedigree and performance
was "garbage" compared to "knowing Christ" (V. 8). Only Jesus loves
us as we are, rescues us, and gives us the power to become more
like Him. No earning required; no scorekeeping possible.

Boasting is bad in itself, but a boast based on false confidence is
tragic. The gospel calls us away from misplaced confidence and into
communion with a Savior who loves us and gave Himself for us.

GLENN PACKIAM

**What would it look like to trust in God's grace today? How can you
live and work from a place of rest and trust in His love for you?**

*Dear Jesus, thank You for Your love for me. I set aside the scorecards
of self-justification. Those are misguided grounds of confidence.*

I am the good shepherd; I know my sheep
and my sheep know me . . . and I lay down my life
for the sheep. [JOHN 10:14–15]

VALIANT ACTIONS

John Harper had no idea what was about to unfold as he and his six-year-old daughter embarked on the *Titanic*. But one thing he knew: he loved Jesus and he was passionate that others know Him too. As soon as the ship hit an iceberg and water started pouring in, Harper, a widower, put his little girl on a lifeboat and headed into the chaos to save as many people as possible. As he distributed life jackets he reportedly shouted, "Let the women, children, and the unsaved into the lifeboats." Until his last breath, Harper shared about Jesus with anyone who was around him. John willingly gave his life away so others could live.

There was One who laid down His life freely two thousand years ago so you and I can live not only in this life but for all eternity. Jesus didn't just wake up one day and decide He would pay the penalty of death for humanity's sin. This was His life's mission. At one point when He was talking with the Jewish religious leaders He repeatedly acknowledged "I lay down my life" (JOHN 10:11, 15, 17, 18). He didn't just say these words but lived them by actually dying a horrific death on the cross. He came so that the Pharisees, John Harper, and we "may have life, and have it to the full" (V. 10).

ESTERA PIROSCA ESCOBAR

How do you reveal that you truly love those around you? How can you show Jesus' love to someone through your actions today?

Jesus, there aren't words grand enough to thank You for demonstrating the greatest act of love there is. Thank You for giving Your life away so I might live. Help me to show Your love to others no matter how much it costs me.

Do not let the sun go down while you are still angry.
[EPHESIANS 4:26]

TURNING FROM CONFLICT

In his graveside tribute to a famous Dutch scientist, Albert Einstein didn't mention their scientific disputes. Instead, he recalled the "never-failing kindness" of Hendrik A. Lorentz, a beloved physicist known for his easy manner and fair treatment of others. "Everyone followed him gladly," Einstein said, "for they felt he never set out to dominate but always simply to be of use."

Lorentz inspired scientists to put aside political prejudice and work together, especially after World War I. "Even before the war was over," Einstein said of his fellow Nobel Prize winner, "[Lorentz] devoted himself to the work of reconciliation."

Working for reconciliation should be the goal of everyone in the church as well. True, some conflict is inevitable. Yet we must do our part to work for peaceful resolutions. Paul wrote, "Do not let the sun go down while you are still angry" (EPHESIANS 4:26). To grow together, the apostle advised, "Do not let any unwholesome talk come out of your mouths, but only what is helpful for building others up according to their needs" (V. 29).

Finally, said Paul, "Get rid of all bitterness, rage and anger, brawling and slander, along with every form of malice. Be kind and compassionate to one another, forgiving each other, just as in Christ God forgave you" (VV. 31–32). Turning from conflict whenever we are able helps build God's church. In this, indeed, we honor Him.   *PATRICIA RAYBON*

How can God help us deal with conflict? To honor Him and your church, what conflict should you let go?

Loving God, when I face conflict, remind my heart to turn my anger over to You.

If anyone is in Christ, the new creation has come:
The old has gone, the new is here! [2 CORINTHIANS 5:17]

HIS DEATH BRINGS LIFE

During her ministry to men incarcerated in South Africa's most violent prison, Joanna Flanders-Thomas witnessed the power of Christ to transform hearts. In *Vanishing Grace,* Philip Yancey describes her experience: "Joanna started visiting prisoners daily, bringing them a simple gospel message of forgiveness and reconciliation. She earned their trust, got them to talk about their abusive childhoods, and showed them a better way of resolving conflicts. The year before her visits began, the prison recorded 279 acts of violence against inmates and guards; the next year there were two."

The apostle Paul wrote, "If anyone is in Christ, the new creation has come: The old has gone, the new is here!" (2 CORINTHIANS 5:17). While we may not always see that newness expressed as dramatically as Flanders-Thomas did, the gospel's power to transform is the greatest hope-providing force in the universe. New creations. What an amazing thought! The death of Jesus launches us on a journey of becoming like Him—a journey that will culminate when we see Him face to face (SEE 1 JOHN 3:1–3).

As believers in Jesus we celebrate our life as new creations. Yet we must never lose sight of what that cost Christ. His death brings us life. "God made him who had no sin to be sin for us, so that in him we might become the righteousness of God" (2 CORINTHIANS 5:21).   *BILL CROWDER*

**How has Jesus' transforming work been evidenced in your life?
What areas are still in need of that "new creation" impact?**

Loving Father, thank You that, because of what Jesus accomplished on the cross, I am a new creation. Forgive me for the times I return to the old things that need to pass away.

Whatever you do, do it all for the glory of God.
[1 CORINTHIANS 10:31]

★ *NOVEMBER TOPIC: SERVICE*

LIVING ON PURPOSE

"**W**e're going on vacation!" my wife enthusiastically told our three-year-old grandson Austin as we pulled out of the driveway on the first leg of our trip. Little Austin looked at her thoughtfully and responded, "I'm not going on vacation. I'm going on a mission!"

We're not sure where our grandson picked up the concept of going "on a mission," but his comment gave me something to ponder as we drove to the airport: *As I leave on this vacation and take a break for a few days, am I keeping in mind that I'm still "on a mission" to live each moment with and for God? Am I remembering to serve Him in everything I do?*

The apostle Paul encouraged the believers living in Rome, the capital city of the Roman Empire, to "never be lacking in zeal, but keep your spiritual fervor, serving the Lord" (ROMANS 12:11). His point was that our life in Jesus is meant to be lived intentionally and with enthusiasm. Even the most mundane moments gain new meaning as we look expectantly to God and live for His purposes.

As we settled into our seats on the plane, I prayed, "Lord, I'm yours. Whatever you have for me to do on this trip, please help me not to miss it."

Every day is a mission of eternal significance with Him!

JAMES BANKS

Have you ever been on a mission?
How can you make life all about God?

Please give me grace to live for You, Jesus, so that I may one day hear You say, "Well done, good and faithful servant!" (MATTHEW 25:23).

Jesus went up on a mountainside and called to him
those he wanted, and they came to him. [MARK 3:13]

SPACE FOR ME

He was an aging military veteran, rough-edged and given to even rougher language. One day a friend cared enough about him to inquire about his spiritual beliefs. The man's dismissive response came quickly: "God doesn't have space for someone like me."

Perhaps that was just part of his "tough-guy" act, but his words couldn't be further from the truth! God creates space *especially* for the rough, the guilt-ridden, and the excluded to belong and thrive in His community. This was obvious from the beginning of Jesus' ministry, when He made some surprising choices for His disciples. First, He chose several fishermen from Galilee—the "wrong side of the tracks" from the perspective of those in Jerusalem. He also selected a tax collector, Matthew, whose profession included extorting from his oppressed countrymen. Then, for good measure, Jesus invited the "other" Simon—"the Zealot" (MARK 3:18).

We don't know much about this Simon (he isn't Simon Peter), but we do know about the Zealots. They hated traitors like Matthew, who got rich by collaborating with the despised Romans. Yet with divine irony, Jesus chose Simon along with Matthew, brought them together, and blended them into His team.

Don't write anyone off as too "bad" for Jesus. After all, He said, "I have not come to call the righteous, but sinners to repentance" (LUKE 5:32). He has plenty of space for the tough cases—people like you and me.   *TIM GUSTAFSON*

Who do you know that you think is unlikely to give their life to Jesus? How might you invite them to consider who Christ is and the space He has for them?

Dear Father, thank You that salvation is available to anyone who puts their faith in Jesus.

Look at the birds of the air; they do not sow or reap
or store away in barns, and yet your heavenly Father
feeds them. [MATTHEW 6:26]

TAUGHT BY TURKEYS

Do you know what a group of turkeys is called? It's called a
rafter. Why am I writing about turkeys? Because I've just
returned from a weekend at a mountain cabin. Each day, I
marveled at the train of turkeys parading past our porch.

I'd never turkey-watched before. They scratched fiercely with
spectacular talons. Then they hunted and pecked at the ground.
Eating, I assume. (Since this was my first turkey-observation time, I
wasn't 100 percent positive.) The scrawny scrubs in the area didn't
look like they could sustain anything. Yet here were these turkeys,
a dozen of them, all of which looked delectably plump.

Watching those well-fed turkeys brought to mind Jesus' words
in Matthew 6:26: "Look at the birds of the air; they do not sow or
reap or store away in barns, and yet your heavenly Father feeds
them. Are you not much more valuable than they?" Jesus uses
God's provision for seemingly worthless birds to remind us of His
care for us. If a bird's life matters, how much more does ours? Jesus
then contrasts fretting about our daily needs (VV. 27–31) with a life in
which we "seek first his kingdom and his righteousness" (V. 33), one
in which we're confident of His rich provision for our needs. Because
if God can care for that rafter of wild turkeys, He can certainly look
after you and me.   *ADAM R. HOLZ*

**Where have you seen God provide for something that you were
worrying about? How might remembering and reflecting on His
provision in the past help us not to be anxious in the future?**

*Father, sometimes I get scared. I worry. I struggle to trust. Thank You
for Your care for me. Help me to remember Your provision in the past
so I'm better able to trust You with future fears.*

Everyone who calls on the name of the Lord
will be saved. [ROMANS 10:13]

ANYONE AND EVERYONE

The country of El Salvador has honored Jesus by placing a sculpture of Him in the center of its capital city. Although the monument resides in the middle of a busy traffic circle, its height makes it easy to see, and its name—*The Divine Savior of the World*—communicates reverence for His supernatural status.

The monument's name affirms what the Bible says about Jesus (1 JOHN 4:14). He's the One who offers salvation to everyone. Jesus crosses cultural boundaries and accepts any sincere person who wants to know Him, regardless of age, education, ethnicity, past sin, or social status.

The apostle Paul traveled the ancient world telling people about Jesus' life, death, and resurrection. He shared this good news with political and religious authorities, soldiers, Jews, gentiles, men, women, and children. Paul explained that a person could begin a relationship with Christ by declaring "Jesus is Lord" and believing that God had indeed raised Him from the dead (ROMANS 10:9). He said, "Anyone who believes in him will never be put to shame. . . . Everyone who calls on the name of the Lord will be saved" (VV. 11, 13).

Jesus isn't a distant image to be honored; we must have a person-to-person connection with Him through faith. May we see the value of the salvation He offers and move forward into a spiritual relationship with Him today.   *JENNIFER BENSON SCHULDT*

How can you get closer to Jesus today? Do you follow Paul's "anyone and everyone" approach to sharing the good news about Jesus?

Jesus, thank You for loving everyone and offering eternal life to anyone who truly wants to know You. Help me to represent You well in the world today.

Give praise to the LORD, proclaim his name;
make known among the nations what he has done.
[ISAIAH 12:4]

GIVING THANKS ALWAYS

I n the seventeenth century, Martin Rinkart served as a clergyman in Saxony, Germany, for more than thirty years during times of war and plague. One year he conducted more than 4,000 funerals, including his wife's, and at times food was so scarce that his family went hungry. Although he could have despaired, his faith in God remained strong and he gave thanks continually. In fact, he poured his gratitude into *"Nun danket alle Gott,"* the song that became the well-loved English hymn, "Now Thank We All Our God."

Rinkart followed the example of the prophet Isaiah, who instructed God's people to give thanks at all times, including when they'd disappointed God (ISAIAH 12:1) or when enemies oppressed them. Even then they were to exalt God's name, making "known among the nations what he has done" (V. 4).

We might give thanks easily during harvest celebrations such as Thanksgiving, when we're enjoying an abundant feast with friends and family. But can we express our gratitude to God in difficult times, such as when we're missing someone from our table or when we're struggling with our finances or when we're locked in conflict with one close to us?

Let's echo Pastor Rinkart, joining hearts and voices as we give praise and thanks to "the eternal God, whom earth and Heaven adore." We can "sing to the LORD, for he has done glorious things" (V. 5). *AMY BOUCHER PYE*

In times of hardship, how do you turn to thanksgiving and praise? What role does God through His Holy Spirit play in this?

Father God, I thank You for Your amazing work in my life. You love me unendingly, more than I can even express.

Look to the LORD and his strength;
seek his face always. [1 CHRONICLES 16:11]

FACING THE BATTLE

Not long ago I met up with a group of friends. As I listened to the conversation, it seemed like *everyone* in the room was facing some significant battle. Two of us had parents fighting cancer, one had a child with an eating disorder, another friend was experiencing chronic pain, and another was facing major surgery. It seemed a lot for a bunch of people in their thirties and forties.

First Chronicles 16 recounts a key moment in Israel's history when the ark of the covenant was brought into the City of David (Jerusalem). Samuel tells us it happened in a moment of peace between battles (2 SAMUEL 7:1). When the ark was in place, symbolizing God's presence, David led the people in a song of praise (1 CHRONICLES 16:8–36). Together the nation sang of God's wonder-working power, His promise-keeping ways, and His past protection (VV. 12–22). "Look to the LORD and his strength," they cried out; "seek his face always" (V. 11). They'd need to, because more battles were coming.

Look to the Lord and His strength. Seek His face. That's not bad advice to follow when illness, family concerns, and other battles confront us, because we haven't been left to fight in our own waning energies. God is present; God is strong; He's looked after us in the past and will do so again.

Our God will get us through. *SHERIDAN VOYSEY*

**What battle do you need God's power to face right now?
How can you hand your struggle to Him?**

Wonder-working God, I hand over this battle to You. I trust in Your strength and Your promises.

All the days ordained for me were written in your
book before one of them came to be. [PSALM 139:16]

BREATH AND BREVITY

Mom, my sisters, and I waited by Dad's bed as his breaths
became shallower and less and less frequent—until they
were no more. Dad was a few days shy of eighty-nine when
he slipped quietly into the life beyond where God awaited him. His
departure left us with a void where he once resided and only
memories and mementos to remind us of him. Yet we have the
hope that one day we'll be reunited.

We have that hope because we believe Dad is with God, who
knows and loves him. When Dad breathed his first breath, God
was there breathing breath into his lungs (ISAIAH 42:5). Yet even
before his first and with every breath in between, God was intimately involved in each detail of Dad's life, just as He is in yours
and mine. It was God who wonderfully designed and "knit" him
together in the womb (PSALM 139:13–14). And when Dad breathed
his last breath, God's Spirit was there, holding him in love and carrying him to be with Him (VV. 7–10).

The same is true for all of God's children. Every moment of our
brief life on Earth is known by Him (VV. 1–4). We're precious to
Him. With each day remaining and in anticipation of the life
beyond, let's join with "everything that has breath" to praise Him.
"Praise the LORD"! (150:6).   *ALYSON KIEDA*

**How does knowing that God is intimately involved in your life give
you hope? How can you use your breath to praise Him?**

*Dear Lord, thank You for creating me and giving me breath—
and for giving me hope. In the sorrow and losses of life,
help me to cling to You.*

On this mountain the LORD Almighty will prepare
a feast of rich food for all peoples. [ISAIAH 25:6]

SWEET AGAIN

R ussian wedding customs are filled with beauty and significance. One such custom takes place during the reception as
the toastmaster proposes a toast in honor of the couple.
Everyone takes a sip from their raised glass and then shouts, *"Gor'ko!
Gor'ko!"* meaning "Bitter! Bitter!" When the guests shout that
word, the newlyweds must rise and kiss each other in order to
make the drink sweet again.

Isaiah prophesies that the bitter drink of desolation, ruin, and
the curse upon the earth (CH. 24) will give way to the sweet hope of
a new heaven and new earth (CH. 25). God will prepare a feast of
rich foods and the finest and sweetest of drinks. It will be a ban-
quet of continual blessing, fruitfulness, and provision for all people
(25:6). There's more. Under the sovereign reign of the righteous
King, death is swallowed up, bitter tears are wiped away, and the
shroud of disgrace is removed (VV. 7–8). And His people will rejoice
because the One they trusted in and waited for will bring salvation
and turn the bitter cup of life sweet again (V. 9).

One day, we'll be together with Jesus at the wedding supper of
the Lamb. When He welcomes His bride (the church) home, the
promise of Isaiah 25 will be fulfilled. The life once bitter will be
made sweet again.   *MARVIN WILLIAMS*

**What makes you long for God to make what is bitter sweet again?
While we wait for Jesus' return, what are some things you can do
to make others' bitter experience sweet again?**

*God, as I witness and experience so much pain, suffering, ruin, and
death, sometimes it's difficult to believe You'll make what is bitter
sweet again. Help me to put my hope in You, the One who's promised
to give me beauty for ashes and joy for mourning.*

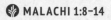

He will purify . . . and refine them like gold and silver.
Then the LORD will have men who will bring offerings
in righteousness. [MALACHI 3:3]

GIVING OUR BEST

We stared at the piles of donated shoes as we entered a local homeless shelter. The director had invited our youth group to help sort through the heaps of used footwear. We spent the morning searching for matches and lining them up in rows across the concrete floor. At the end of the day, we threw away more than half of the shoes because they were too damaged for others to use. Though the shelter couldn't stop people from giving poor quality items, they refused to distribute shoes that were in bad condition.

The Israelites struggled with giving God their damaged goods too. When He spoke through the prophet Malachi, He rebuked the Israelites for sacrificing blind, lame, or diseased animals when they had strong animals to offer (MALACHI 1:6–8). He announced His displeasure (V. 10), affirmed His worthiness, and reprimanded the Israelites for keeping the best for themselves (V. 14). But God also promised to send the Messiah, whose love and grace would transform their hearts and ignite their desire to bring offerings that would be pleasing to Him (3:1–4).

At times, it can be tempting to give God our leftovers. We praise Him and expect Him to give us His all, yet we offer Him our crumbs. When we consider all God has done, we can rejoice in celebrating His worthiness and giving Him our very best.   *XOCHITL DIXON*

Why are you sometimes tempted to give God your leftovers or damaged goods? In what ways will you give Him your best today?

Mighty God, please help me place You first and give You my best.

SPEAKING TO ENCOURAGE

Abraham Lincoln tops the polls as the most popular US president of all time. His troubled presidency came on top of a lifelong struggle with depression, a nervous breakdown, and his neighbors were known to set suicide watches over him in his youth.

So how did he do it? The night he was assassinated, Lincoln's pockets were stuffed with newspaper clippings that praised him, his leadership, and the positive impact he was having.

We all need encouragement. The author of Hebrews says in 10:23–25, "Let us hold unswervingly to the hope we profess, for he who promised is faithful. Consider how we may spur one another on toward love and good deeds, not giving up meeting together, as some are in the habit of doing, but encouraging one another—and all the more as you see the Day approaching."

Ephesians 4:29 says, "Do not let any unwholesome talk come out of your mouths, but only what is helpful for building others up according to their

> *Jesus didn't go it alone—He gathered a group of people.*

needs, that it may benefit those who listen." Imagine what could happen if we were able to live up to that in our homes, churches, and communities?

Don't go it alone. Hebrews 10:25 warns us not to give up meeting together. Jesus didn't go it alone—He gathered a group of people to share life and ministry with, and He asked His closest friends to watch and pray with Him when He needed it most. If Jesus sought out that kind of support, we should as well!

Let's be intentional about encouraging one another as we walk this journey together, so no one has to go it alone.

EXCERPTED FROM WORDS MATTER, *BY **JENNY RAE ARMSTRONG**.*
© OUR DAILY BREAD MINISTRIES.

They sat on the ground with him for seven days
and seven nights. [JOB 2:13]

★ *DECEMBER TOPIC: ENCOURAGEMENT*

BEING THERE

When Jen, a theme park employee, saw Ralph collapse in tears on the ground, she rushed to help. Ralph, a young boy with autism, was sobbing because the ride he'd waited all day to enjoy had broken down. Instead of hurrying him to his feet or simply urging him to feel better, Jen got down onto the ground *with* Ralph, validating his feelings and allowing him the time to cry.

Jen's actions are a beautiful example of how we can come alongside those who are grieving or suffering. The Bible tells of Job's crippling grief after the loss of his home, his herds (his income), his health, and the simultaneous deaths of his ten children. When Job's friends learned of his pain, they "set out from their homes . . . [to go] comfort him" (JOB 2:11). Job sat on the ground in mourning. When they arrived, his friends sat down with him—for seven days—saying nothing because they saw the depth of his suffering.

In their humanness, Job's friends later offered Job insensitive advice. But for the first seven days, they gave him the wordless and tender gift of presence. We may not understand someone's grief, but we don't need to understand in order to love them well by simply being *with* them.   *KIRSTEN HOLMBERG*

Who has been with you in difficult times? Who needs your presence today?

God, I thank You for being with me always—in good times and bad. Help me to offer that gift of presence to those You put in my path.

The virgin will conceive and give birth
to a son. [ISAIAH 7:14]

CHRISTMAS PRESENCE

"**N**o ear may hear His coming, but in this world of sin, where meek souls will receive Him still, the dear Christ enters in." Those words from Phillips Brooks' much-loved hymn "O Little Town of Bethlehem" point to the very heart of Christmas. Jesus came into our broken world to rescue us from our sin and give all who would put their faith in Him a new and vital relationship with God.

In a letter to a friend decades after he wrote the hymn, Brooks poignantly described the outcome of this relationship in his own life: "I cannot tell you how personal this grows to me. He is here. He knows me and I know Him. It is no figure of speech. It is the realest thing in the world, and every day makes it realer. And one wonders with delight what it will grow to as the years go on."

Brooks' calm assurance of God's presence in his life reflects one of the names of Jesus prophesied by Isaiah: "The virgin will conceive and give birth to a son, and will call him Immanuel" (ISAIAH 7:14). The gospel of Matthew gives us the meaning of the Hebrew name Immanuel: "God with us" (1:23).

God drew near to us through Jesus so we could know Him personally and be with Him forever. His loving presence with us is the greatest gift of all.   *JAMES BANKS*

What does it mean to you that God loves you so much He wants to be with you always? How will you draw near to Him today?

Loving God, thank You for giving Yourself to me through Your life on earth, death on the cross, and resurrection. Please help me to live for You today and forever!

Give my son Solomon the wholehearted devotion to keep
your commands, statutes and decrees. ⌈1 CHRONICLES 29:19
⌋

THE PRIVILEGE OF PRAYER

C ountry artist Chris Stapleton's deeply personal song,
"Daddy Doesn't Pray Anymore," was inspired by his own
father's prayers for him. The poignant lyrics reveal the reason
his father's prayers ended: not disillusionment or weariness, but his
own death. Stapleton imagines that now, instead of speaking with
Jesus in prayer, his dad is walking and talking face-to-face with Jesus.

Stapleton's recollection of his father's prayers for him brings
to mind a biblical father's prayer for his son. As King David's life
ebbed away, he made preparations for his son Solomon to take
over as the next king of Israel.

After assembling the nation together to anoint Solomon, David
led the people in prayer, as he'd done many times before. As
David recounted God's faithfulness to Israel, he prayed for the
people to remain loyal to Him. Then he included a personal prayer
specifically for his son, asking God to "give my son Solomon the
wholehearted devotion to keep your commands, statutes and
decrees" (1 CHRONICLES 29:19).

We too have the remarkable privilege to faithfully pray for the
people God has placed in our lives. Our example of faithfulness
can make an indelible impact that will remain even after we're
gone. Just as God continued to work out the answers to David's
prayers for Solomon and Israel after he was gone, so too the
impact of our prayers outlives us.   *LISA M. SAMRA*

**How have someone's prayers made a significant impact on your
life? How might you encourage others with your prayers?**

*Heavenly Father, I bring my loved ones before You and ask that You
would work out Your plans in their lives.*

Let us not love with words or speech
but with actions and in truth. [1 JOHN 3:18]

RELENTLESS LOVE

Heidi and Jeff came home from an overseas work assignment in a hot climate and settled for several months near family in the state of Michigan—just in time for winter. This would be the first time many of their ten children had seen the natural beauty of snow.

But winter weather in Michigan requires a lot of warm outerwear, including coats, mittens, and boots. For a large family, it would be quite an expensive undertaking just to outfit them for the bitterly cold months ahead. But God provided. First, a neighbor brought over footwear, then snow pants, then hats and gloves. Then, a friend urged others at her church to collect a variety of warm clothes in all twelve sizes for each member of the family. By the time the snow arrived, the family had exactly what they needed.

One of the ways we serve God is by serving those in need. First John 3:16–18 encourages us to help others from the abundance of our own possessions. Serving helps us to be more like Jesus as we begin to love and see people as He does.

God often uses His children to fulfill needs and to answer prayers. And as we serve others our own hearts are encouraged as we encourage those we serve. As a result, our own faith will grow as God equips us for service in new ways (V. 18).   *CINDY HESS KASPER*

As you notice the numerous needs of people around you, how can you show God's love in a practical way? How does serving God help your faith to grow?

Father, fill my heart with the willingness to help when I see a need. Help me to give joyfully and serve You with gratitude.

Godliness with contentment is great gain.
[1 TIMOTHY 6:6]

THE YARD-SALE CHRISTMAS

A mom felt she'd been overspending on family Christmas gifts, so one year she decided to try something different. For a few months before the holiday, she scrounged through yard sales for inexpensive, used items. She bought more than usual but for far less money. On Christmas Eve, her children excitedly opened gift after gift after gift. The next day there were more! Mom had felt guilty about not getting new gifts so she had additional gifts for Christmas morning. The kids began opening them but quickly complained, "We're too tired to open any more! You've given us so much!" That's not a typical response from children on a Christmas morning!

God has blessed us with so much, but it seems we're always looking for more: a bigger house, a better car, a larger bank account, or [fill in the blank]. Paul encouraged Timothy to remind people in his congregation that "we brought nothing into this world, and we can take nothing out of it. But if we have food and clothing, we will be content with that" (1 TIMOTHY 6:7–8).

God has given us our very breath and life—besides providing for our needs. How refreshing it might be to enjoy and be content with His gifts and to say, *You've given us so much! We don't need more.* "Godliness with contentment is great gain" (V. 6).

ANNE CETAS

**What are you thankful to God for today?
How might you learn contentment?**

*Father, You've blessed me with so much.
Teach me each day to give thanks.*

This is how we know that we love the
children of God: by loving God and
carrying out his commands. [1 JOHN 5:2]

AUNT BETTY'S WAY

When I was young, whenever my doting Aunt Betty visited, it felt like Christmas. She'd bring Star Wars toys and slip me cash on her way out the door. Whenever I stayed with her, she filled the freezer with ice cream and never cooked vegetables. She had few rules and let me stay up late. My aunt was marvelous, reflecting God's generosity. However, to grow up healthy, I needed more than only Aunt Betty's way. I also needed my parents to place expectations on me and my behavior and hold me to them.

God asks more of me than Aunt Betty. While He floods us with relentless love, a love that never wavers even when we resist or run away, He does expect something of us. When God instructed Israel how to live, He provided Ten Commandments, not ten suggestions (EXODUS 20:1–17). Aware of our self-deception, God offers clear expectations: we're to "[love] God and [carry] out his commands" (1 JOHN 5:2).

Thankfully, "[God's] commands are not burdensome" (V. 3). By the Holy Spirit's power, we can live them out as we experience God's love and joy. His love for us is unceasing. But the Scriptures offer a question to help us know if we love God in return: Are we obeying His commands as the Spirit guides us?

We can *say* we love God, but what we *do* in His strength tells the real story.   *WINN COLLIER*

**When do you find it most difficult to obey God? How does this
connection between obedience and love offer new insight for your
life in Christ?**

*God, I say I love You, but it's hard to love. It's hard to obey. Help me
see the truth and to love You with my actions.*

Help me, LORD my God.
[PSALM 109:26]

PRAYER OF THE BROKEN-DOWN

"Dear Father in heaven, I'm not a praying man, but if you're up there, and you can hear me, show me the way. I'm at the end of my rope." That prayer is whispered by a broken-down George Bailey, the character played by Jimmy Stewart in the classic film *It's a Wonderful Life*. In the now iconic scene, Bailey's eyes fill with tears. They weren't part of the script, but as he spoke that prayer Stewart said he "felt the loneliness, the hopelessness of people who had nowhere to turn." It broke him.

Bailey's prayer, boiled down, is simply "Help me." And this is exactly what's voiced in Psalm 109. David was at the end of his rope: "poor and needy," his "heart . . . wounded" (V. 22), and his body "thin and gaunt" (V. 24). He was fading "like an evening shadow" (V. 23), and sensed himself to be an "object of scorn" in the eyes of his accusers (V. 25). In his extreme brokenness, he had nowhere else to turn. He cried out for the Sovereign Lord to show him the way: "Help me, LORD my God" (V. 26).

There are seasons in our lives when "broken down" says it all. In such times it can be hard to know what to pray. Our loving God will respond to our simple prayer for help.   *JOHN BLASE*

When was the last time you felt broken down by life?
If you have a family member or friend who currently feels that way, how might you help?

Dear Father, some days are hard. They feel hopeless. Turn my heart to You in my brokenness. Give me strength to simply ask for help.

Encourage one another and build each
other up. ⌈1 THESSALONIANS 5:11⌉

★ *DECEMBER TOPIC: ENCOURAGEMENT*
ON THE SAME TEAM

When Philadelphia Eagle's quarterback Carson Wentz returned to the field after healing from a severe injury, the NFL team's backup quarterback, Nick Foles, graciously returned to the bench. Although competing for the same position, the two men chose to support each other and remained confident in their roles. One reporter observed that the two athletes have a "unique relationship rooted in their faith in Christ" shown through their ongoing prayers for each other. As others watched, they brought honor to God by remembering they were on the same team—not just as Eagles quarterbacks, but as believers in Jesus representing Him.

The apostle Paul reminds believers to live as "children of the light" awaiting Jesus' return (1 THESSALONIANS 5:5–6). With our hope secure in the salvation Christ has provided, we can shrug off any temptations to compete out of jealousy, insecurity, fear, or envy. Instead, we can "encourage one another and build each other up" (V. 11). We can respect spiritual leaders who honor God and "live in peace" as we serve together to accomplish our shared goal—telling people about the gospel and encouraging others to live for Jesus (VV. 12–15).

As we serve on the same team, we can heed Paul's command: "Rejoice always, pray continually, give thanks in all circumstances; for this is God's will for you in Christ Jesus" (VV. 16–18).

XOCHITL DIXON

**Who has encouraged you while serving on the same team?
How can you encourage someone who serves alongside you?**

*Jesus, please give me opportunities today to encourage someone
who serves with me.*

Blessed is the one who does not walk
in step with the wicked or stand in the way that sinners
take or sit in the company of mockers. [PSALM 1:1]

GOD'S GUIDANCE

When their bank accidentally deposited $120,000 into their account, a couple went on a shopping spree. They purchased an SUV, a camper, and two four-wheelers in addition to paying off bills. Discovering the deposit error, the bank told the couple to return the money. Unfortunately, the husband and wife had already spent it. They were then charged with felony theft. When the couple arrived at the local court, the husband said to a reporter, "We took some bad legal advice." The two learned that following bad advice (and spending what wasn't theirs) could lead to making a mess of their lives.

In contrast, the psalmist shared wise advice that can help us avoid messing up in life. He wrote that those who find genuine fulfillment—who are "blessed"—refuse to be influenced by the advice of those who don't serve God (PSALM 1:1). They know that unwise, ungodly counsel can lead to unseen dangers and costly consequences. Also, they're motivated by (find "delight" in) and preoccupied with ("meditate on") the timeless and unshakable truths of Scripture (V. 2). They've found that submitting to God's guidance leads to stability and fruitfulness (V. 3).

When we're making decisions, big or small, about our careers, money, relationships, and more, may we seek God's wisdom found in the Bible, godly counsel, and the leading of the Holy Spirit. His guidance is essential and trustworthy for living a fulfilling life and not creating messes.

MARVIN WILLIAMS

Why do you believe Scripture is essential in making godly decisions? Who are your counselors that help you with wise advice?

God, before I seek your advice about things I don't know, help me to practice obedience in the areas I do know and in loving You and others.

Being found in appearance as a man, [Jesus] humbled himself by becoming obedient to death—even death on a cross! [PHILIPPIANS 2:8]

THE TRUE SERVANT

In 27 BC, the Roman ruler Octavian came before the Senate to lay down his powers. He'd won a civil war, become the sole ruler of that region of the world, and was functioning like an emperor. Yet he knew such power was viewed suspiciously. So Octavian renounced his powers before the Senate, vowing to simply be an appointed official. Their response? The Roman Senate honored the ruler by crowning him with a civic crown and naming him the servant of the Roman people. He was also given the name Augustus—the "great one."

Paul wrote of Jesus emptying Himself and taking on the form of a servant. Augustus appeared to do the same. Or *had* he? Augustus only acted like he was surrendering his power but was doing it for his own gain. Jesus "humbled himself by becoming obedient to death—even death on a cross!" (PHILIPPIANS 2:8). Death on a Roman cross was the worst form of humiliation and shame.

Today, a primary reason people praise "servant leadership" as a virtue is because of Jesus. Humility wasn't a Greek or Roman virtue. Because Jesus died on the cross for us, He's the true Servant. He's the true Savior.

Christ became a servant in order to save us. He "made himself nothing" (V. 7) so that we could receive something truly great—the gift of salvation and eternal life.　　　*GLENN PACKIAM*

Why is it true that we're never out of God's reach? What does it mean for you to know that Jesus is the Servant who suffered and died in order to save you?

Dear Jesus, thank You for giving Your life for me. Your servanthood wasn't a show but the reality of Your love for me. Fill my heart with love and gratitude today.

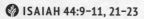
I have swept away your offenses . . .
like the morning mist. [ISAIAH 44:22]

MORNING MIST

O ne morning I visited a pond near my house. I sat on an over-turned boat, thinking and watching a gentle west wind chase a layer of mist across the water's surface. Wisps of fog circled and swirled. Mini "tornadoes" rose up and then exhausted themselves. Before long, the sunlight cut through the clouds and the mist disappeared.

This scene comforted me because I connected it with a verse I'd just read: "I have swept away your offenses like a cloud, your sins like the morning mist" (ISAIAH 44:22). I visited the place hoping to distract myself from a series of sinful thoughts I'd been preoc-cupied with for days. Although I was confessing them, I began to wonder if God would forgive me when I repeated the same sin.

That morning, I knew the answer was yes. Through His prophet Isaiah, God showed grace to the Israelites when they struggled with the ongoing problem of idol worship. Although He told them to stop chasing false gods, God also invited them back to Himself, saying, "I have made you, you are my servant; . . . I will not forget you" (V. 21).

I don't fully grasp forgiveness like that, but I do understand that God's grace is the only thing that can dissolve our sin completely and heal us from it. I'm thankful His grace is endless and divine like He is, and that it's available whenever we need it.

JENNIFER BENSON SCHULDT

How is it possible to abuse God's grace? What steps can you take to break free of sinful habits and experience His forgiveness?

Dear God, thank You for Your gracious presence in my life. I don't want to live in habitual sin. Help me to feel the freedom that comes when I confess my sin and You erase it completely.

Jacob was left alone, and a man wrestled with him
till daybreak. [GENESIS 32:24]

PRAYERFUL WRESTLING

Dennis' life was transformed after someone gave him a New
Testament. Reading it captivated him, and it became his constant companion. Within six months, two life-changing events
occurred in his life. He placed his faith in Jesus for the forgiveness
of his sins, and he was diagnosed with a brain tumor after experiencing severe headaches. Because of the unbearable pain, he
became bedridden and unable to work. One painful, sleepless night
he found himself crying out to God. Sleep finally came at 4:30 a.m.

Bodily pain can cause us to cry out to God, but other excruciating life circumstances also compel us to run to Him. Centuries
before Dennis' night of wrestling, a desperate Jacob faced off with
God (GENESIS 32:24–32). For Jacob, it was unfinished family business.
He had wronged his brother Esau (CH. 27), and he feared that pay-
back was imminent. In seeking God's help in this difficult situation,
Jacob encountered God face-to-face (32:30) and emerged from it a
changed man.

And so did Dennis. After pleading with God in prayer, Dennis
was able to stand up after being bedridden, and the doctor's
examination showed no signs of the tumor. Although God doesn't
always choose to miraculously heal us, we're confident that He
always hears our prayers and will give us what we need for our
situation. In our desperation we offer sincere prayers to God and
leave the results to Him!   *ARTHUR JACKSON*

**What are you struggling with that you could bring before God in
prayer? What are some of the benefits of praying from the depths
of our hearts even when He chooses not to change the situation?**

*Father, help me to see that life's difficulties and challenges are
opportunities for me to seek You in prayer and to grow in my
understanding of who You are.*

His mouth was opened and his tongue set free,
and he began to speak, praising God. [LUKE 1:64]

THE CHRISTMAS GIFT OF SPEECH

A post-surgical stroke had robbed Tom of his ability to speak, and he faced a long rehab journey. Weeks later, we were pleasantly surprised when he showed up at our church's Thanksgiving service. We were even more surprised when he stood up to speak. Searching for what to say, he jumbled his words, repeated himself, and confused days and time. But one thing was clear: he was praising God! It's possible to have your heart break and be blessed at the same moment. This was that kind of moment.

In the "pre-Christmas story" we meet a man who lost the gift of speech. Gabriel the angel appeared to Zechariah the priest and told him he would be the father of a great prophet (SEE LUKE 1:11–17). Zechariah and his wife were elderly, so he doubted it. That's when Gabriel told him he would not speak "until the day this happens" (V. 20).

The day *did* happen. And at the ceremony to name the miracle baby, Zechariah spoke. With his first words he praised God (V. 64). Then he said, "Praise be to the Lord, the God of Israel, because he has come to his people and redeemed them" (V. 68).

Like Zechariah, as soon as he was able, Tom's response was to praise God. Their hearts were inclined toward the One who made their tongues and their minds. Regardless of what faces us this season, we can respond the same way.   *TIM GUSTAFSON*

**How do you respond when a crisis comes? What's your reaction
when you come through it?**

*Thank You, Father, for the gift of speech. In my times of doubt, be
with me to strengthen my faith. Help me learn how to use language
to draw near to and honor You.*

What is mankind that you are mindful
of them? [PSALM 8:4]

WHO YOU ARE

His name is Dnyan, and he considers himself a student of the world. And "this is a very big school," he says of all the cities and towns he's passed through. He began a four-year journey on his bicycle in 2016 to meet and learn from people. When there's a language barrier, he finds that sometimes people can understand just by looking at each other. He also depends on a translation app on his phone to communicate. He doesn't measure his journey in the miles he's traveled or the sights he's seen. Instead, he measures it in the people who've left an imprint on his heart: "Maybe I do not know your language, but I would like to find out who you are."

It's a very big world, yet God knows everything about it and the people in it—fully and completely. The psalmist David was in awe of God when he considered all the works of His hands: the making of the heavens, the moon, and the stars (PSALM 8:3). He wondered, "What is mankind that you are mindful of them, human beings that you care for them?" (V. 4).

God knows you more thoroughly than anyone else possibly can and He cares for you. We can only respond, "LORD, our Lord, how majestic is your name in all the earth!" (VV. 1, 9). *ANNE CETAS*

How do you feel knowing that God knows all about you and loves you? What does believing this truth look like in your life today?

Dear God, it's awesome to realize that You're all-knowing about Your whole creation. I love You for knowing me personally too.

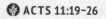

[Barnabas] encouraged them all to remain true to the Lord with all their hearts. [ACTS 11:23]

★ *DECEMBER TOPIC: ENCOURAGEMENT*
TALKING BANANAS

Never give up. Be the reason someone smiles. You're amazing. It isn't where you came from—it's where you're going that counts. Some schoolchildren in Virginia Beach, Virginia, found these messages and more written on bananas in their lunchroom. Cafeteria manager Stacey Truman took the time to write the encouraging notes on the fruit, which the kids dubbed "talking bananas."

This caring outreach reminds me of Barnabas' heart for the "spiritual youngsters" in the ancient city of Antioch (ACTS 11:22–24). Barnabas was famous for his ability to inspire people. Known as a good man, full of faith and the Holy Spirit, he prompted the new believers to "remain true to the Lord with all their hearts" (V. 23). I imagine he spent time with those he wanted to help, saying things like: *Keep praying. Trust the Lord. Stay close to God when life is hard.*

New believers, like children, need loads of encouragement. They're full of potential. They're discovering what they're good at. They may not fully realize what God wants to do in and through them, and often the enemy works overtime to prevent their faith from flourishing.

Those of us who've walked with Jesus for a while understand how hard living for Jesus can be. May all of us be able to give and receive encouragement as God's Spirit guides us and reminds us of spiritual truth.   *JENNIFER BENSON SCHULDT*

**How has God encouraged you in the past?
How might God want to work through you to inspire someone?**

*Heavenly Father, give me someone to encourage today.
Show me what to say and how to meet this person's needs
so that You'll be glorified.*

BIBLE IN A YEAR | AMOS 1–3; REVELATION 6   363

Let all God's angels worship him.
[HEBREWS 1:6]

CHRISTMAS AWE

I was in London one night for a meeting. It was pouring rain, and I was late. I rushed through the streets, turned a corner, and then stopped still. Dozens of angels hovered above Regent Street, their giant shimmering wings stretching across the traffic. Made of thousands of pulsing lights, it was the most amazing Christmas display I'd seen. I wasn't the only one captivated. Hundreds lined the street, gazing up in awe.

Awe is central to the Christmas story. When the angel appeared to Mary explaining she would miraculously conceive (LUKE 1:26–38), and to the shepherds announcing Jesus' birth (2:8–20), each reacted with fear, wonder—and *awe*. Looking around at that Regent Street crowd, I wondered if we were experiencing in part what those first angelic encounters felt like.

A moment later, I noticed something else. Some of the angels had their arms raised, as if they too were gazing up at something. Like the angelic choir that burst into song at the mention of Jesus (VV. 13–14), it seems angels too can be caught up in awe—as they gaze on Him.

"The Son is the radiance of God's glory and the exact representation of his being" (HEBREWS 1:3). Bright and luminous, Jesus is the focus of every angel's gaze (V. 6). If an angel-themed Christmas display can stop busy Londoners in their tracks, just imagine the moment when we see Him face-to-face.   *SHERIDAN VOYSEY*

When was the last time you felt a sense of awe? How can you rekindle a sense of awe over Jesus this Christmastime?

*Father, I worship You. Thank You for the gift
of Your awesome Son.*

Leave them for the poor and for the foreigner
residing among you. [LEVITICUS 23:22]

LEAVE A LITTLE BEHIND

Pennies, nickels, dimes, quarters, and occasionally a half-dollar. That's what you'd find on the nightstand beside his bed. He'd empty his pockets each evening and leave the contents there, for he knew eventually they'd come to visit—*they* being his grandchildren. Over the years the kids learned to visit his nightstand as soon as they arrived. He could have put all that spare change in a coin bank or even stored it away in a savings account. But he didn't. He delighted in leaving it there for the little ones, the precious guests in his home.

A similar mindset is what's expressed in Leviticus 23 when it comes to bringing in the harvest from the land. God, via Moses, told the people something quite counterintuitive: not to "reap to the very edges of your field or gather the gleanings of your harvest" (v. 22). Essentially, He said, "Leave a little behind." This instruction reminded the people that God was behind the harvest in the first place, and that He used His people to provide for those of little account (the strangers in the land).

Such thinking is definitely not the norm in our world. But it's exactly the kind of mindset that will characterize the grateful sons and daughters of God. He delights in a generous heart. And that often comes through you and me.　　　　　　　*JOHN BLASE*

What's your first reaction to the thought of "leaving a little behind"? What's one way you could practice such thankful generosity toward the poor or the strangers in your life?

*Loving God, thank You for Your provision in my life.
Give me eyes to see ways in which I can share with others,
especially those poor and in need.*

God demonstrates his own love for us in this: While we were still sinners, Christ died for us. [ROMANS 5:8]

THE LANGUAGE OF THE CROSS

Pastor Tim Keller said, "Nobody ever learns who they are by being told. They must be shown." In a sense, it's one application of the adage, "Actions speak louder than words." Spouses show their mates that they're appreciated by listening to them and loving them. Parents show their children they're valued by lovingly caring for them. Coaches show athletes they have potential by investing in their development. And on it goes. By the same token, a different kind of action can show people painful things that communicate much darker messages.

Of all the action-based messages in the universe, there's one that matters most. When we want to be shown who we are in God's eyes, we need look no further than His actions on the cross. In Romans 5:8, Paul wrote, "God demonstrates his own love for us in this: While we were still sinners, Christ died for us." The cross shows us who we are: those whom God so loved that He gave His one and only Son for us (JOHN 3:16).

Against the mixed messages and confusing actions of broken people in a broken culture, the message of God's heart rings clear. Who are you? You're the one so loved by God that He gave His Son for Your rescue. Consider the price He paid for you and the wonderful reality that, to Him, you were always worth it. *BILL CROWDER*

How have you been defining your worth? What false messages might you need to discard or reject in exchange for comprehending the value that God places on you?

Father, I can never understand why You would love me so much or give Your Son for my forgiveness. Your love is unsearchable and Your grace is amazing. Thank You for making me Your child!

I have taken away your sin, and I will put fine
garments on you. ⌈ ZECHARIAH 3:4 ⌉

WHO ARE YOU WEARING?

The Argentine women's basketball team came to their tour-
nament game wearing the wrong uniforms. Their navy blue
jerseys were too similar to Colombia's dark blue jerseys, and
as the visiting team they should have worn white. With no time to
find replacement uniforms and change, they had to forfeit the
game. In the future, Argentina will surely double-check what
they're wearing.

In the time of the prophet Zechariah, God showed him a vision
in which the high priest Joshua came before God wearing smelly,
filthy clothes. Satan sneered and pointed. He's disqualified! Game
over! But there was time to change. God rebuked Satan and told
His angel to remove Joshua's grubby garments. He turned to
Joshua, "See, I have taken away your sin, and I will put fine garments on you" (ZECHARIAH 3:4).

We came into this world wearing the stench of Adam's sin,
which we layer over with sin of our own. If we stay in our filthy
clothes, we'll lose the game of life. If we become disgusted with
our sin and turn to Jesus, He'll dress us from head to toe with
Himself and His righteousness. It's time to check, *Who are we
wearing?*

The final stanza of the hymn "The Solid Rock" explains how we
win. "When He shall come with trumpet sound, / Oh, may I then
in Him be found; / Dressed in His righteousness alone, / Faultless
to stand before the throne."

MIKE WITTMER

**Who are you wearing? Are you trusting in your own goodness or
Jesus? Which do you want God and others to notice?**

*Jesus, thank You for providing the way for my sin to be removed and
for Your righteousness to cover me.*

The LORD is my shepherd, I lack nothing.
[PSALM 23:1]

LOOK FOR THE GREEN

The gravelly voiced captain announced yet another delay. Crammed in my window seat aboard a plane that had already sat unmoving for two hours, I chafed in frustration. After a long workweek away, I longed for the comfort and rest of home. How much longer? As I gazed out the raindrop-covered window, I noticed a lonely triangle of green grass growing in the gap of cement where runways met. Such an odd sight in the middle of all that concrete.

As an experienced shepherd, David knew well the need to provide the rest of green pastures for his sheep. In Psalm 23, he penned an important lesson that would carry him forward in the exhausting days of leading as king of Israel. "The LORD is my shepherd, I lack nothing. He makes me lie down in green pastures, . . . he refreshes my soul" (VV. 1–3).

On the concrete jungle of an airport tarmac, delayed from my destination and feeling the lack of comfort and rest, God, my good Shepherd, directed my eyes to a patch of green. In relationship with Him, I can discover His ongoing provision of rest wherever I am—if I notice and enter it.

The lesson has lingered over the years: look for the green. It's there. With God in our lives, we lack nothing. He makes us lie down in green pastures. He refreshes our souls.   *ELISA MORGAN*

Where can you look for the green today? In what ways has God provided a moment of rest when you thought it was impossible?

Loving God, thank You for being my Shepherd and for making me lie down in green pastures to refresh my soul.

The virgin will conceive and give birth to a son,
and will call him Immanuel. [ISAIAH 7:14]

WHAT TO NAME THE BABY

Here's one conversation Mary didn't have to have with Joseph as they awaited the birth of the baby she was carrying: "Joseph, what should we name the baby?" Unlike most people awaiting a birth, they had no question about what they would call this child.

The angels who visited Mary and then Joseph told them both that the baby's name would be Jesus (MATTHEW 1:20–21; LUKE 1:30–31). The angel that appeared to Joseph explained that this name indicated that the baby would "save his people from their sins."

He would also be called "Immanuel" (ISAIAH 7:14), which means "God is with us," because He would be God in human form—deity wrapped in swaddling clothes. The prophet Isaiah revealed additional titles of "Wonderful Counselor," "Mighty God," "Everlasting Father," and Prince of Peace" (9:6), because He would be all of those things.

It's always exciting to name a new baby. But no other baby had such a powerful, exciting, world-changing name as the one who was "Jesus who is called the Messiah" (MATTHEW 1:16). What a thrill for us to be able to "call on the name of our Lord Jesus Christ" (1 CORINTHIANS 1:2)! There's no other name that saves (ACTS 4:12).

Let's praise Jesus and contemplate everything He means to us this Christmas season!   *DAVE BRANON*

**How does reflecting on the name of Jesus encourage you?
Which of His titles from Isaiah 9:6 means the most to you
this season? Why?**

*Thank You, heavenly Father, for sending us One who is our Savior, our
Counselor, our Prince of Peace, and our Messiah. I celebrate His birth
because I know that His life and death and resurrection purchased
for us eternal life.*

BIBLE IN A YEAR | MICAH 4–5; REVELATION 12

Two are better than one, because they have a good
return for their labor. [ECCLESIASTES 4:9]

★ *DECEMBER TOPIC: ENCOURAGEMENT*

TWO ARE BETTER

I n the 1997 Ironman Triathlon in Hawaii, two women fought to
stay on their feet as they hobbled toward the finish line.
Exhausted, the runners persevered on wobbly legs, until Sian
Welch bumped into Wendy Ingraham. They both dropped to the
ground. Struggling to stand, they stumbled forward, only to fall
again about twenty meters from the finish line. When Ingraham
began to crawl, the crowd applauded. When her competitor followed suit, they cheered louder. Ingraham crossed the finish line
in fourth place, and she slumped into the outstretched arms of
her supporters. Then she turned and reached out to her fallen
sister. Welch lunged her body forward, stretching her weary arm
toward Ingraham's hand and across the finish line. As she completed the race in fifth place, the crowd roared their approval.

This pair's completion of the 140-mile swimming, biking, and
running race inspired many. But the image of the weary competitors persevering together remains ingrained in my mind,
affirming the life-empowering truth in Ecclesiastes 4:9–11.

There's no shame in admitting we require assistance in life (V. 9),
especially since we can't *honestly* deny our needs or hide them
from our all-knowing God. At one time or another, we'll all fall,
whether physically or emotionally. Knowing we're not alone can
comfort us as we persevere. As our loving Father helps us, He
empowers us to reach out to others in need, affirming they too
aren't alone.　　　　　　　　　　　　　　　　　XOCHITL DIXON

**How has someone helped you? How can you encourage others
this week?**

*All-powerful God, thank You for reassuring us of Your constant
presence as You help us and give us opportunities to reach out
and help others.*

Because your love is better than life,
my lips will glorify you. [PSALM 63:3]

NO GLITZ, JUST GLORY

Looking at the handmade Christmas ornaments my son, Xavier, crafted over the years and the annual mismatched baubles Grandma had sent him, I couldn't figure out why I was not content with our decorations. I'd always valued the creativity and memories each ornament represented. So, why did the allure of the retail stores' holiday displays tempt me to desire a tree adorned with perfectly matched bulbs, shimmering orbs, and satin ribbons?

As I began to turn away from our humble decor, I glimpsed a red, heart-shaped ornament with a simple phrase scripted on it—*Jesus, My Savior.* How could I have forgotten that my family and my hope in Christ are the reasons I love celebrating Christmas? Our simple tree looked nothing like the trees in the storefronts, but the love behind every decoration made it beautiful.

Like our modest tree, the Messiah didn't meet the world's expectations in any way (ISAIAH 53:2). Jesus "was despised and rejected" (V. 3). Yet, in an amazing display of love, He still chose to be "pierced for our transgressions" (V. 5). He endured punishment, so we could enjoy peace (V. 5). Nothing is more beautiful than that.

With renewed gratitude for our imperfect decorations and our perfect Savior, I stopped longing for glitz and praised God for His glorious love. Sparkling adornments could never match the beauty of His sacrificial gift—Jesus.   *XOCHITL DIXON*

How can you make praising Jesus part of your Christmas celebration? What does His sacrifice on the cross mean to you?

Loving God, please help me see the beautiful love reflected through the magnitude of Your sacrifice.

Peace to those on whom his favor rests.
[LUKE 2:14]

WHEN PEACE BREAKS OUT

O n a cold Christmas Eve in Belgium in 1914, the sound of singing floated from the trenches where soldiers were dug in. Strains of the carol "Silent Night" rang out in German and then in English. Soldiers who earlier in the day had been shooting at each other laid down their weapons and emerged from their trenches to shake hands in the "no man's land" between them, exchanging Christmas greetings and spontaneous gifts from their rations. The ceasefire continued through the next day as the soldiers talked and laughed and even organized soccer matches together.

The Christmas Truce of 1914 that occurred along World War I's Western Front offered a brief glimpse of the peace the angels proclaimed on the first Christmas long ago. An angel spoke to terrified shepherds with these reassuring words: "Do not be afraid. I bring you good news that will cause great joy for all the people. Today in the town of David a Savior has been born to you" (LUKE 2:10–11). Then a multitude of angels appeared, "praising God and saying, 'Glory to God in the highest heaven, and on earth peace to those on whom his favor rests'" (VV. 13–14).

Jesus is the "Prince of Peace" who saves us from our sins (ISAIAH 9:6). Through His sacrifice on the cross He offers forgiveness and peace with God to all who trust in Him.   *JAMES BANKS*

How have you experienced the peace Jesus provides? In what practical way can you share His peace with someone today?

Prince of Peace, rule in my heart today. I praise You for Your perfect peace that this world can never take away!

God so loved the world.
[JOHN 3:16]

JOY TO THE WORLD

Every Christmas we decorate our home with nativity scenes from around the world. We have a German nativity pyramid, a manger scene fashioned out of olive wood from Bethlehem, and a brightly colored Mexican folk version. Our family favorite is a whimsical entry from Africa. Instead of the more traditional sheep and camels, a hippopotamus gazes contently at the baby Jesus.

The unique cultural perspective brought to life in these nativity scenes warms my heart as I ponder each beautiful reminder that Jesus' birth was not just for one nation or culture. It's good news for the whole earth, a reason for people from every country and ethnicity to rejoice.

The little baby depicted in each of our nativity scenes revealed this truth of God's heart for the entire world. As John wrote in relation to Christ's conversation with an inquisitive Pharisee named Nicodemus, "For God so loved the world that he gave his one and only Son, that whoever believes in him shall not perish but have eternal life" (JOHN 3:16).

The gift of Jesus is good news for everyone. No matter where on earth you call home, Jesus' birth is God's offer of love and peace to you. And all who find new life in Christ, "from every tribe and language and people and nation" will one day celebrate God's glory forever and ever (REVELATION 5:9).   *LISA M. SAMRA*

In what unique ways do you celebrate the birth of Jesus? How might the reminder of God's love for the whole world bring joy this Christmas season?

Father, thank You for providing salvation through the gift of Your Son.

When you get there, anoint Hazael king over Aram. [1 KINGS 19:15]

WHO NEEDS ME?

While on a red-eye flight to Washington, DC, opinion writer Arthur Brooks overheard an elderly woman whisper to her husband, "It's not true that no one needs you anymore." The man murmured something about wishing he were dead, and his wife replied, "Oh, stop saying that." When the flight ended, Brooks turned around and immediately recognized the man. He was a world-famous hero. Other passengers shook his hand, and the pilot thanked him for the courage he displayed decades ago. How had this giant sunk into despair?

The prophet Elijah bravely and single-handedly defeated 450 prophets of Baal—or so he thought (1 KINGS 18). Yet he hadn't really done it alone; God was there all along! But later, feeling all alone, he asked God to take his life.

God lifted Elijah's spirits by bringing him into His presence and giving him new people to serve. He must go and "anoint Hazael king over Aram," Jehu "king over Israel," and Elisha "to succeed you as prophet" (19:15–16). Invigorated with renewed purpose, Elijah found and mentored his successor.

Your great victories may lie in the rearview mirror. You may feel your life has peaked, or that it never did. No matter. Look around. The battles may seem smaller, the stakes less profound, but there are still others who need you. Serve them well for Jesus' sake, and it will count. They're your purpose—the reason you're still here.   *MIKE WITTMER*

Who can you serve today for Christ? Why is it so vital for you to reach out to others with God's love?

Holy Spirit, open my eyes to those I can serve for Jesus' sake.

The LORD is compassionate and gracious,
slow to anger, abounding in love. [PSALM 103:8]

A SONG IN THE NIGHT

The sun had long set when our electrical power suddenly went out. I was at home with our two younger children, and this was their first time experiencing a power outage. After verifying that the utility company knew about the outage, I located some candles, and the kids and I huddled together in the kitchen around the flickering flames. They seemed nervous and unsettled, so we began to sing. Soon the concerned looks on their faces were replaced with smiles. Sometimes in our darkest moments we need a song.

Psalm 103 may be one of the psalms prayed or sung after the people of God had returned from exile to a homeland that had been laid waste. In a moment of crisis, they needed to sing. But not just any song, they needed to sing about who God is and what He does. Psalm 103 also helps us remember that He's compassionate, merciful, patient, and full of faithful love (V. 8). And in case we wonder if the judgment for our sin still hangs over our heads, the psalm announces that God isn't angry, He has forgiven, and He feels compassion. These are good things to sing about during the dark nights of our lives.

Maybe that's where you find yourself—in a dark and difficult place, wondering if God really is good, questioning His love for you. If so, pray and sing to the One who abounds in love!

GLENN PACKIAM

How might God's saving acts in Jesus give you a better picture of what He's like? How does He view you?

Dear Jesus, help me to see the love of God revealed in Your life, death, and resurrection. Lift up my weary head that I might sing of Your goodness and faithfulness.

Then this city will bring me renown, joy,
praise and honor. [JEREMIAH 33:9]

REBUILDING THE RUINS

At seventeen, Dowayne had to leave his family's home in Manenberg, a part of Cape Town, South Africa, because of his stealing and addiction to heroin. He didn't go far, building a shack of corrugated metal in his mother's backyard, which soon became known as the Casino, a place to use drugs. When he was nineteen, however, Dowayne came to saving faith in Jesus. His journey off drugs was long and exhausting, but he got clean with God's help and with the support of friends who are believers in Jesus. And ten years after Dowayne built the Casino, he and others turned the hut into a house church. What was once a dark and foreboding place now is a place of worship and prayer.

The leaders of this church look to Jeremiah 33 for how God can bring healing and restoration to people and places, as He's done with Dowayne and the former Casino. The prophet Jeremiah spoke to God's people in captivity, saying that although the city would not be spared, yet God would heal His people and would "rebuild them," cleansing them from their sin (JEREMIAH 33:7–8). Then the city would bring Him joy, renown, and honor (V. 9).

When we're tempted to despair over the sin that brings heart-break and brokenness, let's continue to pray that God will bring healing and hope, even as He's done in a backyard in Manenberg.

AMY BOUCHER PYE

How have you seen God bring restoration in your own life and in the lives of others? How can you pray for His healing this day?

God, thank You for sparking new life in what appeared to be dead. Continue to work in me, that I might share Your saving love with others.

Our struggle is not against flesh and blood,
but … against the spiritual forces of evil in the
heavenly realms. [EPHESIANS 6:12]

UNSEEN REALITIES

I n 1876, men drilling for coal in central Indiana thought they had found the gates of hell. Historian John Barlow Martin reports that at six hundred feet, "foul fumes issued forth amid awesome noises." Afraid they had "bitten into the roof of the devil's cave," the miners plugged the well and scurried back to their homes.

The miners, of course, were mistaken—and some years later, they would drill again and be rich in natural gas. Even though they were mistaken, I find myself a little jealous of them. These miners lived with an awareness of the spiritual world that is often missing from my own life. It's easy for me to live as if the supernatural and the natural rarely intersect and to forget that "our struggle is not against flesh and blood, but . . . against the spiritual forces of evil in the heavenly realms" (EPHESIANS 6:12).

When we see evil winning in our world, we shouldn't give in or try to fight it in our own strength. Instead, we're to resist evil by putting on "the full armor of God" (VV. 13–18). Studying Scripture, meeting regularly with other believers for encouragement, and making choices with the good of others in mind can help us "stand against the devil's schemes" (V. 11). Equipped by the Holy Spirit, we can stand firm in the face of anything (V. 13).   *AMY PETERSON*

How can you cultivate an awareness of the reality of the spiritual world? Is God calling you to "put on" some part of the "armor" Paul describes? What might that look like today?

Help me to remember, God, to walk and serve by faith and in Your power.

The LORD, the LORD, the compassionate and
gracious God, slow to anger, abounding in love
and faithfulness. [EXODUS 34:6]

TRUE SUCCESS

My interview guest politely answered my questions. I had a
feeling, though, that something lurked beneath our interaction. A passing comment brought it out.

"You're inspiring thousands of people," I said.

"Not thousands," he muttered. *"Millions."*

And as if pitying my ignorance, my guest reminded me of his
credentials—the titles he held, the things he'd achieved, the
magazine he'd graced. It was an awkward moment.

Ever since that experience, I've been struck by how God revealed
Himself to Moses on Mount Sinai (EXODUS 34:5–7). Here was the
Creator of the cosmos and Judge of humanity, but God didn't use
His titles. Here was the Maker of 100 billion galaxies, but such feats
weren't mentioned either. Instead, God introduced Himself as "the
compassionate and gracious God, slow to anger, abounding in
love and faithfulness" (V. 6). When He reveals who He is, it isn't His
titles or achievements He lists but the kind of character He has.

As people made in God's image and called to follow His example (GENESIS 1:27; EPHESIANS 5:1–?), this is profound. Achievement is
good, titles have their place, but what really matters is how compassionate, gracious, and loving we're becoming.

Like that interview guest, we too can base our significance on
our achievements. I have. But our God has modeled what true
success is—not what's written on our business cards and resu-
més, but how we're becoming like Him.   *SHERIDAN VOYSEY*

**How tempted are you to base your significance on your
accomplishments? What aspect of God's character needs to grow
in you today?**

Spirit of God, make me compassionate, gracious, patient, and loving!

He himself is our peace.
[EPHESIANS 2:14]

FIREWORKS OF LIFE

O n New Year's Eve, when high-powered fireworks detonate across cities and towns worldwide, the noise is loud on purpose. By their nature, say manufacturers, flashy fireworks are meant to split the atmosphere, literally. "Repeater" blasts can sound the loudest, especially when exploded near the ground.

Troubles, too, can boom through our hearts, minds, and homes. The "fireworks" of life—family struggles, relationship problems, work challenges, financial strain, even church division—can feel like explosions, rattling our emotional atmosphere.

Yet we know the One who lifts us over this uproar. Christ Himself "is our peace," Paul wrote in Ephesians 2:14. When we abide in His presence, His peace is greater than any disruption, quieting the noise of any worry, hurt, or disunity.

This would have been powerful assurance to Jews and gentiles alike. They'd once lived "without hope and without God in the world" (V. 12). Now they faced threats of persecution and internal threats of division. But in Christ, they'd been brought near to Him, and consequently to each other, by His blood. "For he himself is our peace, who has made the two groups one and has destroyed the barrier, the dividing wall of hostility" (V. 14).

As we start a new year, with threats of unrest and division ever rumbling on the horizon, let's turn from life's noisy trials to seek our ever-present Peace. He quiets the booms, healing us.

PATRICIA RAYBON

**What "fireworks" are shattering the calm in your life?
When you give them to God in prayer, what peace do you feel?**

*Comforting God, when life's fireworks shock and unsettle me,
draw me to Your peace.*

Our Daily Bread Ministries

In 1938, our ministry started with a radio program called the Detroit Bible Class. Since then, our audience has grown from a small group of dedicated radio listeners to millions of people around the world who use our Bible-based resources. Over the years, our focus has remained the same: reaching out to people all around the world with the message of God's love.

Our Daily Bread Ministries is a non-denominational, non-profit organization with staff and volunteers in over 37 offices working together to distribute more than 60 million resources annually in 150 countries. Regardless of whether it's a radio broadcast, DVD, podcast, book, mobile app, or website, we provide materials to help people grow in their relationship with God.

Our Daily Bread Publishing

Our Daily Bread Publishing was founded in 1988 as an extension of Our Daily Bread Ministries. Our goal is to produce resources that feed the soul with the Word of God, and we do this through books, music, video, audio, software, greeting cards, and downloadable content. All our materials focus on the never-changing truths of Scripture, so everything we produce shows reverence for God and His wisdom, demonstrates the relevance of vibrant faith, and equips and encourages people in their everyday lives.

🍞 OUR DAILY BREAD MINISTRIES OFFICES

For information on our resources, please write to the office nearest you from the list below, or go to **ourdailybread.org/locations** for the complete list of offices.

AFRICA REGION

KENYA
Our Daily Bread Ministries, PO Box 2761, 00200 City Square, Nairobi
M: +254 717 805557/727 207899
Email: kenya@odb.org

NIGERIA (REGIONAL OFFICE)
Our Daily Bread Ministries, PO Box 80125, Lafiaji Post Office 101006, Lagos State
PH: +234 90 6402 7516 • M: +234 80 5462 7884
Email: nigeria@odb.org

SOUTH AFRICA
Our Daily Bread Ministries, PO Box 2637, Umhlanga Rocks, Durban 4320
PH: +27 31 563 6322 / 825 2001 • FX: +27 31 563 1963
Email: southafrica@odb.org

IBERO-AMERICA & CARIBBEAN REGION

BRAZIL (REGIONAL OFFICE)
Our Daily Bread Ministries, Caixa Postal 4190, 82501-970, Curitiba/PR
PH: +55 41 3257 4028
Email: brazil@odb.org

GUYANA
Our Daily Bread Ministries, PO Box 101070, Georgetown
PH: +592 231 6704
Email: guyana@odb.org

JAMAICA W.I.
Our Daily Bread Ministries, 23 Parkington Plaza, PO Box 139, Kingston 10
PH: +1 876 926 5552
Email: jamaica@odb.org

TRINIDAD & TOBAGO W.I.
Our Daily Bread Ministries, PO Box 4938, Tunapuna, Trinidad W.I.
PH: +1 868 645 7402
Email: trinidad@odb.org

USA
Our Daily Bread, PO Box 2222, Grand Rapids, MI 49501 USA
PH: +1 616 974-2210
Email: odb@odb.org

TOPIC INDEX

JANUARY – DECEMBER 2022

TOPIC INDEX

JANUARY – DECEMBER 2022

TOPIC INDEX

JANUARY – DECEMBER 2022